# The Full Colour Bulldog Handbook

BY

## LINDA WHITWAM

ISBN-13: 979-8645838706

# Acknowledgements

My sincere gratitude to all the Bulldog owners, organisations and canine experts who have contributed to this book. Thanks to: Julie Haigh, Sue Hanson, BCARN and Chicago English Bulldog Rescue, and special thanks to Kathy Jacobsen, without whose expert knowledge and experience this book would not have been possible.

# Copyright

# Contents

**Author's Notes:**

1.  This book has been written in **British English**, except where North Americans have been quoted and the original American English has been preserved.

2.  "He" and "she" are interchanged to make the book relevant to all owners.

# 1. Meet the Bulldog

There are more than 200 breeds registered with the Kennel Clubs and all of them are different — but there is something extra special about the Bulldog.

For a start there's the breed's unique appearance. You could line up 100 non-dog lovers, show them a variety of breeds and every one of them would instantly recognise the Bulldog. The huge distinguished, wrinkled head and powerful body are unmistakable.

.........................................................................................................................................................

Bulldogs have a long and fascinating history dating back hundreds of years to when they were bred for their bravery, tenacity and power to bring down a bull. They have come to symbolise incredible courage and determination, and are the national symbol of Great Britain.

The oldest single breed club in the world is The Bulldog Club, set up in England in 1878.

Over the decades, the Bulldog has been specifically bred to retain his distinctive physical features. What is amazing, however, is that the violent and aggressive nature has been bred out.

*You've heard of a wolf in sheep's clothing? Well, the Bulldog is a sheep in wolf's clothing!*

His nickname is **Bully** - or **Sourmug** - but nothing could be further from the truth. It's true that Bulldogs have retained their stubborn streak, but they are generally the most placid of creatures, happy to snooze the day away next to - and even on top of - their owners.

An adult Bulldog may weigh 40lb to 55lb, but nobody has told him that he is not a lapdog!

He is known for his gentle nature, loves sleeping, and enjoys snuggling up on the couch or his owner's knee. If you don't want yours to do this, train him not to while he is a pup, it may be too late when he is a fully grown adult.

Today the Bulldog is a companion dog without equal. He simply loves to be with his people — so if you are out at work all day, don't get a Bulldog. Go for a breed that is less dependent on humans for its happiness.

Bullies also have a reputation for being wonderful with babies and children. They seem to have a natural affinity and protective instinct towards youngsters. However, a Bulldog is a big, powerful dog who doesn't always know his own strength, and young Bullies are often boisterous, so always supervise their time spent together until the children are old enough to look after themselves.

Bulldogs are very courageous - they won't look to start a fight with other dogs, but will not back down if involved in a confrontation. So, try not to put your Bulldog in a situation where he feels he has to defend himself.

## Temperament and Traits

Your Bulldog's character will depend largely on two things. The first is his temperament, which he inherits and presumably one of the reasons why you have chosen a Bulldog. What many owners do not realise is that as well as being born with those wrinkles and other trademark physical features, your Bully has also inherited his temperament from his parents and ancestors.

Good breeders select their breeding stock based not only on a Bulldog's appearance, but also on what sort of disposition he or she has. And that's another reason to take your time to find a good, responsible breeder. The second factor is environment – or how you bring him up and treat him.

**FACT >** *In other words, it's a combination of NATURE and NURTURE.*

The first few months in a dog's life are so important. Once he has left his mother and littermates, he takes his lead from you as he learns to react to the world around him.

*One essential aspect of nurture is "socialisation," which means: "the process of learning to behave in a way that is acceptable to society."*

Even though Bulldogs are generally placid dogs, it is essential to spend time introducing yours to other animals, humans, loud noises, traffic and new situations from an early age.

A Bulldog comfortable in his surroundings without fear or anxieties is less likely to display unwanted behaviour.

Through your guidance and good socialisation, your Bully learns who he can trust, how much he can get away with, whether to be afraid and so on. Afraid doesn't necessarily mean timid. Often, a dog's reaction when frightened is to come out on the attack, particularly if he feels he can't escape, such as when on the lead or leash.

To say all dogs of the same breed are alike would be akin to saying that all Americans are optimistic and friendly and all Brits are polite and reserved. It is, of course, a huge generalisation. There are grumpy, unfriendly Americans or rude in-your-face Brits! However, it is also true to say that being friendly and optimistic are general American traits, as is being polite in Britain.

It's the same with the Bulldog. Each individual dog is a unique character, but there are certain traits that are common within the breed. So here are the typical Bulldog traits:

- ❖ Most Bulldogs are gentle and placid by nature, they have laid-back personalities
- ❖ They are very loving, loyal and enjoy spending time with their owners
- ❖ They make wonderful companion dogs, provided you can give them the time they need
- ❖ They are patient - especially with children - and dependable
- ❖ They can be attention-seeking and demand your attention for their happiness
- ❖ Despite their physical appearance and nickname, Bullies are not aggressive dogs. They are giant lapdogs
- ❖ If a Bulldog is energetic it is usually in short bursts, as the breed does not have much stamina

- They often have a comical or clownish personality and do funny, illogical things. Some Bullies love to have a mad few minutes and dash round like crazy, grabbing things in their mouths or rolling over on the floor

- They are happy to live indoors most of the time, which makes them one of the few larger dogs suitable for apartment living

- They do not need a lot of exercise – although one daily walk should be the minimum

- They are known for being wonderful with babies and children – although, like any dog, they should be supervised until the child is old enough to look after herself

- They do not like being left alone for long periods

- Bulldogs like to chew, especially when young or bored

- They can be stubborn – or at least strong willed - and some can become dominant if not properly trained and socialised

- A Bulldog is most content and a delight to be with once he knows his place in the household pecking order - and that should be below you

- They do not respond well to heavy-handed or loud, aggressive training techniques, but do better with a patient but firm approach

- Bulldogs do not bark a lot, although many of them "talk," especially when demanding attention. This can sound quite funny, like a parrot being strangled or the warbling of an exotic bird!

- They don't make good guard dogs, although some make better watch dogs and will bark if somebody comes to the door

- They are not aggressive, but are tenacious and courageous and will not back down if pushed into a confrontation

- Most are greedy and prone to obesity

- They overheat easily

- They have big hearts and will respond to anyone who shows them kindness, rather than being one-man or one-woman dogs

- Some can be possessive – you don't own them, they own you!

- They are often good with other dogs and cats, especially if introduced at an early age, although some may be less tolerant of small pets such as hamsters, guinea pigs, etc

- Many Bulldogs suffer from breathing or eye problems, allergies and/or skin problems. They are one of the most expensive breeds when it comes to veterinary bills

- They have a wonderful, quiet dignity – and a high tolerance to pain, so you need to keep an eye on yours for any signs of ill health or discomfort

- They require personal care on an almost daily level

❖ They snore, snuffle, burp, fart and often drool!

If we haven't managed to put you off, then read on and learn more about this wonderful, unique breed and how to fulfil your part of the bargain and take good care of them.

By the way, we asked some Bulldoggers (as the owners are known) to sum up their pets in three words, and this is what they said:

❖ Stubborn, funny, loving

❖ Loving, lovable, expensive

❖ The friendly giant

❖ Worth the effort

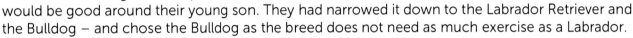

Julie Haigh from Yorkshire, England, added: "They have a giant personality to match their frame and they are the most lovable, sociable, friendly dogs I have ever known."

Julie and her husband were originally looking for a breed with a gentle temperament that would be good around their young son. They had narrowed it down to the Labrador Retriever and the Bulldog – and chose the Bulldog as the breed does not need as much exercise as a Labrador.

Since then the family has never looked back - they got bitten by the Bulldog bug and are now on their third!

## Is a Bulldog the Right Dog for Me?

Many owners forge a bond so deep with their Bulldog that they wouldn't consider any other breed. Bulldogs are not a long-lived breed. If you are lucky, your may have a decade with your Bully, and if you're really lucky, 12 years. But sadly, many do not make it into double figures.

However, taking on a Bulldog is still a big commitment. Before you take the step, make sure it's the right breed for you. Answering the following questions will help you to make up your mind:

1. **Are you looking for a dog to take on daily long walks or go jogging with?**
2. **Do you want to spend a lot of time outdoors with your dog?**
3. **Do you want a dog you can take to agility classes and competitions?**
4. **Do you want to spend hours playing with your dog?**
5. **Are you looking for a guard dog?**
6. **Do you want to breed from your dog?**
7. **Do you live in an extremely hot or cold climate?**
8. **Are you out at work all day?**
9. **Do you have a swimming pool?**
10. **Are you very house-proud or easily embarrassed?**
11. **Are you a first-time dog owner?**

If the answer is YES to any of these questions, then the Bulldog may not be the breed for you – and here's why:

1. Although the "couch potato" reputation is a little unfair as some Bulldogs are quite active, **the breed is regarded as having low to medium energy levels.** They are usually content with short walks. They overheat easily and the shapes of their heads and bodies do not naturally lend them to agility classes, jogging, swimming or other strenuous activity.

2. **The Bulldog spends most of his time indoors.** Unusually for a large dog, he is suited to apartment life, as long as there is regular access to the outdoors. Although Bulldogs are often playful and may start out running around very energetically, they soon run out of steam! The breed does not have the physical stamina for active sports.

3. **Some Bulldogs can compete in activity classes, but they are not known for it.** They lack stamina and can also be a bit stubborn to train. You may have a dog that loves to jump through hoops and over fences – if that's the case, great. But if your Bully doesn't want to do it, you'll have a difficult task to persuade him otherwise.

4. **Many Bulldogs are playful,** some breeders say that the Bulldog is a perpetual child; he never grows up. He may love playing with you and his toys, but it will be in short bursts of high energy activity and he soon tires.

5. **Their appearance alone might scare away any would-be intruders, but that's where it ends.** Over the decades, much of the original aggression has been bred out of the Bulldog. They are generally docile, don't bark much and, although very observant, they are far more likely to watch any burglars walk off with your prize possessions out of a corner of their sleepy eye than try to deter them!

6. **Of all the breeds ever created, the Bulldog is one of the most difficult and complex – not to mention expensive - when it comes to producing puppies,** which is a practice best left to the experts.

7. **People living in extreme climates can have Bulldogs, but it requires a lot of effort on their part to ensure that the dog does not become overheated,** a condition that the breed is prone to. In hot weather they should be in an air conditioned room. Neither can Bulldogs tolerate extremely cold conditions.

8. **Above all, the Bulldog is a companion dog. One left on his or her own will be unhappy** at the separation and may resort to destructive behaviour. If you are out at work all day, maybe you'd be better delaying getting a dog until you have more time for one.

9. **Due to their conformation (body shape) and respiratory system, most Bulldogs cannot swim,** although they often don't realise that. If you have a pool, it would have to be fenced off for the safety of the dog. Some owners buy lifejackets for their Bulldogs.

10. **The vast majority of Bullies - God bless 'em - pass wind and snore!** They are also messy eaters and drinkers, leaving trails across the floor - and they shed hair all year round - but not a lot. If you are extremely house-proud, prim and proper, a less gassy canine with elegant table manners would be a better choice!

11. **The Bulldog has special needs.** Many have health issues as well as an intolerance to temperature fluctuations and excessive exercise. Others need a specialised diet and extra personal daily care to keep them healthy, such as wrinkle and tail cleaning. To make matters worse, they also have an extremely high pain threshold which can mask underlying

problems. For all these reasons, the breed is not recommended for first-time and inexperienced dog owners.

On the other hand, if you answer **YES** to the next set of questions, then the Bulldog could be just the dog for you.

1. Are you looking for a companion dog?

2. Do you want a dog that is good with children or old people?

3. Have you got the finances to cover medical problems that may run into thousands of dollars – or pounds? (Not all conditions may be covered by insurance).

4. Are you prepared to put in the time to train your dog – even if he is a bit stubborn?

5. Are you prepared to clean your dog's eyes, ears, skin folds and tail area regularly – i.e. nearly every day?

6. Does everyone in your house like Bulldogs?

7. Are you around a lot of the time?

**FACT** ❭ *The Bulldog's stand-out feature, apart from his stunning appearance, is his deeply affectionate and relatively undemanding companionship - as long as you are around and he is not left alone for long periods. He will enjoy nothing more than snuggling up and snoring away happily.*

The breed is suitable for the elderly, as most Bulldogs are house dogs that require relatively little exercise, although it all depends on what they have become used to as a puppy. A Bulldog accustomed to two daily walks will come to expect them, whereas another that has only had 20 minutes a day in the park since puppyhood will probably be equally as content.

Bulldogs are renowned for being good with children. They have protective instincts and will take care of them, play with them and patiently allow children to do what children do, which is poke and prod and stroke and play with them.

 *A Bulldog may weigh 50lb or more and can sometimes play rough. If you have small children, train your dog not to be too boisterous around them, and never leave small children and dogs unattended - no matter how gentle the dog is.*

Bulldogs can suffer from a range of inherited illnesses, some of which are due to their trademark large heads and flat faces.

 *Bulldogs are one of the top five most expensive breeds when it comes to veterinary bills.*

Good breeding is helping to improve the health of individual dogs, but you would be a rare owner indeed if you did not need to visit the vet several times during your Bulldog's life - and that's in addition to his annual injections and check-up.

Bulldog training is an art in itself. If you expect your Bully to jump to your every command, you're in for disappointment. Bulldogs prefer to consider the command, and then ruminate on it a little longer...then decide whether or not to respond! Patience is the key if your little treasure is proving to be a tad strong-willed.

Before getting any breed of dog, it is important that all the family wants this new member of the household. There are far too many Bulldogs who become surplus to requirements and end up in rescue shelters or looking for a new home through no fault of their own.

## Becoming a Bulldog Owner

Once you've got a Bulldog, you'd better brush up on a few of the special terms used by lovers of the breed. To begin with, you are not a Bulldog owner, you have become a *Bulldogger!*

Your dog hasn't just got wrinkles, he has got a *roll* or *rope* over his nose, and his cheeks are known as *chops* or *flews.*

A *corkscrew* isn't something with which to open a bottle of wine while you sit back and watch his amusing antics, it's a type of tail to be avoided.

You should also know that many owners succumb to the temptation of becoming wardrobe assistants to their Bulldog - they just can't help but dress up their beloved pets in a variety of outfits.

Most Bulldogs do not object to being put into costumes, but if you do feel compelled to put Buster into a Batman outfit, make sure that it does not restrict his breathing, vision or hearing and that it is not too hot for him. Avoid dangly or small accessories that he could chew and choke on.

One thing the Bulldog does probably better than any other breed is sleep! Any time, any place, anywhere.

He can sleep on his tummy, his side or his back, he loves to doze with his humans, big and small. If you are ever feeling sad, visit YouTube and type in *"Bulldogs sleeping,"* the results are sure to cheer you up.

The Bulldog is a unique breed of dog whose health and happiness rely on a special kind of owner. Are you ready for the challenge? Read on to find out.

# 2. Complete History of the Bulldog

Few breeds have a history as long and as colourful as the Bulldog. To trace its true origins, we have to journey back in time through many centuries and even millennia.

There is some controversy over the exact roots of the breed, with some historians suggesting that the Pug was involved way back in the mists of time to reduce the size of the Bulldog - although this is strongly contested by other experts.

However, we can be pretty sure about the development of the breed over the last century, as there are many literary references and historical documents referring to Bulldogs and *Old English Bulldogs*, a breed that is now officially extinct, but which was the forerunner of today's Bulldog.

## The Beginning

The generally accepted theory is that the Bulldog is one of the breeds descended from the Alaunt, a war dog and protector of livestock and caravans. It was bred by the Alani tribes of the central Asian steppes, who were known as superb warriors, herdsmen and breeders of horses and dogs.

The Alaunt became extinct in the 17th century, but we know it resembled today's Caucasian Shepherd Dog, *pictured,* a breed with primitive origins going back over 2,000 years. The Russian name for the breed is *Volkodav,* which means wolf dog. Some of the Alaunt's ancestors lie with not so much a breed, but a category of dog: the *Mastiff,* which was also known as the *Molosser* or *Molossus.*

The Mastiff originated in ancient times with the Molossis people in the mountainous regions of north west Greece and southern Albania. They were known as ferocious hounds, used by shepherds to guard their flocks in the mountains. Some scholars describe the Molossus as having a wide, short muzzle and a heavy dewlap (similar to modern Mastiff breeds) and believe it was used to fight tigers, lions, elephants, and even men in battle.

A Roman copy of a Greek sculpture of a guard dog known as *The Jennings Dog (pictured below)* is generally considered to represent an ancient Molossus and can be seen at the British Museum in London.

There are many literary references to the Molossus. Former professor of ancient history, Jan Libourel, has written an interesting article for the American Bulldog Review at: http://www.american-bulldog.com/BHCol.html

He says: "The true Molossus dog was undeniably one of the most famous dogs of classical (Greco-Roman) antiquity. It is variously mentioned as a premier hunting dog, an aggressive guard dog and as a guardian and herder of cattle and sheep by many of the greatest writers in Greek and Latin literature over a period of 800 years."

The ancient Greek poet Virgil wrote of Molossus more than 2,000 years ago: "Never, with them on guard need you fear for your stalls a midnight thief, or onslaught of wolves, or Iberian brigands at your back."

Aristotle also mentions them in his History of Animals written in the 4<sup>th</sup> century BC: "Of the Molossian breed of dogs, such as are employed in the chase are pretty much the same as those elsewhere - but the sheep-dogs of this breed are superior to the others in size, and in the courage with which they face the attacks of wild animals."

The poet Grattius, who lived around the time of Jesus, wrote: "..when serious work has come, when bravery must be shown, and the impetuous War-god calls in the utmost hazard, then you could not but admire the renowned Molossians so much."

Today the term *Molosser* is still used by breeders to refer to a group of dogs. There is even a Molosser forum, which lists large breeds including the Bullmastiff, Fila Brasileiro, Spanish Mastiff, Neapolitan Mastiff, Tibetan Mastiff, Great Dane, Dogo Argentino, Boerboel, Dogue de Bordeaux, Cane Corso, and Japanese Tosa Inu. Just to confuse matters, none of these dogs are true "Mastiffs." This word *Mastiff* used in its correct sense today refers only to the English Mastiff.

Although the Bulldog is smaller, it is today still regarded as a Molosser, along with other diminutive breeds such as the American Bulldog, Staffordshire Bull Terrier, Pug and French Bulldog, to name but a few.

······································································································································································

## The Romans

The Romans invaded Britain in 55BC and their historians described the fierce Molossian dogs and the *"pugnace britannicii"* - fighting dogs of Britain - used in battles. These dogs were known as the *"broad-mouthed dogs of Britain"* and according to 1930s Bulldog historian R.H. Voss: "There is very little doubt that they were the original and remote ancestors of our Mastiff and Bulldog."

The Romans were mightily impressed with these fighting dogs, but whether they ever took them back to fight in the Roman amphitheatres is a matter of some conjecture - although it has been stated that they appointed an officer to select British dogs and export them to Rome.

The *"pugnaces"* of Britain were later mentioned around 390AD by the poet Claudian who distinguished them from all other dogs as being able to pull down a bull.

It was around this time that the Alaunt dogs spread from central Asia to Europe with the Western Alani tribes when they invaded Europe. The fierce Alaunts influenced many breeds in France, Spain, Portugal, England and other countries, spreading the use of the Alaunt name.

Because of all the new bloodlines introduced into the original breed, the word *"Alaunt"* came to describe a type of working dog rather than a specific breed.

And through breeding with various scent hounds and sight hounds, the Alaunt became a valued large game hunting dog in Europe, with different types being bred locally for different purposes. It was classified into three distinct types based on their physical appearance and duties:

- ❖ *Alaunt Gentil* was a light greyhound-type hunting dog

- ❖ *Alaunt Vautre (Veantre)* was an aggressive hunting type, also called the running Mastiff, known for hunting boars

- ❖ *Alaunt de Boucherie* was the traditional Mastiff-type used with livestock, which was also crucial in the development of the baiting dogs of France

It is this third type, known as **"the Alaunt Butchers"** in England, which many believe was the ancestor of today's Bulldog and other "bull breeds," as they were used to control and defend herds of cattle. However, some historians, including Jan Libourel, believe that the Bulldog's ancestor was not the huge Mastiff-type of Molossus, but the lighter, faster version used for hunting and herding, more like a greyhound or modern American Pit Bull Terrier.

It is likely that the Bulldog originated from the ancient Alaunt mixed with bloodlines of the fighting dogs of England. However, as you can see from the previous photos, today's Bulldog bears little resemblance to his ancient ancestors. One theory is that the descendants of these large ancient dogs were bred with the Pug to create the smaller breed of Bulldog, but this is hotly disputed by some scholars.

What most breed historians do agree on is that Bulldogs owe their name to the fact that they were once used to guard, control and bait bulls. (To **"bait"** is to taunt or harass).

# Bull-Baiting

Fast forward from the Alani's 4th century western invasion to the 1066 Norman Conquest of England, we can see how the Bulldog's ancestors began to change shape to fulfil a specific function: the baiting of bulls. At this time the training of bulls, bears, horses and other animals for the purpose of baiting them with dogs was practised by jugglers brought from France by the Norman conquerors.

As early as 1154 in the time of Henry II, bear and bull-baiting by dogs was a popular amusement in England. There are also several literary references from the Middle Ages to the sport of bull-baiting and the dogs that took part. Around 1406 the Duke of York wrote **"Mayster of Game"** in which he described the Alaunt, or Allen, as a dog with a large, short and thick head and short muzzle, which was remarkable for his courage. When he attacked an animal he hung on, and this dog was used in bull-baiting.

In the 1570s, physician and naturalist John Caius wrote a book called "**Of Englishe Dogges: The Diuersities, the Names, the Natures, and the Properties**" in which he described the **"Mastvve"** or **"Bandigge,"** (Bandog) as a vast, huge, stubborn, ugly and eager dog with a heavy and burdenous body, serviceable to **"bait and take the bull by the ear."** Two dogs at most were sufficient for that purpose, however untamable the bull might be. It was during the late 1500s that these prized "Bandogs" were exported to Spain to bait bulls there for the amusement of the Spanish aristocracy.

During the reigns of Mary, Elizabeth, James I, and Charles I (1553 to 1649), the baiting of bulls and full-grown bears by dogs was a very popular sport in England.

**FACT** 〉 *It was not until 1631 in the reign of Charles I that the name "Bulldog" was first mentioned.*

This was in a letter written by an Englishman called Prestwich Eaton from St. Sabastian in Spain to his friend George Wellingham in St. Swithin's Lane, London. He asked

for: *"A good Mastive dog, a case of liquor and I beg you to get for me some good bulldoggs"* to be sent out to him. This is proof that the Bulldog and the Mastiff were then becoming separate breeds.

Over the centuries, many crosses were made using Mastiffs and Bandogs, as well as various other breeds. In those days, bull-baiting and bear-baiting was the sport of kings, who used to regale ambassadors and other foreign dignitaries with the sport. There was a theatre built for the purpose in London called the Bankside Bear Garden where very large dogs were used for baiting the bull; historians believe they may have weighed around 90lb.

When James II came to the throne in 1685, the sport was shunned by the nobility. And from then until bull-baiting was banned in 1835, the rules changed so that the dog only had to "pin" the bull, which was now tethered, not roaming free. Specially trained dogs were set upon the bull one at a time, a successful attack resulting in the dog fastening his teeth strongly in the bull's nose. The Bulldog was bred especially for this sport.

The great dogs used when bull-baiting was the sport of kings were no longer wanted, or affordable to the common folk who now ran the sport.

*Much can happen to change any dog by selective breeding and it was in the 18th century that the Bulldog's trademark features emerged and the size of the dog was reduced to around 50lb.*

The following description given by the French Advocate Mission, who lived in England during the late 1600s, is taken from Chamber's Book of Days: "After a coming Bull-baiting had been advertised, the bull, decorated with flowers or coloured ribbons would be paraded round the streets of the town, and the dog which pulled off the favours in the subsequent baiting would be especially cheered by the spectators.

"The parade ended, the bull, with a rope tied round the root of his horns, would be fastened to a stake with an iron ring in it, situated in the centre of the ring."

**FACT** > *This new system of bull-baiting suited a medium-sized, active dog of moderately low stature with well laid-back nose and a protruding underjaw. From early writers' descriptions, we know that the Bulldog had a short muzzle, a massive head and a broad mouth.*

**The big, heavy head and powerful** jaws gave the dogs a vice-like grip on the bull, as well as helping to prevent the enraged beast from shaking the dog around and breaking its back. **The underjaw** projected beyond the upper to enable the dog to grasp the bull and to give him a firmer hold. The thick and strong lower jaw gave **the mouth** the appearance of curving upwards across the middle of the face.

**The top of the nose** inclined backwards to allow free passage of air into the nostrils while still holding on to the bull with its powerful jaws. **The rope** – or fold of skin across the face - channelled the blood away from the Bulldog's eyes. During bull-baiting, the dog would flatten itself to the ground, creeping as close to the bull as possible, then dart out and try to bite the bull on the nose or head. The bull would be tethered by a collar and rope to a stake in the ground. As the dog darted at the bull, the beast would try to catch the dog with his head and horns and throw it into the air.

Most of these fearless dogs were so tenacious that they would hold on to the bitter end and be tossed off rather than let go as the bulls swung them around violently in the air. A great many dogs were killed, more were badly maimed and some held so fast that by the bull swinging them, their teeth were often broken out. Often the men were tossed as well as the dogs.

During my research, I have come across historical reports written at or near the time of bull-baiting events that describe in some detail the gory fates that met these incredibly brave dogs when they refused to give up, even when they were dying. They are distressing to read and I have chosen to omit them.

By the time Queen Anne came to the throne in England in 1702, the cruel blood sport of bull-baiting was practised twice a week at a place called Hockley-in-the-Hole (now Clerkenwell), London.

It was also fairly common in provincial towns. At Stamford in Lincolnshire and Tutbury, Staffordshire, a bull was tied to an iron stake so that it could only move within a 30ft radius. The aim was for the dogs to immobilise the bull. Before the event started, the bull's nose was blown full of pepper to enrage the animal, which was often placed in a hollow in the ground.

Bull baiting may have begun as early as the 13th century in Lincolnshire. The ancient text *"Survey of Stamford"* describes one theory as to how it began in that town: "William, Earl Warren, lord of this town in the time of King John (A.D.1199 to 1216), standing upon the castle walls of Stamford, saw two bulls fighting for a cow in the meadow till all the butchers' dogs, great and small, pursued one of the bulls (being maddened with noise and multitude) clean through the town.

"This sight so pleased the said earl that he gave all those meadows (called the Castle Meadows) where first the bull duel began for a common to the butchers of the town, after the first grass was eaten, on condition they find a mad bull the day six weeks before Christmas Day for the continuance of that sport every year."

**FACT** *Bull-baiting was not only practised as a form of entertainment. In early modern England, many towns had by-laws regulating the sale of meat, which stipulated that bulls' flesh should be baited before any bull was slaughtered and sold!*

The practice was based on what seems to us nowadays a rather strange belief that the meat would be more tender and nutritious if the animal had been baited. This belief was so strong that the meat from a bull that had not been baited was considered improper for consumption, and a butcher who sold it was liable to a penalty.

A graphic description of the Bulldog can be found in the 1800 Cynographia Britannica written by Sydenham Edwards: "...head round and full, muzzle short, ears small... chest wide, body round, with the limbs very muscular and strong; the tail... rarely erected (..). the most striking character is the under-jaw almost uniformly projecting beyond the upper..."

The Bulldog was the breed of choice for dog fighting throughout the 1700s. But in the 1800s, the followers of this barbaric sport wanted a quicker dog in the pit and so crossed the Bulldog with various types of larger terriers used to kill rats and foxes. These dogs became known as Bull Terriers and combined the alertness and speed of the terrier with the indomitable courage and fighting instinct of the Bulldog.

## America and Bull-Baiting

England wasn't the only country to host the bloodthirsty spectacle of bull-baiting; in the 18th century it was also one of America's favourite pastimes. The journal of the American Revolution states that in 1774 the cruel blood sport of bull-baiting had crossed the Atlantic, along with other customs, and was still practised long after the American Revolution ended.

According to Jennie Holliman's **American Sports 1785-1835**: "British troops stationed in America during the Revolution and until 1783 played a part in establishing certain English sports in the States, an impetus being given to bull baiting and cockfighting during this time.

"…For the purpose of the sport, dogs of undisputed pedigree were kept, usually bull dogs. Many butchers kept dogs and buffaloes for animal baiting. The wildest and fiercest bulls of the neighborhood were selected for a bull bait."

Large crowds of spectators gathered behind a circular enclosure as a chained bull would face off against six to eight bull dogs, which oftentimes were immediately killed, Holliman explains.

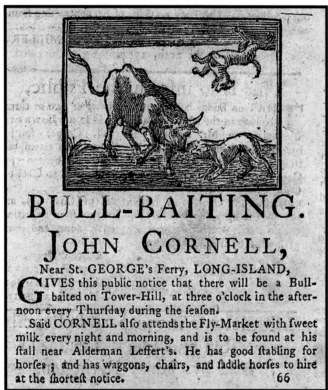

**BULL-BAITING.**

**JOHN CORNELL,**

Near St. GEORGE's Ferry, LONG-ISLAND,
GIVES this public notice that there will be a Bull-baited on Tower-Hill, at three o'clock in the afternoon every Thurſday during the ſeaſon.

Said CORNELL alſo attends the Fly-Market with ſweet milk every night and morning, and is to be found at his ſtall near Alderman Leffert's. He has good ſtabling for horſes; and has waggons, chairs, and ſaddle horſes to hire at the ſhorteſt notice.
66

In his July 28, 1774, **New-York Gazetteer**, printer James Rivington published a bull-baiting advertisement for John Cornell. Apparently the blood sport had such a draw that a "season" of weekly bull-baiting matches was scheduled. **Pictured here is the original public notice.**

However, the Bulldog's early role was not limited to sport in America. In mid-17th century New York, they were used as a part of a city-wide round-up effort led by Richard Nicolls, the first English colonial governor of New York province. Because cornering and leading wild bulls was dangerous, Bulldogs were trained to seize a bull by its nose long enough for a rope to be secured around the animal's neck.

Back in England, bull-baiting began to decline in the early 19th century. In the Parliamentary Record of April 18th, 1800 William Wyndham, the Secretary of War, spoke in defence of the Bulldog in the debate on bull-baiting.

The record states: "He certainly admitted that the practice of bull-baiting was very different from the manly, athletic exercises he had just mentioned, because there was some degree of cruelty in tormenting an animal; but even this had its use; it served to cultivate the qualities and keep up the breed of those useful animals called bull-dogs—a breed which he was sorry to see degenerating very much, so as to be nearly lost.

"England had long been famous for this breed of dog, and they were mentioned by Grattius so early as the days of Augustus; even some of our ships had taken their names from those animals. But the practice of bull-baiting was objected to on the ground of its cruelty, and that too by the very men who gave their sanction to the game laws, and monopolised to themselves the noble practice of shooting."

## Lion-Baiting

One other bizarre sport that was occasionally organised for the amusement of the public was lion-baiting. There were some interesting characters involved in this sport and Bulldog breeding in the

19th century, some of whom appear to have stepped straight out of the pages of a Charles Dickens novel.

Bill George (1802–1881) was a well-known dog dealer who started out as a butcher's boy, then bare-knuckle prize-fighter before becoming apprentice to Old English Bulldog dealer Ben White, from a rough area in north London known as Kensal New Town. Although now officially extinct, in those days the Old English Bulldog was a muscular fighting dog around 15 inches tall weighing some 45lb. It was no doubt the forerunner of today's Bulldog.

> NOTE: The Olde English Bulldogge is an American breed (not recognised by the American Kennel Club) which dates back to the 1970s when David Leavitt, of Coatesville, PA, set about trying to recreate the *"Regency Period Bull Baiter."* His aim was to breed a dog with the look, health and athleticism of the original bull-baiting dogs, but with a mellow temperament.
>
> The foundation crosses were half Bulldog and half a mix of Bullmastiff, American Pit Bull Terrier and American Bulldog. These dogs, although not officially recognised as a breed, do physically look more like the athletic Bulldog of 200 years ago. On January 1st 2014, the United Kennel Club in the USA adopted a Breed Standard for the Olde English Bulldogge.

In 1825, White and George provided the dogs for two lion-baiting contests organised by a promoter called Wombwell. The event, held on July 26th, involved three Old English Bulldogs and a lion named Nero in an enclosure at the Old Factory Yard near Warwick. The dogs were fallow coloured – reddish brown – and were named Captain, Tiger and Turk.

Spectators paid a small fortune to watch the sorry, cruel spectacle. The Bulldogs were incredibly brave, they rushed at Nero, "pinning" him by the nose and face. Although the gently-natured lion repeatedly roared with pain and fended off the dogs with his paws, he refused to bite them.

After two dogs were taken away maimed, Turk, the lightest of the three Old English Bulldogs, showed incredible courage for which the Old English Bulldog was famous in those days:

"Left entirely alone with an animal twenty times its weight, (he) continued the battle with unabated fury and though bleeding all over from the effect of the lion's claws, seized and pinned him by the nose at least half a dozen times; when, at length, releasing himself with a desperate effort, the lion flung his whole weight upon the dog and held him lying between his fore paws for more than a minute, during which time he could have bitten his head off a hundred times over, but did not make the slightest effort to hurt him.

"Poor Turk was then taken away by the dog-keepers, grievously mangled but still alive and seized the lion, for at least the twentieth time, the very same moment that he was released from under him."

The public were outraged at the promotion of such baiting spectacles, and the matter was raised in Parliament and Wombwell's lion baits were the last to be staged in the United Kingdom.

........................................................................................................................................................

## Birth of the Modern Breed

Earlier, in 1802, a bill to abolish bull-baiting was issued in the House of Commons. But the sport continued legally until 1835 when the Cruelty to Animals Act was passed in Parliament outlawing "Blood Sport" in Great Britain – although the practice continued illegally in large towns and cities for about another 45 years.

With the banning of bull-baiting, the Bulldog's work was suddenly over. The breed had also acquired a reputation for being vicious - indeed, it had been bred for its bravery and tenacity, to fight to the death - and the Bulldog rapidly went into decline.

*The Natural History of Dogs, Volume X* printed in 1840, just five years after the banning of bull-baiting, very graphically describes the strength and ferocity of these early Bulldogs. Their bravery and tenacity was second to none. They sometimes wore leather armour for hunting and there is reference to the spiked collar, which has become synonymous with the Bulldog today:

"In stature the present race is of moderate size, but entirely moulded for strength and elasticity; the head is large; the forehead sinks between the eyes, and the line of the nose rises again at a considerable angle; the lower jaw projects beyond the upper, often showing the teeth, which altogether, with the frequent redness about the eyelids, produces a most forbidding aspect; the ears are partially drooping, unless the terrier blood is crossed in the animal; and the tail is carried high.

"The present breed is commonly ochry or reddish buff with the nose and chops alone black. Formerly when the brindled breed, always preferred on the Continent, was ex-ported for strengthening the wolf and boar packs of hounds, the ears were always cropped; and we have seen leather armour, consisting of a breast-piece and cap, with holes for the eyes, made of studded leather, which were used, along with a spiked collar, for some valuable dogs to engage the boar or wolf, and protected them effectually; indeed such a defence, where the breed was scarce, may have been necessary, from the unceremonious mode of attacking and indomitable pertinacity the dogs evince when once excited; never letting go the hold they have, even if mutilated, as if there was some spasm in the jaws to prevent their unlocking.

"The bull-dog differs from all others, even from the mastiff, in giving no warning of his attack by barking; he grapples his opponent without in the least estimating their comparative weight or powers. We have seen one pinning an American bison and holding his nose down, till the animal gradually brought forward its hind feet, and, crushing the dog to death, tore his muzzle out of the fangs, most dreadfully mangled.

"We have known another hallooed on to attack a disabled eagle; the bird, unable to escape, threw himself on the back, and, as the dog sprang at his throat, struck him with his claws, one of which penetrating the skull, killed him instantly, and caused the butcher, his master, the loss of a valued animal, and one hundred dollars in the wager."

**FACT** ❯ *If it had not been for some keen enthusiasts, the breed may have died out completely. But interest remained among some working class men who began carefully breeding Bulldogs with attention to their trademark physical features, but breeding out the dog's aggressive nature.*

They organised small evening shows in public houses, where their dogs paraded on the sanded floors of tap rooms. The landlord usually provided the prizes, though sometimes the working men themselves clubbed together to contribute a handsome silver collar or similar prize. At this time, the

Bulldog was far more of a functional dog than today's Bulldog. It had longer legs, neck and tail, a longer muzzle and was sleeker, more athletic in build. **Crib and Rosa** is an 1817 painting by Samuel Raven **(right)** which depicts two famous Old English Bulldogs. Both dogs had deep chests, extremely well-defined muscle tone, roach backs and low tails.

The painting was frequently referred to by the new Bulldog exhibitors as an ideal form of the breed, and Rosa was regarded as the foundation for the modern Bulldog. Through an engraving, this painting became the best-known and most reproduced painting of any dogs from that period.

In Hugh Dalziels's book (c.1879) *"British Dogs, their Varieties, History, Characteristics, Breeding, Management and Exhibition,"* Mr. F.G.W. Crafer, Honorary Secretary of the Bulldog Club, wrote: "The outline of Rosa, in the well-known print of "Crib and Rosa," is considered to represent perfection in the shape, make, and size of the ideal type of the bulldog.

"The only exception that has ever been taken is that it has been alleged to be deficient in wrinkles about the head and neck, and also in substance of bone in the limbs. This, however, does not alter the fact of its being a correct representation of the true type of the old-fashioned bulldog. Some allowance should be made for her sex - never as grand and well developed as dogs - and her position in the drawing."

This is a description of the ideal body shape of the 19th century Bulldog from the same book: "The body of the dog is (like that of man) broad and deep in the shoulders and chest, and small in the waist, the forelegs appearing short on account of the deep chest and muscular shoulders.

"The back short and strong, long-backed animals being weak, slow, and unwieldy, easily fatigued, and having a loose, shuffling, and disjointed manner of moving. The hind legs large and muscular, with plenty of propelling power and, like the greyhound's, long in proportion to his forelegs, raising the loins into an arch higher than the shoulders, so as to bring his hind legs well under him, and enable him to spring quickly high off the ground. The belly small and well gathered up; and the flank, under the loins, hollow to lighten him as much as possible of useless weight.

"The wrinkles on the head, the length of the tail, the colour, and other minor points much insisted on by modern fanciers, however much to be admired, were, and ought still to be, of secondary importance to (instead of taking precedence of) a correct general formation, and especially of the square protruding lower jaw, the broad mouth, and receding nose."

One of the 19th century Bulldog breeders was Bill George. When his employer, dog dealer Ben White, died in the same year that bull-baiting was outlawed, George bought the premises from his widow and renamed them Canine Castle. Aware that he would have to create a new clientele for the business to continue, George shifted the focus from the Bulldog as a fighter to the Bulldog as a companion animal, giving the breed new life.

In 1840, he imported Big Headed Billy, one of the large Spanish Bulldogs used for bull-baiting on the Iberian peninsula. Billy was brindle pied (white and brindle) in colour and his grandson was George's famous white dog, Dan, which weighed 65 lb and was sold for the huge sum of £100. *This photo* shows one of today's fierce-looking Spanish Bulldogs (still called Alano Espanols) with cropped ears.

The Alano Espanol is believed to be directly descended from the dogs used for bull-baiting in Spain hundreds of years ago. Incredibly it has kept the name Alano, from the Alani tribe that invaded Europe 1,600 years ago.

Today the breed weighs anything up to 90lb and is massively bigger than the (English) Bulldog of the 21st century.

.........................................................................................................................................

## French Bulldogs

Back in the mid-1800s, George was breeding Bulldogs in three sizes. One of these was a new line of *"Toy Bulldogs"* that began to be exhibited once dog shows started in 1860. At the same time, lace workers from Nottingham in England no longer had work at home due to the Industrial Revolution.

Many left and settled in Normandy, France, taking their dogs, including many miniature Bulldogs with them. These dogs sparked a craze, and English breeders like George sent over Bulldogs that they considered to be too small, or with faults such as pricked up ears.

A decade or two later, there were few miniature Bulldogs left in England, such was their popularity in France. These dogs were highly fashionable and sought after by everyone from society ladies to Parisian prostitutes! They also became popular with creative types such as artists, writers and fashion designers.

The small Bulldog type gradually became thought of as a breed, and received a name, the ***Bouledogue Francais*** - or French Bulldog. (In French, *"dogue"* means Mastiff or Molosser). French Bulldogs were introduced to the United States in 1885 when they were imported in order to set up an American-based breeding program. They were mostly owned by society ladies, who first displayed them at the Westminster Kennel Club Dog Show in 1896.

On April 29th, 1899 Country Life Magazine stated: "Some five-and-thirty years ago in fact, [i.e. about 1864], the small-sized or light-weight Bulldog was common in this country; so much so that dogs of the breed that scaled over 28 lb were not encouraged at such shows as Birmingham, which was at that period the most important exhibition of its kind in England.

"Then by some freak of fashion the Toy Bulldog became all the rage in Paris, with the result that the celebrated Bill George, of Canine Castle, Kensal New Town, the most eminent dog dealer of his or any other day, received carte blanche commissions from French customers to procure them light-weight Bulldogs, and by this means England was denuded of all the best specimens."

George became famous for his Bulldogs during his lifetime, being featured in Punch magazine and Charles Dickens is believed to have visited him when researching Bull's Eye, Bill Sikes' Bulldog in Oliver Twist (1837-39).

But the Bulldog's true salvation came with the arrival of the era of the conformation dog show, which began in 1859, although a Bulldog was not present at the first show.

.........................................................................................................................................

## Dog Shows – the Bulldog's Salvation

The breed experienced a new surge of interest and lease of life with the introduction of conformation dog shows. James Hinks is credited with being one of the first Bulldog exhibitors. One of the first shows where he exhibited was held at the Birmingham Agricultural Hall in

December 1860. The show attracted an entry of 40 Bulldogs, including the famous red male, King Dick – also known as Old King Dick - owned by Jacob Lamphier. King Dick had a very successful show career and went on to become the first show champion.

These original show Bulldogs came in three types and sizes:

1. The dog which had been specifically bred to bait the bull from 1735 "when this dog first attained a very definite type" until bull baiting was abolished in 1835 and which since 1835 had maintained its existence by reason, first of a dog fighter and later of pot house shows. These dogs generally varied from 45lb to 50lb in weight, similar to today's Bulldog.

2. The big Mastiff-type dogs (the remnants of the original 90lb Bulldogs), which had by now been reduced to 60lb. These dogs received a stimulus by the importation of the famous Spanish Bulldog, Big-Headed Billy, in 1840.

3. Small dogs weighing 12lb to 25lb which had been produced by inbreeding smaller Bulldogs (and probably by crossing these with Pugs from 1835 to 1845) and which went on to provide the foundation of the French Bulldog.

**FACT** ⟩ *In 1864, the world's first breed club was formed by man called R.S. Rockstro with the motto "Stranglehold," or "Hold Fast," and had about 30 members. Their declared aim was: "The perpetuation and improvement of the Old English Bulldog."*

Unfortunately, the club only lasted three years, but this was long enough for the ***Philo-Kuon*** Breed Standard to be written, named after the nom-de-plume of its author, Samuel Wickens. ***Philo kuon*** means "dog lover" in Greek.

The original Bulldog was a ferocious fighting dog, and the breeders who stuck to the Philo Kuon standard bred a dog that retained some of these pugilistic qualities, but which were also suitable as companions. These dogs would attack on command and became known as excellent family protectors, but they were also easy to control.

The printed Philo Kuon Breed Standard stated: "The English Bulldog is a majestic, ancient animal, very scarce, much maligned and as a rule, very little understood. .........but brought up in kindness, constant communication and attention from the owner, the dog is calm and docile, but if it is on the circuit without attention, it becomes far less sociable and obedient, but excited, can burn up so much that it becomes very dangerous for the environment. Dogs of this breed are excellent guards, excellent swimmers, are very valuable for breeding with terriers, Pointer, hounds, Greyhound, etc, to give them courage and endurance. This is the most bold and determined animal."

"Venturesome, daring and fearless, he will fight to the last drop of blood. This noble dog becomes degenerate abroad – in truth he is a national animal, and is perfectly identified with old England – and he is a dog of which Englishmen may be proud."

*Picture: T. Wood's portrait of Captain G. Holdworth's white Bulldog, Sir Anthony born 1872. His sire was Crib by Duke II out of Rush, his dam was Meg by Old King Dick out of Old Nell. Sir Anthony took first prize in the Open Class at the Crystal Palace, 1874.*

The Philo Kuon standard also stated that the Bulldog should be least 20lb (9kg) and rarely exceed 60lb (27kg). Owners tested these athletic Bulldogs extensively in various activities, such as throwing wooden planks into a churning ocean from 15ft cliffs.

The Philo-Kuon Bulldogs would plunge off the cliffs into white caps and drag the planks to shore! It is interesting that the Bulldog was a good swimmer. The heavy body and short legs of today's Bulldog means that most can't swim.

**FACT** ⟩ *The Philo-Kuon Bulldog was used to create many fine bull breeds around the world. English breeders sold top dogs to the Germans, and the modern Boxer is at least 50% descended from Philo-Kuon bloodlines.*

Among historians, there is some confusion about the dog Crib. Some saying that all Bulldogs were based on Rosa from Samuel Raven's 1817 painting, and others saying that the modern Bulldog was based on Crib. And if you read that Sir Anthony was sired by Crib, you might wonder how a dog that was painted in 1817 lived to father another dog some 56 years later, a remarkable feat - even for a determined Bulldog!

The answer, I believe, is simple - there were two Cribs; the name was not uncommon among Bulldogs at that time. And in fact, the conformation of the modern Bulldog is based on the ideals of Rosa in the early painting as well as the bloodlines of the champion show dog of the 1870s called Crib. This dog was also known as Turton's Crib after its owner, Mr. T. Turton.

The dog is listed in the "English Bulldog Pedigree Database" (an unofficial register for mainly Bulldog bloodlines in Europe) as being born in 1871 and bred by Fred Lamphier, son of the famous Bulldog breeder Jacob Lamphier.

Turton's Crib, *pictured,* was never beaten in the show ring and went on to become English Champion. Four of the Bulldog's foundation bloodlines originated with Crib. These were through the following dams:

❖ **Rose,** (owned by Mr. Berrie) who gave rise to the Monarch champion show dogs

❖ **Meg** (owned by Fred Lamphier), whose bloodlines produced the brindle male Tiger, that in turn bred the champions Richard the Lionheart, Redova, the white bulldog Sir Anthony (pictured on the pervious page) and many others

❖ **Miss Smiff** (owner P. Rust), who bred Sancho Panza, L'Ambassador, the first champion of the American-bred champion Rodney Stone, and many others

❖ **Kit** (owner V. Beckett), bred the champion lines of Dryads and Dimbulah

Amongst the finest champions and stud dogs of the day were: Mr. Raper's Tiger - full brother to Sir Anthony, Mr. Berrie's Monarch, Mr. Shirley's Sancho Panza, Mr. Pearl's Duke, Mr. Benjamin's Smasher, Mr. Shaw's Sepoy, Mr. Verinder's Slenderman, Mr. Ball's Lord Nelson, Capt. Holdsworth's Doon Brae, Mr. Webb's Faust, and especially Mr. Donkin's Byron *(pictured)* and Mr. Raper's Richard Coeur de Lion.

BULLDOG.
Mr. B. H. Donkin's BYRON. Sire, Mr. Gibbon's Dan, out of Rose, by Tiger out of Rush ; Tiger by Crib.

They were particularly admired: "for their possession of the broad lower jaw, with the six front teeth in an even row - the chief bulldog point to be produced and transmitted, and in which too many of Crib's descendants show a deplorable deficiency."

# The Original Breed Standard

April 4th, 1873 saw the formation of The Kennel Club. One of its priorities was the Kennel Club Stud Book, or pedigree register, and the Bulldog was listed in the first-ever version. The first Bulldog ever listed register was Adam (Adamo), born 1864, belonging to Mr. R. Heathfield and bred by Jacob Lamphier.

Imports of Spanish Bulldogs continued, boosting numbers and making the large Bulldogs even bigger, although only four or five kennels used these imported studs. These Spanish dogs incensed the Bulldog breeders of England, who swore by their by-now 50lb dogs. This was one of the main factors that led to the formation of The Bulldog Club, the world's oldest single breed association, at the Blue Post Inn on London's Oxford Street in 1875.

The Club held its annual exhibition of Bulldogs in London, offering trophies and medals for competitions among members in other cities. The new Bulldog Club drew up a Breed Standard very similar to the original Philo Kuon Breed Standard below, which remained largely unchanged in the UK for over a century.

> *The UK Bulldog Breed Standard was slightly revised in 2008 to soften some of the Bulldog's trademark features to improve the health of the breed.*

The ultimate aim of the original Breed Standard was to preserve the distinctive features of the Bulldog, which had been bred for a specific purpose over centuries.

Even though that purpose was now defunct, the Bulldog had a unique and distinctive look that enthusiasts were keen to preserve. They also set about breeding the aggression out of the dog – a task at which they were particularly successful.

Here is the original 1870s Breed Standard laid down by the Bulldog Club. The number in brackets is the maximum number of points out of 100 that the show judges of the day could award for perfection. You will see that great importance was placed on the size of the head, and also that black, once a popular Bulldog colour, was no longer desirable:

1. **General appearance. (10)** – The general appearance of the bulldog is that of a smooth coated thick set dog, rather low in stature, about 18in. high at the shoulder, but broad, powerful, and compact. Its head strikingly massive, and very large in proportion to the dog's size. Its face extremely short, with nose almost between the eyes. Its muzzle very broad, blunt, truncated, and inclined upwards. Its body short and well knit; the limbs stout and muscular. Its hind quarters very high and strong, but rather lightly made in comparison with its massive fore parts. The dog conveys an impression of determination, strength, and activity, similar to that suggested by the appearance of a thick set Ayrshire or Highland bull.

2. **Skull. (15)** The head (or skull) should be very large - the larger the better - and in circumference should measure round in front of the ears at least the height of the dog at the shoulder. Viewed from the front, it should be very high from the corner of the lower jaw to the apex of the skull; it should also be broad and square. The cheeks should be well rounded, and extend sideways beyond the eyes. Viewed at the side, the head should be very high, and very short from its back to the point of the nose. The forehead should be flat, neither prominent, rounded, nor overhanging the face; and the skin upon it and about the head very loose, hanging in large folds or wrinkles.

3. **Stop. (5)** The temples or frontal bones should be very prominent, broad, square, and high, causing a groove between the eyes. This indentation is termed the 'Stop,' it should be both broad and deep, and extended up the middle of the forehead, dividing the head vertically, and be traceable at the top of the skull.

4. **Eyes. (5)** The eyes (seen from the front), should be situated low down in the skull, as far from the ears as possible. Their corners should be in a straight line at right angles with the stop, and quite in front of the head. They should be as wide apart as possible, provided their outer corners are within the outline of the cheeks. They should be quite round in shape, of moderate size, neither sunken nor prominent, and in colour should be as dark as possible, showing no white when looking directly forward.

5. **Ears. (5)** The ears should be set on high, i.e., the front inner edge of each ear should (as viewed from the front) join the outline of the skull at the top corner of such outline, so as to place them as wide apart and as high and far from the eyes as possible. In size they should be small and thin. The shape termed 'rose ear' is the most correct. The 'rose ear' folds inwards at its back, the upper or front edge, curving over outwards and backwards, showing part of the inside of the burr.

6. **Face. (5)** The face, measured from the front of the cheek bone to the nose, should be as short as possible; its skin should be deeply and closely wrinkled. The muzzle should be short, broad, square, not pointed, turned upwards, and very deep from the corner of the eye to the corner of the mouth. The nose should be large, broad, and black its top should be deeply set back, almost between the eyes. The distance from the inner corner of the eye (or from the centre of the stop between the eyes) to the extreme tip of the nose should not exceed the length from the tip of the nose to the edge of the under lip. The nostrils should be large, wide, and black, with a well-defined straight line between them.

*Picture: "Six Bulldogs, end of 19th Century," by Ward Binks.*

7. **Chop. (5)** The flews, called the 'chop,' should be thick, broad, pendent, and very deep, hanging completely over the lower jaw at the side (not in front). They should join the under lip in front and quite cover the teeth, which should not be seen when the mouth is closed.

8. **Mouth. (5)** The jaws, more especially the lower, should be broad, massive, and square, not in any way pinched or pointed, the canine teeth, or tusks, wide apart. The lower jaw should project considerably in front of the upper, and turn up. It should be very broad and square, and have the six small front teeth between the canines in an even row. The teeth should be large and strong.

9. **Neck and Chest. (5)** The neck should be moderate in length, rather short than long, very thick, deep, and strong. It should be well arched at the back, with much loose, thick, and wrinkled skin hanging about the throat, forming a double dewlap on each side from the lower jaw to the chest. The chest should be very wide laterally, round, prominent, and deep, making the dog appear very broad and short-legged in front.

10. **Shoulders. (5)** The shoulders should be broad, slanting, deep, and very powerful.

11. **Body. (5)** The barrel should be capacious, round, and deep. It should be very deep from the top of the shoulders to its lowest part, where it joins the chest, and be well let down between the fore legs. It should be large in diameter, and round

behind the fore legs (not flat-sided, the ribs being well rounded). The body should be well ribbed up behind, with the belly tucked up, and not pendulous.

12. **Back. (5)** The back should be short, broad, and strong, very broad at the shoulders and comparatively narrow at the loins. There should be a slight fall in the back close behind the shoulders (its lowest part), whence the spine should rise to the loins (the top of which should be higher than the top of the shoulder), thence curving again more suddenly to the tail, forming an arch - (a distinctive characteristic of the breed) - termed 'roach back,' or, more correctly, 'wheel back.'

13. **Tail. (5)** The tail, termed the 'stern,' should be set on low, jut out rather straight, and then turn downwards, the end pointing horizontally. It should be quite round in its whole length, smooth, and devoid of fringe or coarse hair. It should be moderate in length - rather short than long - thick at the root, and tapering rather quickly to a fine point. It should have a downward carriage (not having a decided upward curve at the end or being screwed or deformed), and the dog should, from its shape and position, not be able to raise it over his back.

14. **Fore Legs. (5)** The fore legs should be very stout and strong, set wide apart, thick, muscular, and straight, with well-developed calves, presenting a rather bowed outline, but the bones of the legs should be large and straight, not bandy or curved. They should be rather short in proportion to the hind legs, but not so short as to make the back appear long, or to detract from the dog's activity and so cripple him.

15. The elbows should be low and stand well away from the ribs. The ankles, or pasterns, should be short, straight, and strong. The fore feet should be straight, and turn very slightly inwards; they should be of medium size, and moderately round. Toes short, compact, and thick, being well split up, making the knuckles prominent and high.

16. **Hind Legs. (5)** The hind legs should be large and muscular, and longer in proportion than the fore legs, so as to elevate the loins. The hocks should be very slightly bent and well let down, so as to be long and muscular from the loins to the point of the hock. The lower part of the leg should be short, straight, and strong. The stifles should be round, and turn slightly outwards away from the body. The hocks are thereby made to approach each other, and the hind feet to turn outwards. The latter, like the fore feet, should be round and compact, with the toes short, well split up and the knuckles prominent. From his formation, the dog has a peculiar heavy, slouching, and constrained gait, appearing to walk with short quick steps on the tips of his toes, his hind feet not be lifted high, but appearing to skim the ground, and often running with the one shoulder rather advanced, similar to the manner of a horse in cantering.

17. **Size. (5)** The most desirable size for the bulldog, and at which excellence is mostly attained, is about 50lb.

18. **Coat and Colour. (5)** The coat should be fine in texture, short, close, and smooth (hard only from its shortness and closeness, not wiry or woolly). The colour should be whole or smut, that is, a whole colour with a black mask or muzzle. It should be brilliant and pure of its sort. As 'a good horse cannot be of a bad colour,' the same may be said of the dog if perfect in other points. The colours, in their order of merit, if bright and pure, are, first smuts, and whole brindles, reds, white, with their varieties, as whole fawns, fallows, etc.; second, pied and mixed colours. Black, which was once most esteemed, is now considered undesirable.

# The Bulldog Arrives in the United States

In the late 1870s and 1880s, Bulldogs began to be imported to the United States. One of the first dogs to be shown was Donald, a brindle-and-white exhibited by Sir William Verner in the 1880 New York dog show. According to the famous judge Enno Meyer: *"Donald lacked somewhat in substance, but he had a rather good head."*

The leading imported Bulldogs of the day were two littermates: Colonel John E. Thayer's Robinson Crusoe and his sister and English champion, Britomartis. She took first place at the New York shows from 1885 to 1890, and Robinson Crusoe was the first national champion in 1888.

Another very famous dog of the period was Handsome Dan, *pictured.* In 1889, Andrew B. Graves saw a Bulldog sitting in front of a New Haven blacksmith shop. Graves was an Englishman in the Yale class of 1892 and a member of the crew team as well as a footballer.

He offered $50 for the dog, the blacksmith countered with $75 and they settled on $65. Graves cleaned up the dog and named him "Handsome Dan." The dog followed him everywhere around campus, including to sporting events, and the Yale students quickly adopted him as their mascot.

**FACT** ❭ *Handsome Dan is believed to be the first live mascot in the world. Since the original, a further 16 dogs have held the position of Yale mascot.*

Dan's modern successors are selected on the basis of their ability to tolerate bands and children, cleanliness and, most importantly, their negative reaction to the colour crimson and tigers - the symbols of rivals Harvard and Princeton!

On April 1, 1890, The Bulldog Club of America was founded in the Mechanics Hall, Boston, by H.D. Kendall of Lowell, Massachusetts. Its aim was the "Unification of efforts to support the deliberate and serious breeding of bulldogs in America, preserving the purity of form, to improve the quality of the local population, as well as to put an end to the unwanted bias, in the public mind in relation to this wonderful breed" and to encourage "the thoughtful and careful breeding of the English Bulldog in America."

The Club was originally composed of a small group of men in the north eastern United States, but membership soon grew country-wide. Six years later, members came to the conclusion that the English Breed Standard was not sufficiently clear, and so they wrote their own version for America, which, with a few minor refinements, is today's AKC Breed Standard. In 1950 the structure of The Bulldog Club of America was revamped to make it a national organisation.

In the 1890s, the only major dog show in America was the Westminster Kennel Club's annual event held at the old Madison Square Garden in New York City. For the first 10 to 15 years, the Bulldog entry was an indifferent collection entered by scattered breeders, generally running from five to 10 exhibits in all.

But in 1891, the newly-formed Bulldog Club of America backed the show in an organised fashion. The Club offered the unheard of total of 16 cups, medals, and cash prizes for the breed, and the Bulldog entry jumped to 51, several times the number of specimens ever before exhibited at a single dog show.

At this time, American bloodlines relied on the importation of pedigree champions from top producers in England. Three of the most famous were imported by R.B. Sawyer; they were:

**Harper,** a male from the champion British Monarch; the arrival of this great dog caused a sensation in Bulldog circles as well as receiving considerable attention in the press. Harper became the first winner of one of two historic silver trophies awarded by the BCA, the Parke Cup (renamed the Grand Trophy).

The females **Graven Image** and **Holy Terror** were also brought in, *pictured with another top dog, Bathos, to the right of them.*

In 1901, Richard Croker's newly-imported champion Rodney Stone won the Grand Trophy, and he became the first Bulldog ever to command a price of $5,000, when he was bought by controversial Irish-American political figure Richard Croker. The BCA's introduction of prestigious trophies and prizes triggered the heyday for Bulldog showing, which culminated in 1904 when Bulldogs led the entries at all the major USA dog shows.

The great champion La Roche won the Grand Trophy in 1905 and repeated the win in 1906. In 1913, Strathway Prince Albert, the only Bulldog ever to win Best in Show at Westminster, won the cup and returned to win it again in both 1914 and 1915.

The Bulldog Club of America initially hampered efforts to establish other Bulldog clubs in order to maintain a monopoly on the breed. Regional organisations were denied recognition and there were many heated debates. These finally culminated in the successful recognition of the Philadelphia Bulldog Club in 1907.

During these early days, there were many scandals and allegations of fraud and rigged prize-giving in the United States! After several unsuccessful attempts, the Chicago Bulldog Club was finally allowed to conduct its own show in 1916, followed in 1923 by the Pacific Coast Club.

THE BULLDOGS THE GRAVEN IMAGE, HOLY TERROR, AND BATHOS.

In 1972, the BCA first published a quarterly magazine entitled *"The Bulldogger"* which is the name now given to fans of the breed. Today the organisation has eight regional divisions.

Incidentally, the American Bulldog has an entirely different - and even longer - history in the Americas. In the Depression of the early 1700s, British immigrants arrived, bringing their dogs with them. Many of them settled on farms in Georgia and used their Bulldogs as versatile working dogs to protect property, pen cattle and even to hunt wild boar. The farmers selected the biggest and strongest dogs to breed from.

## The Bulldog's Changing Temperament

Although the ideal size and shape of the Bulldog was hotly contested by the various fanciers and breeders in the mid to late 19th century, it is clear that their efforts to rid the Bulldog of its ferocity and aggression and turn it into a companion dog were highly successful.

It is interesting to note two things: firstly, that the Bulldog's character trait of being wonderful with children dates back more than 125 years. Secondly, in the 19th century, the Bulldog was still regarded as an excellent guard dog.

F.G.W. Crafer wrote about the Bulldog of the day in *"British Dogs; Their Varieties, History, Characteristics, Breeding, Management and Exhibition"* published around 1879. He says: "…it may be said that the manners also make the dog; if a dog is capable of being trained to the perfection of canine intelligence and fidelity, he ought not to be undeservedly condemned. There are many people who can testify and prove that the bulldog can be so trained "precisely."

"Several owners of bulldogs have assured me that in their opinion it is the only kind of dog that can with perfect safety be trusted alone to the mercy of children, than which there can hardly be a greater trial of patience and good temper. Having from my earliest recollection been accustomed to dogs, and having possessed specimens of almost every breed of dog, I consider myself, from experience, competent to contradict the statements made to the disparagement of this breed, whose cause I now advocate.

"In proof I can show one which for nine years has been the constant companion and playfellow of my only child. It succeeded in my household a fine Mount St. Bernard, and has proved itself in every way fully, if not more than, equal to any of its predecessors in endurance, fidelity, and sagacity (wisdom).

"When first brought home the dog was chained to a kennel in the garden, whence my little child, then not three years old, brought it indoors to play with. It has since remained always loose in the house, and has, with others of the same breed, daily sustained trials which none but a bulldog could endure without showing its teeth.

**Dryad and British Monarch, 1891 pencil drawing**

"Food or bones can be taken away from them without any exhibition of ill temper, whilst they are as good watch dogs as possible, and under the most complete control. I could adduce plenty of little anecdotes in proof of the bulldog's intelligence; but as every dog owner can do the same of his own dog, and not having space for such, I will only repeat that there are many people who can corroborate my assertion that the bulldog is inferior to no other dog, and that ferocity is not natural to this more than any other breed."

He goes on to criticise the 19th century breeders for not paying as much attention to the colour of Bulldogs as to the other features of the dog: "It is a matter of surprise that bulldog breeders have not the good taste to take the same pains to study the art of breeding for colour which they take to produce the broad mouth, short face, and other points by which the dog is judged.

"By so doing they would remove the prejudice impressed on the admirers of other breeds by the pied specimens. The colour is the most conspicuous point to a casual observer, and when a bulldog is white and unevenly pied with brindled patches and a patch over one eye and ear, and appears red and raw round its eyes, and wherever its coat is thin, it is no wonder that fanciers of Pomeranians, Italian greyhounds, and other breeds so diametrically opposed, should decline to admit the bulldog's claim to beauty.

"But when of uniform colour brindle, red, or fawn the bulldog is in many respects more attractive than several other canine pets; for example, the modern King Charles spaniel, and if its colour be whole and a "smut," like the pug whose 'Mouth was black as a bulldog's at the stall,' it is in every way to be preferred to that dog, being handsomer as well as more useful, faithful, and intelligent. White animals have not generally as strong constitutions as dark coloured ones, and are, therefore, much more liable to disease. When bred together they frequently produce "ricketty" or deaf whelps."

**FACT** > *In many modern dog breeds, the white gene is still associated with deafness.*

In a testament to the Bulldog's guarding abilities, Mr. Crafer said that a Staffordshire farmer had written in a newspaper that: "Two good bulldogs always loose in his yard do much more towards making his neighbours honest than all the parson's preaching.

"The bulldog has been described as stupidly ferocious, but this is untrue, he being an excellent watch and as a guard unequalled . . . far from quarrelsome. ... If once the pure breed is allowed to drop, the best means of infusing fresh courage into degenerate breeds will be finally lost ... for I believe that every kind of dog possessed of very high courage owes it to a cross with the bulldog. ... I am sure my brother sportsmen will see the bad taste of running down a dog which with all its faults is not only the most courageous dog, but the most courageous animal in the world. I think this alone is sufficient testimony in the bulldog's favour, and fully endorse the words of the poet Smart:

> *Well! of all dogs, it stands confessed, Your English bulldogs are the best!*
> *I say it and will set my hand to it; Cambden records it, and I'll stand to it."*

................................................................................................................................................

## The Great Bulldog Race

Towards the end the 19<sup>th</sup> century, there was much discussion as to exactly how the Bulldog should look. We know that there were three sizes of Bulldogs, although eventually the very small type was dropped, and it was around this time that the term *"sourmug"* was used for the first time to describe a particular type of Bulldog.

The sourmug had an extremely short muzzle and its legs were bowed. Its chest was so wide that it was no longer highly mobile, but moved in a less agile manner. In short, it looked much more like today's Bulldog. The Philo-Kuon breeders, who were breeding towards the idealised athletic conformation of Rosa, declared it an abomination against nature. However, the sourmug-type began to have increased success in the show ring when competing against the Philo-Kuon ideal.

There was much bad feeling between the two groups, with the breeders of sourmugs accusing the Philo-Kuon fanciers of being unpatriotic, as some were using the Spanish Bulldog (whose bloodlines actually originated in England) to breed a larger dog. There was also criticism that some Philo-Kuon Bulldogs were aggressive and would attack cats and other dogs. However, others were mellower and, with training, made excellent guard dogs that would attack a person or animal on command, but which remained easy for the owner to control.

**FACT >** *The event that followed was to determine the look of today's Bulldog. In 1893, the two top Bulldogs of the day were King Orry (pictured) and Dockleaf, and it was decided to hold a 10-mile race to see which dog would win.*

Dockleaf, was a three-year-old sourmug owned by Mr. Sam Woodiwiss and was condemned as a deformed "cripple" by his detractors, yet he won prize after prize at dog shows, becoming the English champion. The four-year-old King Orry (next page), owned by Mr. George Murrell, was reminiscent of the original fighting Bulldogs, being lighter boned with a sleeker, more athletic body and smaller head.

Rawdon Lee describes the background to the race *in "The History of Modern Dogs of Great Britain and Ireland (Nonsporting Division)"* (1894):

"I must write of dogs as I find them at the present time, and, to show the state to which an endeavour to breed for exaggeration in certain points has brought the bulldog, reproduce the following account of a walking match between two crack bench winners, which took place in the summer of 1893.

"There had been a brindled dog shown with extraordinary success at that time, for which his owner, Mr. S. Woodiwiss, was reported to have given £250—the greatest amount of money ever paid for a dog of this variety. In the opinion of many persons he was so much a cripple as to be unable to stand properly in the ring, which was a fact.

"However, the judges under whom the dog in question came, appeared blind to his defects, and time after time he was placed over more perfect animals. Then a match was made between Dockleaf *(pictured)* the dog above alluded to, and another well-known prize-winning bulldog, called King Orry owned by Mr. G. R. Murrell."

Here is his account of the race: "Each dog (is) to be led and make the best of the way from the Roebuck Hotel, Lewisham, to Bromley Town Hall and back, the distance being about ten miles. The competitors might have as much rest as appeared desirable, but 'lifting' from the ground was disqualification.

"At seven o'clock, when the start was made, a big crowd was in attendance, a portion of which accompanied the dogs on their journey. King Orry went off with the lead, and was nearly 400 yards ahead when a mile or more had been traversed.

"Soon after Dockleaf showed signs of fatigue, but continued on his journey to a couple of miles from the start, when, being fairly beaten.

"Mr. Woodiwiss withdrew him from further competition; his opponent was then far in front, and 'going well'. Mr. Murrell's dog, after a rest of seven minutes, arrived at Bromley Town Hall, and then set off on the return journey, Lewisham being duly reached at 9.25 p.m.

"Both animals had been in training for the match, and the winner showed no signs of distress after the accomplishment of what some modern admirers of the bulldog consider a great feat, but which we consider any bulldog ought to do equally satisfactorily.

"The loser occupied a trifle under forty minutes in covering his two miles, and, exclusive of stoppages, the winner progressed at the rate of some four and a half miles in the hour."

Although beaten, the sourmug breeders and supporters of Dockleaf retaliated, saying that perhaps the new sourmug was no ball of fire, but at least it was not polluted with Spanish blood and a media campaign was directed against the Philo-Kuon breeders and King Orry. The Press campaign and anti-Spanish feelings were very strong and resulted in a moral victory for the pro-Dockleaf campaign.

It was, therefore, Dockleaf – and not King Orry - that breeders chose as the ideal conformation and which forms the basis of Bulldogs today. The drawings of Rosa and Crib were torn from the Breed Standard and ground under a boot heel as the victorious sourmug breeders had their final revenge for being humiliated in the race.

At the turn of the 19th century there were almost no Philo-Kuon Bulldogs left in England. The result of this was that within 20 years of the Kennel Club being formed and an official Breed Standard being laid down, the supremely athletic Bulldog had been so interbred that it was no longer able to walk more than a couple of miles without difficulty.

........................................................................................................................................................................

## Controversy

The new Bulldog was not without its detractors. Many dog fanciers and experts were saddened at the changes within the breed and the fact that the national dog of England, once known for its immense bravery, strength and athleticism, had become a physical weakling.

Even in these early days, difficulties with breathing, stamina and whelping (giving birth to puppies) were recorded. One such was Edgar Farman, Honorary Member of the Bulldog Club and Editor of the Kennel Gazette, who said in his book *"The Bulldog - A Monograph,"* *(The Stock Keeper Co, Ltd 1899)*: "He is a manufactured article, a mass of show points."

In *"The Book Of Dogs– An Intimate Study Of Mankind's Best Friend"* (National Geographic Society, 1919) Ernest Baynes and Louis Fuertes wrote: "The bulldog of today is a grotesque deformity – short-legged, short-winded, short-lived, and barely able to reproduce its kind.

"It is chiefly useful for infusing courageous blood into other breeds, for adding variety to a dog show, and as an example (to be avoided) of what can be done by senseless breeding to spoil a perfectly good dog. But they haven't quite spoiled him, for he still retains his old-time dauntless courage, and he has a homely smile that would melt the hearts of even the few unfortunates who boast that they hate dogs.

"And here is an appropriate place to register a friendly protest against the arbitrary fixing of points for which dog owners must breed in order to win at the dog shows.

"There is tendency in the very proper enthusiasm over dog shows and show dogs to forget that the primary object of breeding most dogs is to produce animals which are useful in different fields of activity, and not to conform to a particular standard unless that standard is the one most likely to develop dogs fitted in mind and body for the work required of them."

"With the idea of making as ugly and surly looking a beast as possible, the present (interpretation of the) standard for the bulldog demands a type that is all but unfitted for existence."

*Pictured here* is J. Hay Hutchison's illustration from *"The Perfect Bulldog in Word and Picture; A Guide for Exhibitors, Breeders and Judges,"* printed in the Illustrated Kennel News, London, 1908.

It is a dog like this which retains the stand-out features of the Bulldog, but in a rather more athletic form, that some modern Bulldog breeders are working towards.

## The Modern Era

In the 20th century, the Bulldog increased in popularity, not only in Britain, but also in Europe, Russia, North and South America, Australia, New Zealand, South Africa and Japan.

During the Second World War, the Bulldog once again came to the fore, as it was portrayed on posters and photographs as the indomitable national dog of Britain.

Since 2000, the Bulldog has enjoyed a further resurgence, becoming one of the most popular dogs in both the USA and UK.

*Photo: Venus, mascot of the 1941 Royal Navy destroyer HMS Vansittart.*

It is not only the breed's unique look that has attracted new "bulldoggers," but also the modern Bulldog's reputation as having an agreeable and gentle temperament and being an excellent companion dog for all ages, but second to none when it comes to children.

Today, the Bulldog is no longer classed as a working or sporting dog, but in the Non-Sporting Group by the AKC and the Utility Group in the UK.

Numerous references were used in the research of this history, in particular:

- **The R.H. Voss article "Our Dogs" magazine, Dec. 15, 1933, University of California Digital Library**

- **"British Dogs: Their Varieties, History, Characteristics, Breeding, Management, And Exhibition," Hugh Dalziel**

- **"The History of Modern Dogs of Great Britain and Ireland (Nonsporting Division" (1894), Rawdon Lee**

- **"The Perfect Bulldog in Word and Picture; A Guide for Exhibitors, Breeders and Judges"**

- **"The Book Of Dogs – An Intimate Study Of Mankind's Best Friend" (National Geographic Society, 1919)**

- **"The Bulldog - A Monograph"**

- **Wikipedia**

- **Chest of Books www.chestofbooks.com**

- **"American Sports 1785-1835," Jennie Holloman**

- **"The Natural History of Dogs, Volume X"**

March 27, 1943

# 3. Breed Standard

The **Breed Standard** is what makes a Great Dane a Great Dane and a Chihuahua a Chihuahua. It is a blueprint not only for the appearance of each breed, but also for character and temperament, how the dog moves and what colours are acceptable. In other words, it ensures that a Bulldog looks and acts like a Bulldog.

In the UK, the Bulldog is in the *Utility Group* and in the US, it's in the *Non-Sporting Group,* which is ironic, as the Bulldog was originally a sporting dog.

The Breed Standard is laid down by the breed societies. In the UK it's the Kennel Club, and in the USA it's the AKC (American Kennel Club) that keeps the register of pedigree (purebred) dogs.

Dogs entered in conformation shows run under Kennel Club and AKC rules are judged against an ideal list of attributes. Breeders approved by the Kennel Clubs agree to produce puppies in line with the Breed Standard and maintain certain welfare conditions.

Responsible breeders select only the finest dogs for reproduction, based on the health, looks and temperament of the parents and their ancestors. They do not simply take any available male and female and allow them to randomly breed.

The Breed Standard can vary over time and from country to country, and this is certainly true of the Bulldog, whose Breed Standard has changed dramatically over the last 50 years.

In the UK, the Kennel Club has revised its list of ideal attributes following public pressure from the media who heavily criticised the breeding guidelines for some dogs - including the Bulldog - for causing health problems.

The new Bulldog standard in Britain calls for a "relatively" short face, a slightly smaller head and less-pronounced facial wrinkling. The Bulldog Club of America (BCA), which owns the copyright to the American Breed Standard, still calls for a "massive, short-faced head," a "heavy, thick-set, low-swung body," a "very short" face and muzzle and a "massive" and "undershot" jaw.

## Breed Watch

In 2014 the Kennel Club (UK) launched its **Breed Watch Fit For Purpose** campaign. It identified a number of breeds and designated them as Category Three: *"Breeds where some dogs have visible conditions or exaggerations that can cause pain or discomfort."*

The Bulldog is on this list, along with the following breeds: Basset Hound, Bloodhound, Chow, Clumber Spaniel, Dogue de Bordeaux, German Shepherd, Mastiff, Neapolitan Mastiff, Pekingese, Pug, Shar-Pei, and Saint Bernard.

The KC states: "The Kennel Club works closely with the clubs for these breeds in identifying key issues to be addressed within the breed, obtaining the opinion of breed experts on the issues identified, advising on how breed clubs can effectively address health and conformational issues and investigating how the Kennel Club can assist."

Points of concern with the Bulldog for special attention by judges are:

- ❖ Dogs showing respiratory distress, including difficulty in breathing or laboured breathing
- ❖ Excessive amounts of loose facial skin with conformational defects of the upper and/or lower eyelids so that the eyelid margins are not in normal contact with the eye when the dog is in its natural pose (e.g. they turn in, or out, or both abnormalities are present).
- ❖ Hair loss or scarring from previous dermatitis
- ❖ Heavy over-nose wrinkle (roll)
- ❖ Inverted tail
- ❖ Lack of tail
- ❖ Pinched nostrils
- ❖ Significantly overweight
- ❖ Sore eyes due to damage or poor eyelid conformation
- ❖ Tight tail
- ❖ Unsound movement

This is the KC's description of the Bulldog:

"One of Britain's oldest indigenous breeds, the Bulldog is known as the national dog of Great Britain and is associated throughout the world with British determination and the legendary John Bull. The Bulldog was first classified as such in the 1630s, though there is earlier mention of similar types referred to as bandogs, a term reserved today for a type of fighting dog.

"Used originally for bull-baiting, the Bulldog also fought its way through the dog pits, but after 1835 it began to evolve into the shorter-faced, more squat version we know today. It entered the show ring in 1860 and the ensuing years saw a big personality change.

"The pugilistic expression of this delightfully ugly dog belies his loving, affectionate nature to family and friends. He has a reputation for tenacity and is very courageous, strong and powerful. Although he is a little bit stubborn by nature, he is good-tempered with children, of whom he is also very protective.

"The impression he gives of being slow and sluggish is completely contradicted by the great bursts of speed that he can and does produce when the occasion demands. His mood can be dignified, humorous or comical, and he has many endearing ways."

# UK Breed Standard

**General Appearance -** Smooth-coated, fairly thick set, rather low in stature, broad, powerful and compact. Head, fairly large in proportion to size but no point so much in excess of others as to destroy the general symmetry, or make the dog appear deformed, or interfere with its powers of motion. Face relatively short, muzzle broad, blunt and inclined upwards although not excessively so. Dogs showing respiratory distress highly undesirable.

Body fairly short, well knit, limbs stout, well-muscled and in hard condition with no tendency towards obesity. Hindquarters high and strong. Bitches not so grand or well developed as dogs.

**Characteristics -** Conveys impression of determination, strength and activity.

**Temperament -** Alert, bold, loyal, dependable, courageous, fierce in appearance, but possessed of affectionate nature.

**Head and Skull -** Skull relatively large in circumference. Viewed from front appears high from corner of lower jaw to apex of skull; also broad and square. Cheeks well rounded and extended sideways beyond eyes.

Viewed from side, head appears very high and moderately short from back to point of nose. Forehead flat with skin on and about head slightly loose and finely wrinkled without excess, neither prominent nor overhanging face. From defined stop, a furrow extending to middle of skull being traceable to apex.

Face from front of cheek bone to nose, relatively short, skin may be slightly wrinkled. Muzzle short, broad, turned upwards and deep from corner of eye to corner of mouth. Nose and nostrils large, broad and black, under no circumstances liver colour, red or brown.

Distance from inner corner of eye (or from centre of stop between eyes) to extreme tip of nose should not be less than distance from tip of the nose to edge of the underlip. Nostrils large wide and open, with well-defined vertical straight line between. Flews (chops) thick, broad and deep, covering lower jaws at sides, but joining underlip in front.

Teeth not visible. Jaws broad, strong and square, lower jaw slightly projecting in front of upper with moderate turn up. Over nose wrinkle, if present, whole or broken, must never adversely affect or obscure eyes or nose. Pinched nostrils and heavy over nose roll are unacceptable and should be heavily penalised.

Viewed from front, the various properties of the face must be equally balanced on either side of an imaginary line down centre.

**Eyes -** Seen from front, situated low down in skull, well away from ears. Eyes and stop in same straight line, at right angles to furrow. Wide apart, but outer corners within the outline of cheeks. Round, of moderate size, neither sunken nor prominent, in colour very dark – almost black – showing no white when looking directly forward. Free from obvious eye problems.

**Ears -** Set high – i.e. front edge of each ear (as viewed from front) joins outline of skull at top corner of such outline, so as to place them as wide apart, as high and as far from eyes as possible. Small and thin. "Rose ear" correct, i.e. folding inwards back, upper or front inner edge curving outwards and backwards, showing part of inside of burr.

**Mouth -** Jaws broad and square with six small front teeth between canines in an even row. Canines wide apart. Teeth large and strong, not seen when mouth closed. When viewed from front under jaw directly under upper jaw and parallel.

**Neck -** Moderate in length, thick, deep and strong. Well arched at back, with some loose skin about throat, forming slight dewlap on each side.

**Forequarters** - Shoulders broad, sloping and deep, very powerful and muscular giving appearance of being "tacked on" body. Brisket round and deep. Well let down between forelegs. Ribs not flat-sided, but well rounded.

Forelegs very stout and strong, well developed, set wide apart, thick, muscular and straight, bones of legs large and straight, not bandy nor curved and short in proportion to hindlegs, but not so short as to make back appear long, or detract from dog's activity. Elbows low and standing well away from ribs. Pasterns short, straight and strong.

**Body** - Chest wide, prominent and deep. Back short, strong, broad at shoulders. Slight fall to back close behind shoulders (lowest part) whence spine should rise to loins (top higher than top of shoulder), curving again more suddenly to tail, forming slight arch – a distinctive characteristic of breed. Body well ribbed up behind with belly tucked up and not pendulous.

**Hindquarters** - Legs large and muscular, slightly longer in proportion than forelegs. Hocks slightly bent, well let down; legs long and muscular from loins to hock. Stifles turned very slightly outwards away from body.

**Feet** - Fore, straight and turning very slightly outward; of medium size and moderately round. Hind, round and compact. Toes compact and thick, well split up, making knuckles prominent and high.

**Tail** - Set on low, jutting out rather straight and then turning downwards. Round, smooth and devoid of fringe or coarse hair. Moderate in length – rather short than long – thick at root, tapering quickly to a fine point. Downward carriage (not having a decided upward curve at end) and never carried above back.

Lack of tail, inverted or extremely tight tails are undesirable.

**Gait/Movement** - Appearing to walk with short, quick steps on tips of toes, hind feet not lifted high, appearing to skim ground, running with one or other shoulder rather advanced. Soundness of movement of the utmost importance.

**Coat** - Fine texture, short, close and smooth (hard only from shortness and closeness, not wiry).

**Colour** - Whole or smut, (i.e. whole colour with black mask or muzzle). Only whole colours (which should be brilliant and pure of their sort) viz., brindles, reds with their various shades, fawns, fallows etc., white and pied (i.e. combination of white with any of the foregoing colours).

Dudley, black and black with tan highly undesirable.

**Size** - Dogs: 25 kg (55 lb); bitches: 23 kg (50 lb).

**Faults** - Any departure from the foregoing points should be considered a fault and the seriousness with which the fault should be regarded should be in exact proportion to its degree and its effect upon the health and welfare of the dog.

**Note** - Male animals should have two apparently normal testicles fully descended into the scrotum.

# US Breed Standard

In the US, the Bulldog is in the Non-Sporting Group, alongside such other breeds as the Bichon Frise, Boston Terrier, Chinese Shar-Pei, Chow Chow, Dalmatian, Finnish Spitz, French Bulldog, Lhasa Apso, Poodle, Tibetan Spaniel and Tibetan Terrier. The Bulldog has been in the top five or six most popular dogs in the US for many years.

According to the AKC, non-sporting dogs are a diverse group. They are a varied collection in terms of size, coat, personality and overall appearance.

The AKC states: "Known for their loose-jointed, shuffling gait and massive, short-faced head, the Bulldog is known to be equable, resolute and dignified. A medium-sized dog, they are not your typical lap dog, but would like to be!

"They are one of the most popular breeds according to AKC Registration Statistics, due to their lovable and gentle dispositions and adorable wrinkles. The Bulldog may be brindle, white, red, fawn, fallow or piebald.

"Bulldogs are recognised as excellent family pets because of their tendency to form strong bonds with children. They tend to be gentle and protective. The breed requires minimal grooming and exercise. Their short nose makes them prone to overheating in warm weather, so make sure to provide a shady place to rest."

Here is the full US Breed Standard, it is one of the most detailed you will ever read:

**General Appearance -** The perfect Bulldog must be of medium size and smooth coat; with heavy, thick-set, low-swung body, massive short-faced head, wide shoulders and sturdy limbs. The general appearance and attitude should suggest great stability, vigour and strength. The disposition should be equable and kind, resolute and courageous (not vicious or aggressive), and demeanour should be pacific and dignified. These attributes should be countenanced by the expression and behaviour.

**Size, Proportion, Symmetry** – *Size* -The size for mature dogs is about 50 pounds; for mature bitches about 40 pounds.

*Proportion* -The circumference of the skull in front of the ears should measure at least the height of the dog at the shoulders.

*Symmetry* - The "points" should be well distributed and bear good relation one to the other, no feature being in such prominence from either excess or lack of quality that the animal appears deformed or ill-proportioned.

*Influence of Sex* - In comparison of specimens of different sex, due allowance should be made in favour of the bitches, which do not bear the characteristics of the breed to the same degree of perfection and grandeur as do the dogs.

**Head -** *Eyes and Eyelids* -The eyes, seen from the front, should be situated low down in the skull, as far from the ears as possible, and their corners should be in a straight line at right angles with the stop.

They should be quite in front of the head, as wide apart as possible, provided their outer corners are within the outline of the cheeks when viewed from the front. They should be quite round in form, of moderate size, neither sunken nor bulging, and in colour should be very dark.

The lids should cover the white of the eyeball, when the dog is looking directly forward, and the lid should show no "haw."

*Ears* -The ears should be set high in the head, the front inner edge of each ear joining the outline of the skull at the top back corner of skull, so as to place them as wide apart, and as high, and as far from the eyes as possible. In size they should be small and thin.

The shape termed "rose ear" is the most desirable. The rose ear folds inward at its back lower edge, the upper front edge curving over, outward and backward, showing part of the inside of the burr. (The ears should not be carried erect or prick-eared or buttoned and should never be cropped).

*Skull* - The skull should be very large, and in circumference, in front of the ears, should measure at least the height of the dog at the shoulders. Viewed from the front, it should appear very high from the corner of the lower jaw to the apex of the skull, and also very broad and square. Viewed at the side, the head should appear very high, and very short from the point of the nose to occiput. The forehead should be flat (not rounded or domed), neither too prominent nor overhanging the face.

*Cheeks* -The cheeks should be well rounded, protruding sideways and outward beyond the eyes.

*Stop* -The temples or frontal bones should be very well defined, broad, square and high, causing a hollow or groove between the eyes. This indentation, or stop, should be both broad and deep and extend up the middle of the forehead, dividing the head vertically, being traceable to the top of the skull.

*Face and Muzzle* - The face, measured from the front of the cheekbone to the tip of the nose, should be extremely short, the muzzle being very short, broad, turned upward and very deep from the corner of the eye to the corner of the mouth.

*Nose* - The nose should be large, broad and black, its tip set back deeply between the eyes. The distance from bottom of stop, between the eyes, to the tip of nose should be as short as possible and not exceed the length from the tip of nose to the edge of underlip. The nostrils should be wide, large and black, with a well-defined line between them. Any nose other than black is objectionable and a brown or liver-coloured nose shall **disqualify**.

*Lips* - The chops or "flews" should be thick, broad, pendant and very deep, completely overhanging the lower jaw at each side. They join the underlip in front and almost or quite cover the teeth, which should be scarcely noticeable when the mouth is closed.

*Bite – Jaws* - The jaws should be massive, very broad, square and "undershot," the lower jaw projecting considerably in front of the upper jaw and turning up.

*Teeth* - The teeth should be large and strong, with the canine teeth or tusks wide apart, and the six small teeth in front, between the canines, in an even, level row.

**Neck, Topline, Body -** *Neck* - The neck should be short, very thick, deep and strong and well arched at the back.

*Topline* - There should be a slight fall in the back, close behind the shoulders (its lowest part), whence the spine should rise to the loins (the top of which should be higher than the top of the shoulders), thence curving again more suddenly to the tail, forming an arch (a very distinctive feature of the breed), termed "roach back" or, more correctly, "wheel-back."

*Body* -The brisket and body should be very capacious, with full sides, well-rounded ribs and very deep from the shoulders down to its lowest part, where it joins the chest. It should be well let down between the shoulders and forelegs, giving the dog a broad, low, short-legged appearance.

*Chest* - The chest should be very broad, deep and full.

*Underline* -The body should be well ribbed up behind with the belly tucked up and not rotund.

*Back and Loin* -The back should be short and strong, very broad at the shoulders and comparatively narrow at the loins.

*Tail* - The tail may be either straight or "screwed" (but never curved or curly), and in any case must be short, hung low, with decided downward carriage, thick root and fine tip. If straight, the tail should be cylindrical and of uniform taper. If "screwed," the bends or kinks should be well defined, and they may be abrupt and even knotty, but no portion of the member should be elevated above the base or root.

**Forequarters** – *Shoulders* - The shoulders should be muscular, very heavy, widespread and slanting outward, giving stability and great power.

*Forelegs* - The forelegs should be short, very stout, straight and muscular, set wide apart, with well-developed calves, presenting a bowed outline, but the bones of the legs should not be curved or bandy, nor the feet brought too close together.

*Elbows* - The elbows should be low and stand well out and loose from the body.

*Feet* - The feet should be moderate in size, compact and firmly set. Toes compact, well split up, with high knuckles and very short stubby nails. The front feet may be straight or slightly out-turned.

**Hindquarters** – *Legs* - The hind legs should be strong and muscular and longer than the forelegs, so as to elevate the loins above the shoulders. Hocks should be slightly bent and well let down, so as to give length and strength from the loins to hock. The lower leg should be short, straight and strong, with the stifles turned slightly outward and away from the body. The hocks are thereby made to approach each other, and the hind feet to turn outward.

*Feet* - The feet should be moderate in size, compact and firmly set. Toes compact, well split up, with high knuckles and short stubby nails. The hind feet should be pointed well outward.

**Coat and Skin** – *Coat* - The coat should be straight, short, flat, close, of fine texture, smooth and glossy. (No fringe, feather or curl). *Skin* - The skin should be soft and loose, especially at the head, neck and shoulders.

*Wrinkles and Dewlap* - The head and face should be covered with heavy wrinkles, and at the throat, from jaw to chest, there should be two loose pendulous folds, forming the dewlap.

**Colour of Coat** - The colour of coat should be uniform, pure of its kind and brilliant. The various colours found in the breed are to be preferred in the following order:

1.   Red brindle
2.   All other brindles
3.   Solid white
4.   Solid red, fawn or fallow
5.   Piebald
6.   Inferior qualities of all the foregoing

**Note:** A perfect piebald is preferable to a muddy brindle or defective solid colour. Solid black is very undesirable, but not so objectionable if occurring to a moderate degree in piebald patches.

The brindles to be perfect should have a fine, even and equal distribution of the composite colours. In brindles and solid colors a small white patch on the chest is not considered detrimental. In piebalds the colour patches should be well defined, of pure colour and symmetrically distributed.

**Gait -** The style and carriage are peculiar, his gait being a loose-jointed, shuffling, sidewise motion, giving the characteristic "roll." The action must, however, be unrestrained, free and vigorous.

**Temperament -** The disposition should be equable and kind, resolute and courageous (not vicious or aggressive), and demeanor should be pacific and dignified. These attributes should be countenanced by the expression and behavior.

In the show ring, here is how the judging points are awarded:

**Disqualification**
Brown or liver-coloured nose.

**Approved July 20, 1976. Reformatted November 28, 1990**

# 4. Finding Your Puppy

If you haven't got your puppy yet, then read this chapter before you commit to anything; it will help you find a healthy, happy puppy with a good temperament. If you already have yours, skip to the next chapter.

Once you've decided that the Bulldog is your ideal dog, the best way to select a puppy is with your HEAD - and not with your heart! You'll soon find hundreds of Bulldog puppies advertised - but it requires a lot more time and research to find a first-rate breeder with healthy pups.

With their beautiful, wrinkly faces, velvety bodies and playful personalities, there are few more appealing things on this Earth than a Bulldog puppy. If you go to view a litter, the pups are sure to melt your heart and it is extremely difficult – if not downright impossible - to walk away without choosing one.

 *The Bulldog has more health issues than most breeds. A priority should be to buy a puppy that breathes easily from bloodlines free from genetic diseases.*

If you haven't yet chosen your pup and take only one sentence from this entire book, it is this:

## FIND AN ETHICAL BREEDER WHO PRODUCES HEALTHY BULLDOGS, FIT FOR FUNCTION, FROM HEALTH-TESTED PARENTS

 – even if that means paying more than you wanted. It'll be worth it. The main reason for Bulldogs ending up in rescue is health issues.

Find a breeder who knows Bulldogs inside out and who does not breed lots of different types of dogs. After all, apart from getting married or having a baby, getting a puppy is one of the most important, demanding, expensive and life-enriching decisions you will ever make.

Bulldogs will love you unconditionally - but there is a price to pay. In return for their devotion, you have to fulfil your part of the bargain.

In the beginning, you have to be prepared to devote much of your day to your new puppy. You have to feed her several times a day and housetrain virtually every hour, you have to give her your attention and start to gently introduce the rules of the house. You also have to be prepared to part with hard cash for regular healthcare and pet insurance.

If you are unable to devote the time and money to a new arrival, if you have a very young family, a stressful life or are out at work all day, then now might not be the right time to consider getting a puppy. Bulldogs are stay-at-home people-loving dogs.

If left alone too long, behaviour issues result. This is a natural reaction and is not the dog's fault; she is simply responding to an environment that is failing to meet her needs.

Pick a healthy pup and he or she could live for up to 10 years; if you're very lucky, maybe even double figures - so this is certainly a long-term commitment. Before taking the plunge, ask yourself some questions:

## Have I Got Enough Time?

In the first days after leaving her mother and littermates, your puppy will feel very lonely and probably even a little afraid. Spend time with your new arrival to make her feel safe and sound. Ideally, for the first few days you will be around all of the time to help her settle and to start bonding.

If you work, book time off if you can - although this is more difficult for some of our American readers who get short vacations - but don't just get a puppy and leave her all alone in the house a couple of days later.

Housetraining, or potty training, starts the moment your pup arrives home. Then, after the first few days and once she's feeling more settled, make time for short sessions of a few minutes of behaviour training. Bulldog puppies can be boisterous and clumsy, and this energy can become mischievous if not channelled.

You'll also have to find time to slowly start the socialisation process by taking her out of the home to see new places, strangers, other animals, loud noises, busy roads, etc. - but make sure you CARRY her until the vaccinations have taken effect.

*Start socialisation as soon as possible; that critical window up to four months of age is when she is at her most receptive to all things new.*

The more positive experiences she is introduced to at this early stage, the better, and good breeders will already have started the process. Once she has had the all-clear after vaccinations, get into the habit of taking her for a short walk every day – increase it as she gets older. While the

garden or yard is fine, new surroundings stimulate interest and help to stop puppies becoming bored.

Make time right from the beginning to get your pup used to being handled, gently brushed, ears checked, and later having her teeth touched and cleaned.

We recommend you have your pup checked out by a vet within a couple of days of arriving home - but don't put your puppy on the clinic floor where she can pick up germs from other dogs. Factor in time to visit the vet's surgery for annual check-ups as well as vaccinations, although most now last several years – check with your vet.

## How Long Can I Leave My Puppy?

This is a question we get asked a lot and one that causes much debate among new owners. All dogs are pack animals; their natural state is to be with others. So being alone is not normal for them - although many have to get used to it.

Another issue is the toilet; Bulldog puppies have tiny bladders. Forget the emotional side of it, how would you like to be left for eight hours without being able to visit the bathroom? So how many hours can you leave a dog alone?

 *UK rescue organisations will not allow anybody to adopt who is intending to leave the dog alone regularly for more than four or five hours a day.*

Solitary dogs get sad and bored and, in the case of dogs like the Bulldog that love companionship, they can become destructive. A lonely Bulldog may display signs of unhappiness by barking, chewing, aggression, digging, eliminating, disobedience or just being plain sad and disengaged.

 *In terms of housetraining, a general rule of thumb is that a puppy can last without urinating for one hour or so for every month of age, sometimes longer.*

So, provided your puppy has learned the basics, a three-month-old puppy should be able to last for three hours or a little longer without needing to go. Of course, until housetraining kicks in, young puppies just pee at will!

A puppy or fully-grown Bulldog must NEVER be left shut in a crate all day. It is OK to leave her in a crate if she is happy there, but the door should never be closed for more than two or three hours. A crate is a place where a puppy or adult should feel safe, it's not a cage.

## A Dog or a Bitch (Male or Female)?

*The differences within the sexes are greater than the differences between the sexes*. In other words, you can get a dominant female and a submissive male, or vice versa. There are, however, some general traits that are more common with one sex or another.

Bulldogs are sociable dogs and, unless they have had a bad experience, are not normally aggressive. However, un-neutered males – referred to as *dogs* – are more likely to display aggression if confronted by aggression from other male dogs. The Bulldog will not pick a fight, but he will defend himself and whatever he regards as his territory – and this may include you or your children. An entire (un-neutered) male is also more likely to wander off on the scent of a female.

**FACT** ⟩ If it is the classic beefy look of the Bulldog you love, then the huge head and chunky build are more apparent in the male; females tend to be slightly smaller.

If you take a male Bulldog for a walk, he may well stop at every lamp-post, trash can and interesting blade of grass to leave his mark by urinating. A female will tend to urinate far less frequently.

Female dogs, or bitches, generally tend to be less aggressive towards other dogs, except when they are raising puppies. With some breeds, families consider a female if they have young children, as she may be more tolerant towards young creatures. However, virtually all Bulldogs, regardless of their gender, love children.

Female Bulldogs can be messy when they come into heat every six to nine months, due to the blood loss. If your princess is not spayed, you will also have the nuisance of becoming a magnet for all the free-wandering male dogs within a mile or more radius.

If you plan to have two or more Bulldogs living together, the neutering or spaying issue will have to be addressed. You can't expect an un-neutered male and unspayed female to live together.

## Other Pets

If you already have other pets in your household, spend time to introduce them gradually to each other. If you have other dogs, supervised sessions from an early age will help the dogs to get along and chances are they will become the best of friends. Bulldogs are generally placid by nature and do well with other pets, provided the introductions are done properly and early.

*With another dog, introduce the two on neutral territory, rather than in a place that one dog regards as her own. You don't want the established dog to feel she has to protect her territory.*

Walking the dogs on leashes parallel to each other away from the home is also a good idea to get them used to each other.

Cats can sometimes be more of a problem; most dogs' natural instinct is to chase a cat. However, it's also true that most Bulldogs are not like Spike - the Bully in the Tom and Jerry cartoons who spent his life chasing Tom - and many live very happily alongside other pets, including cats.

Bulldogs love attention and may see the cat as a threat, and in a minority of cases it may take a long time (if ever) to accustom them to small pets.

Your chances of success are greater if your cat is strong-willed and your dog is docile - fortunately most Bulldogs are! If your cat is timid and your dog is alert, young and active, then it's a bit more difficult.

Supervised sessions and patience are the answer. A pup may tease a cat, but in the end, she will probably learn to live with it. Make sure the cat does not attack the puppy, as he could scratch her eyes. Take the process slowly, if your cat is stressed and frightened he may decide to leave.

Our feline friends are notorious for abandoning home because the food and facilities are better down the road! Wait until you know that they can get on together before leaving them alone.

If your Bulldog insists on tormenting or barking at the cat, use **Redirection** training. Get your dog to focus on you and give her something she likes – playtime, stroking, a long-lasting treat. Talk in a positive encouraging manner and reward her for being quiet and ignoring the cat.

Initially, allow them to occupy the same space for limited periods only, while you use the Redirection to get your Bulldog used to the cat being around. For a dog to get on with a cat, you are asking her to forget some of her natural instincts and to respond to your training. But, with time, patience and initial partial separation, it can be done - even with the most stubborn of Bulldogs

**FACT** > *The fact that a dog has lived with one cat will not guarantee that she will tolerate a different, strange cat. Many Bulldogs will have no problems at all with a cat in the home and will even protect them, but meeting a strange cat outside the home can be a completely different matter!*

A lot depends on the temperament of the individual dog and at what age she is introduced to the other animal(s) – the earlier, the better.

## Family and Children

What about the other members of your family, do they all want the puppy as well? A puppy will grow into a dog that will become a part of your family for many years to come. If you have children, they will, of course, be delighted.

One of the wonderful things about Bulldogs is how good they are with children; many seem to have a natural affinity or attraction to kids and babies - they get excited when they see them and love to be around them.

Bulldogs are often child-like themselves, they have been described as: *"Little humans trapped in fur!"* While many love toddlers and children, some may take a little longer to adapt to another child in the house.

 *If yours is reluctant to have anything to do with your baby or kids, take things slowly. Bulldogs are stubborn and don't like having things forced on them.*

It is **highly unlikely** that a Bulldog will attack a small child, but the two should never be left alone. Many teething Bulldogs have shark-like tendencies and love nothing more than nipping flesh – it's a great game!

Introduce the two slowly, perhaps on the floor at the Bulldog's level, but don't force them together. You can leave an item of clothing or towel belonging to the child next to the dog, so she gets used to the scent.

When my friend Julie first took her Bulldog, Winston, to the playground with her young son, Winston thought he was in Seventh Heaven, he just loved being with children so much. If you want to see just how good Bulldogs can be with youngsters, type *"Bulldogs with children"* into Google or YouTube for some really heart-warming videos.

Children shouldn't be allowed to constantly pester your new Bulldog. Puppies need enough time to sleep – which is most of the time in the beginning. Sleep is as important for puppies as it is for babies. One of the reasons some Bullies are rehomed is that the owners are unable to cope with the demands of small children AND a dog.

Dogs are hierarchical, in other words, there is a pecking order. Although Bulldogs are not regarded as one-person dogs, there is usually one human that the puppy will regard as pack leader (alpha), usually the person who feeds her or who spends most time with her.

Puppies will often regard children as being on their own level, like a playmate, and so they might chase, jump and nip at them with their powerful jaws and sharp teeth. This is not aggression; this is normal play for puppies. Be sure to supervise play time and make sure the puppy doesn't get too boisterous; when she's 40lb or 50lb and roughhousing, she can cause some damage.

 *Train your Bulldog to be gentle with your children and your children to be gentle with your dog.*

## Older People

If you are older or have elderly relatives living with you, the good news is that Bulldogs are great company. They love to be with people and are affectionate in a laid back way. Nobody has told the Bulldog that she is not a lapdog and is happiest when snoozing on a chair - or on you.

Bear in mind that strong dogs may be too much for a senior citizen, especially if they haven't been trained properly. They may pull on the leash or be boisterous or destructive in the house (the dog, not the old person!)

If you are older and are thinking of getting a puppy, make sure your energy levels are up to it. Are you fit enough to take your Bulldog for at least one walk away from the home every day? Can you devote time and energy to training? Bulldogs are very powerful, and the last thing you want is an out-of-control adolescent rampaging through the house or pulling you over when on a walk.

Some Bulldogs will survive perfectly well by only going out into the garden or yard, but there is no substitute in most dogs' minds for a walk away from the home at least once a day – even a short one. Take out the leash and see how your dog reacts, you'll soon find out if she'd rather go for a walk.

Dogs can be great for older people. In his late 80s. my father walked his dog for at least an hour a day, spread over two walks - even in the rain or snow. It was good for him and good for the dog, it kept both of them fit and socialised!

They got fresh air, exercise and the chance to communicate with other dogs and their humans. His dog died last year, but he still walks every day with a friend and her dog.

Dogs are also great company at home – you're never alone when you've got a dog. Many older people get a puppy after losing a loved one -a husband, wife or previous much-loved dog. A dog gives them something to care for and love, as well as a constant companion.

Remember that health may become an issue with some Bulldogs, so it's important to be able to afford annual pet insurance or veterinary fees.

## Single People

Many single adults own dogs, but if you live alone, having a puppy will require a lot of dedication from you. There will be nobody to share the tasks of daily care, exercise and training, so taking on a dog requires a huge commitment and a lot of your time if the dog is to have a decent life.

If you are out of the house all day as well, it is not really fair to get a puppy, or even an adult dog. Left alone all day, Bulldogs feel isolated, bored and sad. However, if you work from or are at home for all or part of the day, then great! Bulldogs make excellent companions. If you're still determined to have a Bully when you're out for several hours at a time, here are some useful points:

# Top 10 Tips For Working Bulldog Owners

**1. Employ a dog walker, come home during your lunch break or drop your dog off at doggie day care,** if you can afford it.

**2. Do you know anybody you could leave your dog with during the day?** Consider leaving the dog with a friend, relative or elderly neighbour who would welcome the companionship of a Bulldog without the full responsibility of ownership.

**3. Take her for a walk before you go to work** – even if this means getting up at the crack of dawn – and spend time with her as soon as you get home. Exercise generates serotonin in the brain and has a calming effect. A dog that has been exercised will be less anxious and more ready for a good nap.

**4. Leave her in a place of her own where she feels comfortable.** If you use a crate, leave the door open, otherwise her favourite dog bed or chair. If possible, leave her in a room with a view of the outside world. This will be more interesting than staring at four blank walls.

**5. VERY IMPORTANT: Make sure that the place where you leave her does not get too hot during the day and there are no cold draughts.** Your dog can die if she overheats; she may need an air-conditioned room in very hot weather.

**6. Food and drink.** Put food down at specific meal times. If the food is there all day, she may become a fussy eater or "punish" you for leaving her alone by refusing to eat. Make sure she has access to water at all times. Dogs do not have many sweat glands, so they pant to cool down, but this is much less efficient than sweating and they can die without water.

**7. Leave toys for her to play with to prevent boredom and destructive chewing -** the favourite occupation of a bored Bulldog or one suffering from separation anxiety. Stuff a Kong toy, *pictured,* with treats to keep her occupied for a while. You can even smear the inside with peanut butter or another favourite treat to keep her occupied for longer.

**8. Consider getting a companion for your Bulldog** - another dog or even a cat. This will involve even more of your time and twice the expense, and if you have not got time for one dog, you have hardly time for two. A better idea is to find someone you can leave the dog with during the day.

**9. Consider leaving a radio or TV on very softly in the background.** The "white noise" can have a soothing effect on some pets. If you do this, select your channel carefully – try and avoid one with lots of bangs and crashes or heavy metal music!

**10. Stick to the same routine before you leave your dog home alone.** This will help her to feel secure. Before you go to work, get into a daily habit of getting yourself ready, then feeding and exercising your Bulldog. Dogs love routine. But don't make a huge fuss of her when you leave, this can also stress the dog; just leave the house calmly.

Similarly, when you come home. Your Bulldog will feel starved of attention and be pleased to see you. Greet her normally, but try not to go overboard by making too much of a fuss as soon as you walk through the door. Give her a pat and a stroke then take off your coat and do a few other things before turning your attention back to her.

Lavishing your Bulldog with too much attention the second you walk through the door may encourage demanding behaviour or *separation anxiety.*

## Plan Ahead

Choosing the right breeder is one of the most important decisions you will make. Like humans, your puppy will be a product of her parents and will inherit many of their characteristics.

 *Natural temperament and how healthy your puppy will be now and throughout her life will depend to quite a large extent on the genes of her parents.*

Responsible breeders DNA test their breeding dogs. They reduce genetic illnesses by screening and NOT breeding from the ones with faulty genes -and only breed from dogs with good temperaments.

Expect to pay around $2,500 to $4,000 in the US for a Bulldog from a recognised AKC breeder who fully health tests her breeding stock, and £2,000 to £3,000 or more from a UK Kennel Club Assured Breeder who carries out DNA genetic health testing.

 **FACT** ⟩ *Bulldogs are notoriously difficult to breed, females should not have more than two or three litters maximum, they are often poor mothers and the litters are small. Add to this the cost of DNA health screening for the dam and sire and you suddenly see why well-bred Bulldog puppies are so expensive!*

Anything less than the above figures means corners have been cut somewhere – and it's usually health-testing.

★ *In the case of Bulldogs, health tests include eyes, heart, spine, patellas, hips, BOAS (Brachycephalic Obstructive Airway Syndrome), thyroid and HUU (Hyperuricosuria) – exact details are in Chapter 11. Bulldog Health.*

**BE PATIENT.** Start looking months before your planned arrival. There is usually a waiting list for Bulldog pups from health-tested parents and expert breeders, so once you know you can afford a well-bred Bulldog, get your name on a list.

Phone or email your selected breeder or breeders to find out about future litters and potential dates, but don't commit until you've asked lots of questions.

Good breeders will also ask a lot of questions about you, your household and living conditions and how you will take care of and train their much-loved puppy. Visit the breeder personally at least once.

With the distances sometimes involved, this is not always possible in the USA, so speak at length on the phone to the breeder and ask lots of questions and ask for week-by-week photos of the puppies.

Some American breeders may arrange escorted *"Nanny Transport"* to safely deliver the pup to your home, or an agreed meeting place. If you are satisfied with the answers to your questions, and have checked the Puppy Contract and Health Guarantee on offer, then go ahead and put your name down on the waiting list.

Bulldogs should be at least eight weeks old before they leave the breeder. Puppies need this time to physically develop and learn the rules of the pack from their mothers and littermates. In some US states it is illegal to sell a puppy younger than eight weeks.

A healthy Bulldog will be your irreplaceable companion for up to a decade, so why buy one from a pet shop or general ad? Would you buy an old car or a house with potential structural problems just because it looked pretty in a website photo or was cheap? The answer is probably no, because you know you'd have stress and expense at some point in the future.

# Buyer Beware

Good breeders do not sell their dogs on general purpose websites, Gumtree, eBay, Craig's List or Freeads, in car parks or somebody else's house. Puppies in pet shops often come from puppy mills.

A couple of years ago, the UK Government considered banning the sale of puppies in pet shops – sadly, so far, nothing has happened. If you are looking at dogs on Pets4Homes in the UK, follow their guidelines carefully, check the health screening and see the pup with her mother.

There is a difference between *a hobby breeder* and a *backyard or backstreet breeder*. Both may breed just one or two litters a year and keep the puppies in their homes, but that's where the similarity ends. In the UK, *hobby breeders* often don't have a website and you will probably find out about them via word of mouth.

Good hobby breeders are usually breed enthusiasts or experts; sometimes they show their pedigree dogs. They carry out health tests and lavish care and love on their dogs. They are not full-time professional dog breeders. **NOTE:** While it is often a good sign in the UK, the term *"hobby breeder"* can have negative implications in the USA.

*Backyard breeders* are often breeding family pets. They have less knowledge about the breed, pay little attention to the health and welfare of their dogs and are doing it primarily for extra cash. They may be very nice people, but avoid buying a dog from them.

**FACT** *All good breeders - professional or hobby - have in-depth knowledge of the Bulldog, they take measures to prevent potential health issues being passed on to puppies, and are passionate about the breed.*

Here are four reasons for buying from a good breeder:

1. **HEALTH:** Bulldogs have many potentially inheritable health issues. Screening breeding stock and NOT breeding from those that fail the health tests is the best way of preventing genetic disorders from being passed on.

2. **SOCIALISATION:** Scientists and dog experts now realise that the critical socialisation period for dogs is up to the age of four months. An unstimulated puppy is likely to be less well-adjusted and more likely to have fear or behaviour issues as an adult. Good breeders start this process, they don't just leave the puppies to their own devices for eight weeks.

3. **TEMPERAMENT:** Good breeders select their breeding stock based not only on sound structure and health, but also on temperament. They will not breed from an aggressive or overly anxious Bulldog.

4. **PEACE OF MIND:** Most good breeders give a genetic health guarantee with their puppy, often from a year to two or three years. Some even give a lifetime genetic guarantee. Many also agree to take the dog back at any time in its life if things don't work out - although you may find it too hard to part with your beloved Bully by then.

# Spotting Bad Breeders

Getting a puppy is such an emotional decision - and one that should have a wonderfully positive impact on you and your family's life for up to a decade. Unfortunately, the high price of Bulldog puppies has resulted in unscrupulous people producing litters primarily for the money.

This section helps you avoid the pitfalls of getting a puppy from a puppy mill, a puppy broker (somebody who makes money from buying and selling puppies), a backyard breeder or even an importer. You can't buy a Rolls Royce or a Lamborghini for a couple of thousand pounds or dollars - you'd immediately suspect that the *"bargain"* on offer wasn't the real thing. No matter how lovely it looked, you'd be right - and the same applies to Bulldogs.

## Become Breeder Savvy

- ❧ Avoid websites where there are no pictures of the owners, home or kennels

- ❧ If the website shows lots of photos of cute puppies with little information about the family, breeding dogs, health tests and environment, click the **X** button

- ❧ Don't buy a website puppy with a shopping cart symbol next to her picture

- ❧ See the puppies with their mother face-to-face. If this is not possible due to distances, speak at length on the phone with the breeder and ask lots of questions

- ❧ You hear: *"You can't see the parent dogs because......"* ALWAYS ask to see the parents and, as a minimum, see the mother and how she looks and behaves with the pups. If the pups are really hers, she will interact with them.

- ❧ Good breeders are happy to provide lots of information and at least one reference before you commit

- ❧ If the breeder is reluctant to answer your questions, look elsewhere

- ❧ Pressure selling: on the phone, the breeder doesn't ask you many questions and then says: *"There are only X many puppies left and I have several other buyers interested."* Walk away

- ❧ You hear *"Our Bulldog puppies are cheaper because*...." Walk away

- ❧ Ask to see the other puppies from the litter

- ❧ The mother is not with the puppies, but brought in to meet you

- ❧ The puppies look small for their stated age

- ❧ If the breeder says that the dam and sire are Kennel Club or AKC registered, ask to see the registration papers

- ❧ Photographs of so-called *"champion ancestors"* do not guarantee the health of the puppy

*Look beyond the cute, fluffy exterior. The way to look INSIDE the puppy is to see the parents and, most importantly, check what health tests have been carried out. "Vet checked" does NOT mean the pup or parents have passed any genetic health tests*

- The person you are buying the puppy from did not breed the dog themselves. Deal with the breeder, not an intermediary

- The place you meet the puppy seller is a car park, somebody else's house or place other than the puppies' home

- The seller tells you that the puppy comes from top, caring breeders from your or another country. Good breeders don't sell their puppies through brokers

- Ask to see photos of the puppy from birth to present day

- Be wary of *"rare colours"* or *"rare markings."* Make sure health and welfare boxes are ticked

- Price – if you are offered a very cheap Bulldog, he or she almost certainly comes from dubious stock and you will likely face issues in the future – usually health-related

- Beware of imported Bulldogs! There is a huge dog export trade from some countries, especially in Central and Eastern Europe. These dogs are often poor specimens raised in unacceptable conditions with little socialisation. They often go on to develop health or behaviour problems

- If you get a rescue Bulldog, make sure it is from a recognised rescue group and not a *"puppy flipper"* who may be posing as a do-gooder, but is in fact getting dogs (including stolen ones) from unscrupulous sources

- NEVER buy a puppy because you feel sorry for it; you are condemning other dogs to a life of misery

- If you have any doubt, go with your gut instinct and **WALK AWAY** - even if this means losing your deposit. It will be worth it in the long run

One UK breeder adds: "Avoid websites that want money straight away to go on their waiting list. Feedback or reviews may not be genuine, so always ask if you can be put in contact with a few of them and ask lots of questions to see if the info adds up. My reviewers are always open for contact.

"If there are a lot of different breeds on the website, then you know they are breeding on a big scale, which means there is no attention to detail or one-to-one rearing. This is why puppies often develop behavioural problems that are hard to reverse. Your gut instinct is a good one to follow if something is just not right or adding up when looking through any website."

 *Bad breeders do not have two horns coming out of their heads! Most will be very friendly when you phone or visit - after all, they want to make the sale. It's only later when problems develop.*

## Puppy Mills and Farms

Unscrupulous breeders are everywhere. That's not to say there aren't some excellent Bulldog breeders out there; there certainly are. You have to do your research to find them.

While new owners might think they have bagged a cheap puppy, it often turns out to be false economy in the case of Bulldogs, and emotionally disastrous when the puppy develops health problems due to poor breeding, or behavioural problems due to poor temperament or lack of socialisation.

The UK's Kennel Club says as many as one in four puppies bought in the UK may come from puppy farms - and the situation is no better in North America. The KC Press release states: "As the popularity of online pups continues to soar:

🐾 Almost one in five pups bought (unseen) on websites or social media die within six months

🐾 One in three buys online, in pet stores and via newspaper adverts - outlets often used by puppy farmers – this is an increase from one in five in the previous year

🐾 The problem is likely to grow as the younger generation favour mail order pups, and breeders of fashionable breeds flout responsible steps

"We are sleepwalking into a dog welfare and consumer crisis as new research shows that more and more people are buying their pups online or through pet shops, outlets often used by cruel puppy farmers, and are paying the price with their pups requiring long-term veterinary treatment or dying before six months old."

The KC research found that:

🐾 One third of people who bought their puppy online, over social media or in pet shops failed to experience "overall good health" with their puppy

🐾 Some 12% of puppies bought online or on social media end up with serious health problems that require expensive on-going veterinary treatment from a young age

Caroline Kisko, Kennel Club Secretary, said: "Whilst there is nothing wrong with initially finding a puppy online, it is essential to then see the breeder and ensure that they are doing all of the right things. This research clearly shows that too many people are failing to do this, and the consequences can be seen in the shocking number of puppies that are becoming sick or dying."

Marc Abraham, TV vet and founder of Pup Aid, added: "Sadly, if the *"buy it now"* culture persists, then this horrific situation will only get worse. There is nothing wrong with sourcing a puppy online, but people need to be aware of what they should then expect from the breeder.

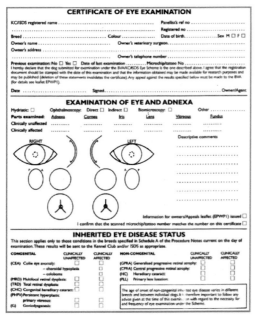

"For example, you should not buy a car without getting its service history and seeing it at its registered address, so you certainly shouldn't buy a puppy without the correct paperwork and health certificates and without seeing where it was bred."

*Pictured is a UK BVA Eye Certificate.*

"However, too many people are opting to buy directly from third parties, such as the internet, pet shops, or from puppy dealers, where you cannot possibly know how or where the puppy was raised.

"Not only are people buying sickly puppies, but many people are being scammed into paying money for puppies that don't exist, as the research showed that 7% of those who buy online were scammed in this way."

The KC has a lot of info on the dos and don'ts of buying a puppy at www.thekennelclub.org.uk/paw

Now you know what to avoid, what should you look out for? Read on to find out:

........................................................................................................

# Top 10 Signs of a Good Breeder

1. **His or her breeding dogs are health tested** with certificates to prove it.

2. **The area where the puppies are kept is clean and the puppies look clean.**

3. **Their Bulldogs appear happy and healthy.** The pups have clean eyes, ears, nose and bum (butt) with no discharge. They are alert, excited to meet new people and don't shy away from visitors.

4. **You see the puppy interact with the mother and other puppies.** The breeder encourages you to spend time with the puppy's parents - or at least the mother - when you visit and he or she is happy for you to visit more than once.

5. **Good breeders are very familiar with Bulldogs,** although some may also have one other breed – lots of breeds is a warning sign.

6. **They feed their adults and puppies high quality dog food** and give you some to take home and guidance on feeding and caring for your puppy. They will also be available for advice afterwards.

7. **They provide you with a written Puppy Contract, Health Guarantee and Puppy Pack or Going Home Bag** with items to help the pup's transition. They will show you records of the puppy's visits to the vet, vaccinations, worming medication, etc. and explain what other vaccinations your puppy will need.

8. **They don't always have pups available, but keep a list of interested people** for the next available litter. They don't over-breed, but do limit the number of litters from their dams.

9. **They will, if asked, provide references** from other people who have bought their puppies; call at least one.

10. **And finally ... good Bulldog breeders want to know their beloved pups are going to good homes and will ask YOU a lot of questions about your suitability as owners.**

When visiting puppies, take your time to have a good look around and go inside and outside. Are the breeders happy to show you around everywhere or a bit secretive? You will probably know if it's right or not when you see the surroundings. Walk away promptly if you have any doubts.

It's a massive decision, you want to make sure that the puppy you choose will be healthy and happy. If you think it could be a puppy mill, report it to the relevant authorities.

 *Take your puppy to a vet to have a thorough check-up within 48 hours of purchase. If your vet is not happy with the pup's condition, return her - no matter how painful it may be. Keeping an unhealthy puppy will only lead to further distress and expense.*

## Where to Find a Good Breeder

An excellent place to source a reputable breeder is the relevant breed club in your region or country. A full list of UK regional clubs is on the Kennel Club website. Type *"Kennel Club Bulldog*

*Dog Clubs'* into an online search engine to see them all, as well as a list of Bulldog rescue organisations.

Nationally, there is The British Bulldog Club at www.britishbulldogclub.com and on Facebook at www.facebook.com/groups/638841699530800 and The Bulldog Club Incorporated at www.bulldoginc.co.uk

The Bulldog Breed Council has lots of information for new and potential owners at www.bulldogbreedcouncil.co.uk

In the US, the AKC national club is the Bulldog Club of America at www.bulldogclubofamerica.org and details of regional clubs are at www.bulldogclubofamerica.org/about-bca/local-member-clubs

The UK Kennel Club and AKC also have lists of breeders. In the UK, look for an *Assured Breeder* and in the AKC "Find a Puppy" or "Marketplace" section, try and stick to *Breeders of Merit* or *Breeders with H.E.A.R.T.* as the AKC does not carry out checks on the others.

 *The fact that a puppy is registered with the Kennel Club or AKC does NOT mean that the parents have been screened for hereditary diseases, or that you have any guarantee of a healthy pup. A Kennel Club or AKC certificate simply means that the puppy's family tree can be traced back several generations. Always ask to see health certificates.*

Here are some other places to search:

1. Visit dog shows or canine events where Bulldogs are participating and talk to competitors and breeders.

2. Get a recommendation from somebody who has a Bulldog that you like - but make sure her dogs are tested.

3. Ask your vet for details of local, ethical Bulldog breeders.

4. Search the internet - there are dozens out there; use the advice in this chapter to find a reputable breeder.

5. If you are in the UK, visit the Bulldog stand at Discover Dogs during the annual Crufts dog show in early March.

# Questions to Ask a Breeder

Here's a reminder of the questions you should be asking. The Kennel Club also has a three-minute YouTube video entitled *The Dos and Don'ts of Buying a Puppy* at: www.youtube.com/watch?v=1EhTu1TQcEc

1. **Have the parents been health screened?** Ask to see certificates and what guarantees the breeder is offering in terms of genetic illnesses. How long do these guarantees last – 12 weeks, a year, a lifetime? It varies, but reputable breeders will definitely give some form of guarantee, and this should be stated in the Puppy Contract.

2. **What veterinary care have the pups had so far?** Ask to see records of flea treatments, wormings, vaccinations and microchipping, which is compulsory in the UK.

3. **Are you registered with the Kennel Club in the UK, AKC in the US, or a member of a Bulldog breed club?** Not all good Bulldog breeders are members, but this is a good place to start.

4. **How long have you been breeding Bulldogs?** You are looking for someone who has a track record with the breed.

5. **Can you put me in touch with someone who already has one of your puppies?**

6. **How many litters has the mother had?** Females should not have litters until they are two years old, and a female Bulldog should not have more than three litters maximum in her lifetime. Check the age of the mother.

7. **What happens to the mother once she has finished breeding?** Are they kept as part of the family, rehomed in loving homes or sent to animal shelters?

8. **Do you breed any other types of dog?** Buy from a specialist, preferably one who does not breed lots of other types of dog - unless you know they have a good reputation.

9. **What is so special about this litter?** You are looking for a breeder who has used good breeding stock and his or her knowledge to produce handsome, healthy dogs with good temperaments.

10. **What do you feed your adults and puppies**? A reputable breeder will feed a top quality dog food and advise that you do the same.

11. **What is the average lifespan of your dogs?** Bulldog lifespan is short and pups that a) breathe easily and b) have been bred from healthy stock generally live longer.

12. **How socialised and housetrained is the puppy?** Good breeders often start the socialisation and potty training process before they leave.

13. **How would you describe the temperament of the parents?** Try to interact with both parents, or at least the mother.

14. **Why aren't you asking me any questions?** A good breeder is committed to making a good match between the new owners and their puppies. If the breeder spends more time discussing money than the welfare of the puppy, draw your own conclusions as to what their priorities are – and they probably don't include improving the breed. Walk away.

## Choosing a Healthy Bulldog

Once you've selected your breeder and a litter is available, you then have to decide WHICH puppy to pick, unless the breeder has already earmarked one for you after asking lots of questions. Here are some pointers on puppy health:

1. Your chosen puppy should have **a well-fed appearance.** She should not, however, have a distended abdomen (pot belly) as this can be a sign of worms or other illnesses. The ideal puppy should not be too thin either; you should not be able to see her ribs.

2. **The puppy should breathe freely** without snorting and snuggling.

3. **Her nose should be cool, damp and clean** with no discharge.

4. **The pup's eyes should be bright and clear** with no discharge or tear stain. Steer clear of a puppy that blinks a lot, this could be the sign of a problem.

5. **The pup's ears should be clean** with no sign of discharge, soreness or redness and no unpleasant smell.

6. **Check the puppy's rear end** to make sure it is clean and there are no signs of diarrhoea.

7. While you're there, **check what type of tail the pup has.** Avoid buying a pup with an inverted tail, a very tight corkscrew tail or no tail at all. Bacteria gets trapped near the anus in these types of tails and it's very hard, if not impossible, to clean up. In extreme cases, the tail has to be amputated to avoid recurring infections. A tiny corkscrew tail that looks like it is turning back into the body could also be a sign of the spinal condition hemivertebrae. The tail, whether straight or screw, should be flexible.

8. **The pup's coat should look clean,** feel soft - and puppies should smell good! The coat should have no signs of ticks or fleas. Red or irritated skin or bald spots could be a sign of infestation or a skin condition. Also, check between the toes of the paws for signs of redness or swelling.

9. **The puppy should be alert** and curious about you and her surroundings, not timid.

10. **Gums should be clean and pink.**

11. **Choose a puppy that moves freely** without any sign of injury or lameness. It should be a fluid movement, not jerky or stiff, which could be a sign of joint problems.

12. When the puppy is distracted, clap or make a noise behind her - not so loud as to frighten her - to **make sure she is not deaf.**

13. Finally, **ask to see veterinary records** to confirm your puppy has been wormed and had her first vaccinations.

If you get the puppy home and things don't work out for whatever reason, good breeders will also take the puppy back — either within a limited time frame or for the whole life of the puppy - although if it is more than one year later, you cannot expect to be financially reimbursed.

# Choosing the Right Temperament

You've decided on the Bulldog because you really like the way these dogs look, their temperament and maybe because they are one of the very few impressive-looking breeds that doesn't need a huge amount of exercise.

**Individuals -** The first thing to remember is that while different Bulldogs may share many characteristics and temperament traits, each puppy also has her own individual character, just like humans.

The generally placid temperament of the Bulldog suits most people. However, if you are buying a puppy, visit the breeder more than once to see how your chosen pup interacts and get an idea of her character in comparison to her littermates. If you are rescuing or adopting an adult dog, you may also have to deal with health or behaviour issues which may arise.

Some Bulldog puppies will run up to greet you, pull at your shoelaces and playfully bite your fingers. Others will be more content to stay in the bed sleeping. Watch their behaviour and energy levels. Which puppy will be most suitable?

**Submissive or Dominant? -** A submissive dog will by nature be more passive, less energetic and also possibly easier to train. A dominant dog will usually be livelier. They may also be more stubborn and need more time and patience when training or socialising with other dogs.

There is no good or bad, it's a question of which type of character will best suit you and your lifestyle. Here are a couple of quick tests to try at the breeder's to see if your puppy has a submissive or dominant personality:

- Roll the Bulldog puppy gently on to her back in the crook of your arm (or on the floor). Then rest a hand on the pup's chest and look into her eyes for a few seconds. If she immediately struggles to get free, she is considered to be **dominant**. A puppy that doesn't struggle, but is happy to stay on her back may have a more **submissive** character

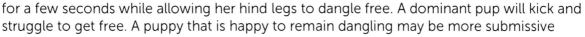

- A similar test is the suspension test. Gently lift the puppy at arm's length under the armpits for a few seconds while allowing her hind legs to dangle free. A dominant pup will kick and struggle to get free. A puppy that is happy to remain dangling may be more submissive

Here are some other useful signs to look out for:

- Watch how she interacts with other Bulldog puppies in the litter. Does she try and dominate them, does she walk away from them or is she happy to play with her littermates? This may give you an idea of how easy it will be to socialise her with other dogs

- After contact, does the pup want to follow you or walk away from you? Not following may mean she has a more independent nature

- If you throw something for the puppy is she happy to retrieve it for you or does she ignore it? This may measure their willingness to work with humans

❧ If you drop a bunch of keys behind the puppy, does she act normally or does she flinch and jump away? The latter may be an indication of a timid or nervous disposition. Not reacting could also be a sign of deafness

Decide which temperament would fit in with you and your family and the rest is up to you.

A Bulldog that has constant positive interactions with people and other animals during the first four months of life will be a happier, more stable dog. In contrast, a puppy plucked from her family and isolated at home alone for weeks on end will be less happy, less socialised and may develop behaviour problems later.

Puppies are like children. Being properly raised contributes to their confidence, sociability, stability and intellectual development. The bottom line is that a pup raised in a warm, loving environment with people is likely to be more tolerant and accepting and less likely to display poor behaviour.

## Puppy Contracts

Most good breeders provide their puppy parents with a Puppy Contract. This protects buyer and seller by providing information on the puppy until she leaves the breeder. You should also have a health guarantee for a specified time period. A Puppy Contract will answer such questions as:

❧ Whether the puppy is covered by breeder's insurance and can be returned if there is a health issue within a certain period of time

❧ Microchipping, vaccinations and details of worming treatments

❧ What health issues the pup and parents have been screened for

❧ What the puppy is currently being fed and if any food is being supplied

❧ Whether the pup was born by Caesarean section

❧ Details of the dam and sire

It's not easy for caring breeders to part with their puppies after they have lovingly bred and raised them, and so many supply extensive care notes for new owners, which may include details such as:

❧ The puppy's daily routine

❧ Feeding schedule

❧ Future vaccination schedule

❧ General puppy care

❧ Toilet training

❧ Socialisation

The Royal Society for the Prevention of Cruelty to Animals (RSPCA) has a downloadable puppy contract, *pictured,* endorsed by vets and animal welfare organisations; you should be looking for something similar from a breeder.

Type *"RSPCA Puppy Contract"* into Google or read it in full at: https://puppycontract.rspca.org.uk/home

In the US, type *"AKC Preparing a Puppy Contract"* into Google, or visit: www.akc.org/expert-advice/dog-breeding/preparing-a-contract-for-puppy-buyers

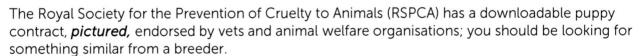

# 5. Bringing Puppy Home

Getting a new puppy is so exciting. You can't wait to bring the little fella home. Before that happens, you probably dream of all the things you are going to do together; going for walks in the countryside, playing games, making new friends in the park then falling asleep together on the sofa.

Your pup has, of course, no idea of your big plans, and the reality when he or she arrives can be a big shock for some owners!

Bulldog puppies are wilful little critters with minds of their own and powerful jaws with teeth like sharks. They leak at both ends, chew anything in sight, constantly demand your attention, nip the kids or anything else to hand, cry or whine and don't pay a blind bit of notice to your commands... There is a lot of work ahead before the two of you develop that unique bond!

Your pup has to learn what you require from him before he can start to meet some of your expectations - and you have to learn what your pup needs from you.

.........................................................................................................................................

Once your new arrival lands in your home, your time won't be your own, but you can get off to a good start by preparing things before the big day. Here's a list of things to think about getting beforehand - your breeder may supply some of these:

## Puppy Checklist

- ✓ A dog bed or basket
- ✓ Bedding – a Vetbed or Vetfleece would be a good choice, you can buy one online
- ✓ A towel or piece of cloth that has been rubbed on the puppy's mother to put in the bed
- ✓ A puppy gate or pen to initially contain the pup in one area of the house
- ✓ A collar or puppy harness with identification tag and leash
- ✓ Food and water bowls, preferably stainless steel
- ✓ Puppy food – find out what the breeder is feeding and stick with that to start with
- ✓ Puppy treats, healthy ones like carrots or apple are best, no rawhide
- ✓ Newspapers, and a bell if you decide to use one, for potty training
- ✓ Poop bags
- ✓ Toys and chews suitable for puppies
- ✓ A puppy coat if you live in a cool climate
- ✓ A crate if you decide to use one
- ✓ Old towels for cleaning and drying your puppy and partially covering the crate

**AND PLENTY OF TIME!**

Later on, you'll also need grooming brushes, flea and worming products and maybe a travel crate. Many good breeders provide Puppy Packs to take home; they contain some or all of the following items:

- ✓ Registration certificate
- ✓ Pedigree certificate
- ✓ Buyer's Contract
- ✓ Information pack with details of vet's visits, vaccinations and wormings, parents' health certificates, diet, breed clubs, etc.
- ✓ Puppy food
- ✓ ID tag/microchip info
- ✓ Blanket that smells of the mother and litter
- ✓ Soft toy that your puppy has grown up with, possibly a chew toy as well
- ✓ Four or five weeks' free insurance

 **FACT** ⟩ *In the UK, all puppies have to be microchipped BEFORE they leave the breeder by law - and that must be at eight weeks or older.*

# Puppy Proofing Your Home

A few adjustments will be needed to make your home safe and suitable. Puppies are small bundles of instinct and energy when they are awake, with little common sense and even less self-control.

Young Bulldogs love to play. They may have bursts of energy before they run out of steam and spend much of the rest of the day sleeping. As one breeder says: *"They have two speeds – ON and OFF!"*

Puppies love to investigate with their noses and mouths. Check your garden or yard, make sure there are no poisonous or low plants with sharp leaves or thorns that could cause eye injuries. There are literally dozens of plants harmful to a puppy if ingested, including azalea, daffodil bulbs, lily, foxglove, hyacinth, hydrangea, lupin, rhododendron, sweet pea, tulip and yew.

The Kennel Club has a list of some of the most common ones, type *"Kennel Club poisonous plants"* into Google or visit: http://bit.ly/1nCv1qJ The ASPCA has an extensive list for the USA at: http://bit.ly/19xkhoG or Google *"ASPCA poisonous plants."*

Fence off any sharp plants, such as roses, that can injure a dog's eyes. Make sure every little gap has been plugged in any fences. You'd be amazed at the tiny spaces determined puppies can escape through - and your new arrival won't have any road sense.

Puppies are little chew machines and puppy-proofing your home involves moving anything sharp, breakable or chewable - including your shoes. Lift electrical cords, mobile phones and chargers, remote controls, etc. out of reach and block off any off-limits areas of the house, such as upstairs or your bedroom, with a child gate or barrier, especially as he may be shadowing you for the first few days.

Create an area where your puppy is allowed to go, perhaps one or two rooms, preferably with a hard floor that is easy to clean. Keep the rest of the house off-limits, at least until the pair of you have mastered potty training.

This area should be near the door to the garden or yard for toileting. Restricting the puppy's space also helps him to settle in. He probably had a den and small space at the breeder's. Suddenly having the freedom of the whole house can be quite daunting - not to mention messy!

You can buy a purpose-made dog barrier or use a sturdy baby gate, which may be cheaper. Choose one with narrow vertical gaps or mesh, and check that your puppy can't get his head stuck between the bars, or put a covering or mesh over the bottom of the gate initially. You can also make your own barrier, but bear in mind that cardboard, fabric and other soft materials will get chewed.

 **FACT** ⟩ *A puppy's bones are soft, and studies have shown that if pups go up and down stairs regularly, or jump on and off furniture, they can develop joint problems later in life.*

**Don't underestimate your puppy! Young Bulldogs are very determined, so choose a barrier higher than you think necessary.**

The puppy's designated area or room should not be too hot, cold or damp and free from draughts. Bulldogs, and particularly puppies, are sensitive to temperature fluctuations and don't do well in very hot or very cold conditions. If you live in a hot climate, your pup may need air conditioning in the summertime.

Just as you need a home, so your puppy needs a den; a haven where your pup feels safe. Young puppies sleep for 18 hours or more a day at the beginning; this is normal. You have a couple of options; you can get a dog bed or basket, or you can use a crate, which can also speed up potty training. **See Chapter 7. Crate Training and Housetraining** for getting your Bulldog used to being in a crate.

It may surprise American readers to learn that common practice in the UK is to contain the puppy in the kitchen or utility room until he's housetrained, and later to allow the dog to roam around the house at will. Some owners do not allow their dogs upstairs, but many do.

Some owners prefer to create a safe penned area for their pup, rather than a crate, while others use both a pen and a crate. You can make your own barriers or buy a manufactured heavy duty metal playpen, *pictured, next page.* A fabric pen will not be robust enough for a Bulldog.

The time any young children spend with the puppy should be limited to a few short sessions a day. Plenty of sleep is **essential** for the normal development of a young dog. You wouldn't wake a baby every hour or so to play, and the same goes for puppies.

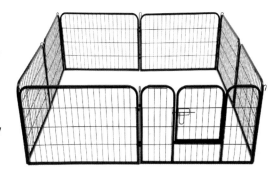

Wait a day or two before inviting friends round to see your handsome new puppy. However excited you are, your new arrival needs a few days to get over the stress of leaving mother and siblings and start bonding with you.

While confident, well-socialised puppies may settle in right away, other puppies may feel sad and a little afraid. Make the transition as gentle and unalarming as possible. For young Bulldogs to grow into well-adjusted adult dogs, they have to feel comfortable and relaxed in their new surroundings, and understand their place in the household.

After a few sleep-deprived nights followed by days filled with entertaining your little puppy and dealing with chewed shoes, nipping and a few housetraining "accidents," your nerves might be a tiny bit frayed! Try to remain calm and patient... it may take a little time for you both to get on the same wavelength.

**FACT** ❯ *This early period is a very important time for your puppy - how you react and interact with each other during these first few days and weeks will help to shape your relationship and your Bulldog's character for the rest of his life.*

## Bones, Chew Treats and Toys

Like babies, puppies like to explore the world with their mouths, and some Bulldogs go through a *"shark phase"* where they bite everything in sight - so chew treats and toys are a must!

There are some things you can't move out of puppy's way, like kitchen cupboards, doors, sofas, fixtures and fittings, so try not to leave your pup unattended for any length of time where he can chew something that is hard to replace.

**Tip** *Avoid giving old socks, shoes or slippers, or your pup will naturally come to think of your footwear as fair game!*

You can give a Bulldog puppy *a raw bone* to gnaw on - NEVER cooked bones as these can splinter. Avoid poultry and pork bones, and ribs - especially pork ribs - are too high in fat.

Big knuckle bones and marrow bones are a good choice - the bone should be too large for the puppy to swallow. Puppies should be supervised and the bone removed after an hour or so. Don't feed a puppy a bone if there are other dogs around, it could lead to food aggression.

**FACT** ❯ *Raw bones contain bacteria, and families with babies or very young children shouldn't feed them indoors. Keep any bones in a fridge or freezer and always wash your hands after handling them.*

Alternatives to real bones or plastic chew bones are natural *reindeer antler* chew toys *(pictured),* which have the added advantage of calcium, although they are hard and have been known to crack teeth.

Natural chews preferred by some breeders include ears, dried rabbit pelt and tripe sticks – all excellent for teething puppies - once you have got over the smell!

*Rawhide chews are not recommended as they can get stuck in a dog's throat or stomach, but bully sticks (pictured) are a good alternative.*

Made from a bull's penis(!) they can be a good distraction from chewing furniture, etc. and help to promote healthy teeth and gums. Bully sticks are highly digestible, break down easily in the stomach and are generally considered safe for all dogs. They are made from 100% beef, normally contain no additives or preservatives, come in different sizes and dogs love 'em. **NOTE: Puppies should be supervised while eating bully sticks or any other treats.**

Dental sticks are good for cleaning your dog's teeth, but many contain preservatives and don't last very long with a determined chewer. One that does last is the **Nylabone Dura Chew Wishbone,** made of a type of plastic infused with flavours appealing to dogs. Get the right size and throw it away if it starts to splinter after a few weeks.

 Another long-lasting treat option is the **Lickimat (pictured),** which you smear with a favourite food. This inexpensive mat, available online, will keep your puppy occupied for some time – although they can leave a bit of a mess. Other choices include **Kong toys,** which are pretty indestructible, and you can put treats (frozen or fresh) inside to keep your dog occupied while you are out. All of these are widely available online, if not in your local pet store.

As far as toys go, the **Zogoflex Hurley and** the **Goughnut** are both strong and float, so good for swimmers – and you'll get your money back on both if your Bulldog destroys them! For safety, the Goughnut has a green exterior and red interior, so you can tell if your dog has penetrated the surface - as long as the green is showing, you can let your dog "goughnuts."

A natural hemp or cotton tug rope is another option, as the cotton rope acts like dental floss and helps with teeth cleaning. It is versatile and can be used for fetch games as well as chewing.

**FACT ❯** *Puppies' stomachs are sensitive, so be careful what goes in. Even non-poisonous garden plants can cause intestinal blockages and/or vomiting. Like babies, pups can quickly dehydrate, so if your puppy is sick or has watery poop for 48 hours or more, seek medical advice.*

# The First Few Days

Before you collect your puppy, let the breeder know what time you will arrive and ask her not to feed the pup for a couple of hours beforehand - unless you have a very long journey, in which case he will need to eat something. If he hasn't just eaten, he will be less likely to be car sick and hungry when he lands in his new home. The same applies to an adult dog moving to a new home.

When you arrive, ask for an old towel or toy that has been with the pup's mother – you can leave one on an earlier visit to collect with the pup. Or take one with you and rub the mother with it to collect her scent and put this with the puppy for the first few days.

Get copies of any health certificates relating to the parents and a Contract of Sale or Puppy Contract that outlines everyone's rights and responsibilities – see **Chapter 4. Finding Your Puppy** for details. It should also state that you can return the puppy if there are health issues within a certain time frame – although if you have picked your puppy carefully, it should not come to this.

The breeder will also give you details of worming and any vaccinations, as well as an information sheet.

Find out exactly what the breeder is feeding and how much; dog's digestive systems cannot cope with sudden changes in diet - unless the breeder has deliberately been feeding several different foods to her puppies to get them used to different foods. In the beginning, stick to whatever the pup is used to; good breeders send some food home with the puppy.

## The Journey Home

Bringing a new puppy home in a car can be a traumatic experience. Your puppy will be sad at leaving his mother, brothers and sisters and a familiar environment. Everything will be strange and frightening and he may whimper and whine or even bark on the way home.

If you can, take somebody with you on that first journey – some breeders insist on having someone there to hold and cuddle the pup to make the journey less stressful for the pup.

Under no circumstances have the puppy on your lap while driving. It is simply too dangerous - a

Bulldog puppy is extremely cute, wriggly and far too distracting. Have an old towel between your travel companion and the pup as he may quite possibly pee - the puppy, not the passenger!

If you have to travel any distance, take a crate – either a purpose-made travel crate or a wire crate that he will use at home. Travel crates can be soft canvas or hard plastic. A plastic one should have holes in the sides to allow air flow.

Cover the bottom of the crate with a waterproof material and then put a comfortable blanket on top. You can put newspapers in half of the crate if the pup is partly housetrained. Don't forget to allow the pup to relieve himself beforehand.

 *If your journey is more than a couple of hours, take water to give him en route. He may need the toilet, but don't let him outside on to the ground as he is not yet fully vaccinated.*

## Arriving Home

As soon as you arrive home, let your puppy into the garden or yard, and when he "performs," praise him for his efforts. These first few days are critical in getting your puppy to feel safe and confident in his new surroundings. Spend time with the latest addition to your family, talk to him often in a reassuring manner. Introduce him to his den and toys, slowly allow him to explore and show him around the house – once you have puppy-proofed it.

Bulldog puppies are extremely curious - and amusing, you might be surprised at their reactions to everyday objects. Puppies explore by sniffing and mouthing, so don't scold for chewing. Instead, put objects you don't want chewed out of reach and replace them with chew toys. Some Bulldog puppies can be more "shark-like" than others; if yours is like a Hammerhead, make sure he has safe toys to chew!

Bulldogs usually get on well with other animals. However, it is important to introduce them to each other in the right conditions. Do it slowly and in supervised sessions on neutral territory or outdoors where there is space so neither feels threatened - preferably once the pup has got used to his new surroundings, not as soon as you walk through the door.

Gentleness and patience are the keys to these first few days, so don't over-face your pup. Have a special, gentle puppy voice and use his new name frequently in a pleasant, encouraging manner.

 *NEVER use his name to scold or he will associate it with bad things. The sound of his name should always make him want to pay attention to you as something good is going to happen - praise, food, playtime, and so on.*

Resist the urge to keep picking your puppy up – no matter how irresistible he is! Let him explore on his own legs, encouraging a little independence.

One of the most important things at this stage is to ensure that your puppy has enough sleep – **which is nearly all of the time** - no matter how much you want to play with or cuddle him. If you haven't decided what to call your new puppy yet, "Shadow" might be a good suggestion, as he will follow you everywhere!

Our website receives emails from worried new owners. Here are some of the most common concerns:

❧ My puppy won't stop crying or whining

❧ My puppy is shivering

❧ My puppy won't eat

❧ My puppy is very timid

❧ My puppy follows me everywhere, he won't let me out of his sight

❧ My puppy sleeps all the time, is this normal?

These behaviours are quite common at the beginning. They are just a young pup's reaction to leaving his mother and littermates and entering into a strange new world. It is normal for puppies to sleep most of the time, just like babies. It is also normal for some puppies to whine during the first couple of days.

**FACT** ❯ *Bulldog puppies from breeders who have already started socialising and housetraining will already have some idea about what is expected of them. They are likely to settle in quicker than those left to their own devices away from the family.*

Make your new pup as comfortable as possible, ensuring he has a warm (but not too hot), quiet den away from draughts, where he is not pestered by children or other pets. Handle him gently, while giving him plenty of time to sleep. If you have children teach them how to handle the pup safely.

 *Some breeders recommend keeping the pup in a crate near your bed for the first couple of nights, so he knows he is not alone. If he makes sad little whimpering noises or barks, talk softly and gently stroke him. Resist the urge to pick him up every time or he learns that crying always gives him the reward of your attention.*

A puppy will think of you as his new mother and it is quite normal for him to want to follow you everywhere, but after a few days start to leave your pup for short periods of a few minutes, gradually building up the time. A puppy unused to being left alone at all can grow up to have separation anxiety.

If your routine means you are normally out of the house for a few hours during the day, get your puppy on a Friday or Saturday so he has at least a couple of days to adjust to his new surroundings. A far better idea is to book time off work to help your puppy to settle in, if you can, or if you don't work, leave your diary free for the first couple of weeks.

Helping a new pup to settle in is virtually a full-time job. This can be a frightening time for some puppies. Is your puppy shivering with cold or is it nerves? Avoid placing him under stress by making too many demands. If he leaves his food, take it away and try it later. Don't leave it down all of the time or he may get used to turning his nose up at it. If your puppy is crying, it is probably for one of the following reasons:

-  He is lonely
- He is hungry
- He wants attention from you
- He needs to relieve himself

If it is none of these, then physically check him over to make sure he hasn't picked up an injury. Try not to fuss too much! If he whimpers, reassure with a quiet word. If he cries loudly and tries to get out of his allotted area, he may need to go to the toilet. Even if it is the middle of the night, get up and take him outside. Praise him if he performs.

The strongest bonding period for a puppy is between eight and 12 weeks of age. The most important factors in bonding with your puppy are TIME and PATIENCE, even if he makes a mess in the house or chews things. Spend time with your pup and you will have a loyal friend for life.

**FACT** ❯ *Bulldogs are very focused on their human and that emotional attachment may grow to become one of the most important aspects of your life – and certainly his.*

## Where Should the Puppy Sleep?

Where do you want your new puppy to sleep? In the beginning, you cannot simply allow a pup to wander freely around the house. Ideally, he will be in a contained area, such as a pen, possibly a crate, at night. While it is not acceptable to shut a dog in a cage all day, you can keep your puppy in a crate at night until housetrained. Some adult dogs still prefer to sleep in a crate.

You also have to consider whether you want the pup to permanently sleep in your bedroom or elsewhere. If it's the bedroom, don't let him jump on and off beds or couches, or race up and down stairs until he has stopped growing, as this can cause joint damage.

 *Some breeders recommend putting the puppy in a crate (or similar) next to your bed for the first two or three nights before moving him to the permanent sleeping place. Knowing you are close and being able to smell you will help overcome initial fears.*

He may still cry when you move him further away or out of your bedroom, but that should soon stop - you just have to block your ears for a couple of nights! He will have had those few days to get used to his new surroundings and feeling safe with you.

Eight or nine-week-old puppies can't go through the night without needing to pee (and sometimes poo); their bodies simply aren't up to it. To speed up housetraining, consider getting up in the night from Day One for the first week or so to let your pup outside for a pee. Just pick him up, take him outside with the minimum of fuss, praise the pee and put him back into the crate. After that, set your alarm for an early morning wake-up call.

NOTE: *While I and many breeders recommend getting up in the night in the beginning, a few breeders are against it, as they don't believe it speeds up housetraining. Ask your own breeder's advice on this one.*

We don't recommend letting a new pup sleep on the bed. He will not be housetrained and also a puppy needs to learn his place in the household and have his own special place. It's up to you whether to let him on the bed or not when he's older, but my advice is: if you value a good night's sleep, don't!

If you do allow your dog to sleep in the bedroom but not on the bed, be aware that most fully-grown Bulldogs snuffle, snore, fart and - if not in a crate - pad around the bedroom in the middle of the night and come up to the bed to check you are still there - or see if you want to play! None of this is conducive to a good night's sleep.

While it is not good to leave a dog alone all day, it is also not healthy to spend 24 hours a day together, as a dog can become too dependent. While this is very flattering for you, it actually means that the dog is less sure of himself when you are not there. The last thing you want on your hands is an anxious Bulldog.

A Bulldog puppy used to being on his own every night is less likely to develop attachment issues, so consider this when deciding where he should sleep.

# Vaccinations and Worming

It is a good idea to have your Bulldog checked out by a vet soon after picking him up. In fact, some Puppy Contracts stipulate that the dog should be examined by a vet within a couple of days.

This is to everyone's benefit and, all being well, you are safe in the knowledge that your puppy is healthy, at least at the time of purchase. Keep your pup on your lap away from other dogs in the waiting room as he will not yet be fully protected against canine diseases.

## Vaccinations

All puppies need immunisation and currently the most common way of doing this is by vaccination. An unimmunised puppy is at risk every time he meets other dogs as he has no protection against potentially fatal diseases – and it is unlikely a pet insurer will cover an unvaccinated dog.

It should be stressed that vaccinations are generally quite safe and side effects are uncommon. If your Bulldog is unlucky enough to be one of the **very few** that suffer an adverse reaction, here are some signs to look out for; a pup may exhibit one or more of these:

**MILD REACTION** - Sleepiness, irritability and not wanting to be touched. Sore or a small lump at the place where he was injected. Nasal discharge or sneezing. Puffy face and ears.

**SEVERE REACTION** - Anaphylactic shock. A sudden and quick reaction, usually before leaving the vet's, which causes breathing difficulties. Vomiting, diarrhoea, staggering and seizures.

*A severe reaction is rare.* There is a far greater risk of your Bulldog either being ill and/or spreading disease if he does not have the injections.

The usual schedule is for the pup to have the first vaccination at eight or nine weeks of age, usually before leaving the breeder. This gives protection from a number of diseases in one shot.

In the UK these are Distemper, Canine Parvovirus (Parvo), Infectious Canine Hepatitis (Adenovirus) and Leptospirosis. Most vets also recommend vaccinating against Kennel Cough (Bordetella). In the US this is known as DHPP. Puppies in the US also need vaccinating separately against Rabies. There are optional vaccinations for Coronavirus (not the COVID-19 strain!) and - depending on where you live and if your dog is regularly around woods or forests - Lyme Disease.

A puppy requires a second vaccination two to four weeks later. He is clear to mix with other animals two weeks after the second vaccinations.

- ❧ **Boosters for Distemper, Parvo and Canine Hepatitis are every three years**
- ❧ **Boosters for Leptospirosis are every year**

Leptospirosis is a bacterial infection that attacks the body's nervous system and organs. It is spread through infected rat urine and contaminated water, so dogs are at risk if they swim in or drink from stagnant water or canals. Outbreaks can often happen after flooding.

Diseases such as Parvo and Kennel Cough are highly contagious and you should not let your new arrival mix with other dogs - unless they are your own and have already been vaccinated - until two weeks after his last vaccination, otherwise he will not be fully immunised. Parvovirus can also be transmitted by fox faeces.

The vaccination schedule for the USA is different, depending on which area you live in and what diseases are present. The recommended ones are:

- ❧ **6-8 weeks - Distemper, Parainfluenza (normally organised by the breeder)**
- ❧ **8-12 weeks - DHPP (Distemper, Adenovirus Parainfluenza and Parvovirus)**
- ❧ **12-24 weeks – Rabies**
- ❧ **14-16 weeks DHPP**

Full details can be found by typing *"AKC puppy shots"* into Google, which will take you to this page: www.akc.org/expert-advice/health/puppy-shots-complete-guide

Avoid taking your new puppy to places where unvaccinated dogs might have been, like the local park. This does not mean that your puppy should be isolated - far from it. This is an important time for socialisation. It is OK for the puppy to mix with other dogs that you 100% know are up-to-date with their vaccinations and annual boosters. Perhaps invite a friend's dog round to play in your yard or garden.

Once your puppy is fully immunised, you have a window of a few weeks when it's the best time to introduce him to as many new experiences as possible - dogs, people, traffic, noises, other animals, etc. This critical period before the age of four to five months is when he is at his most receptive to socialisation. It is important that all of the experiences are **positive** at this stage of life; don't frighten or over-face your little puppy. Socialisation should not stop after a few months, but should continue for the rest of your dog's life.

The vet should give you a record card or send you a reminder when a booster is

due, but it's also a good idea to keep a note of the date in your diary – or in the **Pet Tracker** at the back of this book.

Tests have shown that the Parvovirus vaccination gives most animals at least seven years of immunity, while the Distemper jab provides immunity for at least five to seven years. In the US, many vets now recommend that you take your dog for a titer test once he has had his initial puppy vaccinations and one-year booster.

## Titres (Titers in the USA)

Some breeders and owners feel strongly that constantly vaccinating our dogs is having a detrimental effect on our pets' health. Many vaccinations are now effective for several years, yet some vets still recommend annual "boosters."

One alternative is **titres.** The thinking behind them is to avoid a dog having to have unnecessary repeat vaccinations for certain diseases as he already has enough antibodies present. Known as a **VacciCheck** in the UK, where they are still relatively new, they are more widespread in the USA.

To **"titre"** is to take a blood sample from a dog (or cat) to determine whether he has enough antibodies to guarantee immunity against a particular disease, usually Parvovirus, Distemper and Adenovirus (Canine Hepatitis). If so, then an annual injection is not needed. Titering is not recommended for Leptospirosis, Bordetella or Lyme Disease, as these vaccines provide only short-term protection. Many US states also require proof of a Rabies vaccination.

The vet can test the blood at the clinic without sending off the sample, thereby keeping costs down for the owner. A titre for Parvovirus and Distemper currently costs around $100 or less in the US, and a titre test in the UK costs as little as £40.

Titre levels are given as ratios and show how many times blood can be diluted before no antibodies are detected. So, if blood can be diluted 1,000 times and still show antibodies, the ratio would be 1:1000, which is a strong titre, while a titre of 1:2 would be "weak."

- ❧ A *strong (high) titre* means that your dog has enough antibodies to fight off that specific disease and is immune from infection

- ❧ A *weak titre* means that you and your vet should discuss revaccination - even then your dog might have some reserve forces known as *"memory cells"* that will provide antibodies when needed

🅣🅘🅟 *If you are going on holiday and taking your Bully to kennels, check whether the kennel accepts titre records; many don't as yet.*

One UK breeder said: "Most people don't realise that there are tests you can do to ensure that you don't over-vaccinate or over-worm your dog. It is well known that, although very rare, all

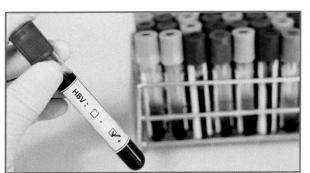

vaccinations can have potential adverse reactions. These can range from mild problems such as cystitis to a severe autoimmune disease. There are also a lot of discussions going on as to whether the over-vaccination of dogs may be linked to the increased rates of cancers.

"When my puppies go to their new homes, I tell all my owners to follow their vet's advice about worming and vaccinating, as the last thing new owners require is to be at odds with their vets.

"However, a few owners do express concern about all the chemicals we are introducing into our puppies' lives and if they do, I explain how I try to give my dogs a chemical-free life, if possible, as adult dogs. All dogs must have their puppy vaccinations.

"Instead of giving my adult dogs their core vaccinations for Canine Distemper, Parvovirus and Adenovirus (Hepatitis) every three years, I just take my dogs down to the local vet and ask them to do something called a titre test, also known as a VacciCheck.

"They take a small amount of blood and send it to a lab and the lab checks for antibodies to the diseases. If they have antibodies to the diseases, there is no reason to give dogs a vaccination. If a puppy has its puppy vaccinations, it is now thought that the minimum duration of immunity is between seven and 15 years.

"However, you should note that there is a separate vaccination for Leptospirosis and Canine Parainfluenza, which is given annually. Leptospirosis is recommended by the BSAVA (British Small Animal Veterinary Association). Leptospirosis is more common in tropical areas of the world and not that common in England. In order to make a decision about whether to give this to your dog annually, you need to talk to your vet and do some research yourself so you can make an informed decision. It may be that Leptospirosis is a problem in your area.

"We vaccinate our children up to about the age of 16. However, we don't vaccinate adults every one to three years, as it is deemed that the vaccinations they receive in childhood will cover them for a lifetime. This is what is being steadily proved for dogs and we are so lucky that we can titre test our dogs so we don't have to leave it to chance."

Another breeder added: "I do not vaccinate my dogs beyond the age of four to five years, I now have them titre tested. Every dog I have titre tested aged five to 10 years has been immune to the diseases vaccinated against when younger. I believe many vets over-vaccinate."

The (UK) Kennel Club now includes titre testing information into its Assured Breeder Pack, but has yet to include it under its general information on vaccines on its website. Type *"Titer testing Embrace Pet Insurance"* into Google for more info.

## Worming

All puppies need worming (technically, deworming). A good breeder will give the puppies their first dose of worming medication at around two weeks old, then probably again at five and eight weeks before they leave the litter – or even more often. Get the details and inform your vet exactly what treatment, if any, your pup has already had.

The main worms affecting puppies are roundworm and tapeworm. In certain areas of the US, the dreaded heartworm can also pose a risk. If you live in an affected area, discuss the right time to start heartworm medication when you visit your vet for puppy vaccinations – it's usually from a few months old.

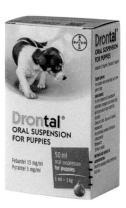

The pill should be given every month when there is no heavy frost (frost kills mosquitos that carry the disease); giving it all year round gives the best protection. The heartworm pill is by prescription only and deworms the dog monthly for heartworm, round, hook, and whip worm.

Roundworm can be transmitted from a puppy to humans – often children - and can in severe cases cause blindness, or miscarriage in women, so it's important to keep up to date with worming.

 *Worms in puppies are quite common, often picked up through their mother's milk. If you have children, get them into the habit of*

*washing their hands after they have been in contact with the puppy – lack of hygiene is the reason why children are susceptible.*

Most vets recommend worming a puppy once a month until he is six months old, and then around every two to three months. If your Bulldog goes in woods and fields on his walks, it is important to stick to a regular worming schedule, as he is more likely to pick up worms than one that spends most time indoors or in the yard.

Fleas can pass on tapeworms to dogs, but a puppy would not normally be treated unless it is known for certain he has fleas - and then only with caution. You need to know the weight of your puppy and then speak to your vet about the safest treatment to get rid of the parasites.

It is not usually worth buying a cheap worming or flea treatment from a supermarket, as they are usually far less effective than more expensive vet-recommended preparations, such as Drontal.

📌 *Buy age-appropriate worming treatments.*

Several people living in the US have contacted our website claiming the parasite treatment *Trifexis* has caused health issues in their dogs. http://www.max-the-schnauzer.com/trifexis-side-effects-in-schnauzers.html

Breeders must worm their puppies as they are all born with worms picked up from the mother's milk. However, there are ways to reduce worming treatments for adult dogs.

Following anecdotal reports of some dogs experiencing side effects with chemical wormers, more owners are looking to use natural wormers on their dogs. If you go down this route, check exactly which worms your chosen herbal preparation deals with – it may not be all of them.

A method of reducing worming medication by testing your dog's stools is becoming more popular. You send a small sample of your dog's poop off in an envelope every two to three months. If the result is positive, your dog needs worming, but if negative, no treatment is necessary.

In the UK this is done by veterinary labs like Wormcount www.wormcount.com and similar options are available in the USA – there is even a *"fecal worm test"* available at just over $20 from Amazon.com.

**A Bulldog has a relatively sensitive system, so anything that reduces the amount of chemicals going into your dog should at least be considered.**

# 6. Feeding A Bulldog

Your Bulldog may look like a tough guy or gal, but that sturdy exterior is covering a delicately balanced interior. And to keep their whole biological machine in good working order, Bullies need the right fuel, just like finely-tuned sports cars.

Feeding the correct diet is more important with Bulldogs than with most other breeds, which is why good breeders provide new owners with a feeding chart and a quantity of puppy food. The correct diet in the right quantities is an essential part of keeping your Bulldog fit and healthy.

Many Bulldogs react to certain foods. The wrong food can result in allergic reactions, dermatitis, kidney stones, indigestion, flatulence, joint problems and even heart issues.

Bulldogs have a tendency to gulp their food; they will eat just about anything if left to their own devices and they put on weight easily. So, it's up to you to monitor their intake and weight.

The topic of feeding your dog the right diet is something of a minefield. Owners are bombarded with endless choices and countless adverts from dog food companies, all claiming that theirs is best.

There is not one food that will give every single Bully the brightest eyes, shiniest coat, most energy, best digestion, least gas, longest life and stop him from scratching or having skin problems. Dogs are individuals, so you could feed a quality food to a group of dogs and find that most of them thrive on it, some do not so well, while a few may get an upset stomach or even an allergic reaction.

The question is: *"Which food is best for my Bulldog?"*

If you have been given a recommended food from a breeder, rescue centre or previous owner, it is best to stick to this. A good breeder will know which food their Bulldogs do well on. If you do decide - for whatever reason - to change diet, then this must be done gradually.

**FACT** ❯ *There are many different qualities of manufactured food. Often, you get what you pay for. A more expensive food is more likely to provide better nutrition - in terms of minerals, nutrients and high quality meats – than cheap ones, which usually contain a lot of grain.*

Dried foods, or kibble, tend to be less expensive than other foods. They have improved a lot over the last few years and some of the more expensive ones are now a good choice for a healthy, complete diet. Dried foods also contain the least fat and the most preservatives.

Some quality dried foods are also *"hypoallergenic,"* which means *"less likely to cause an allergic reaction."* Our dogs have generally done well on hypoallergenic kibble, but not all dogs thrive on dried food. It is a question of each owner finding the best food for their dog. If you got your Bulldog from a good breeder, he or she should be able to advise you on this.

*Beware of buying a food just because it is described as "premium." Many manufacturers blithely use this word, but there are no official guidelines as to what "premium" means.*

Always check the ingredients on any food sack, packet or can to see which ingredients are listed first, and it should be meat or poultry, not corn or grain. If you are in the USA, look for a dog food that has been endorsed by AAFCO (Association of American Feed Control Officials). In general, tinned foods are 60-70% water. Often semi-moist foods contain a lot of artificial substances and sugar, which is maybe why some dogs seem to love them!

## Life Stages

All Bulldog puppies should stay with their mothers and littermates until at least eight weeks old. Initially, pups get all their nutrients from their mother's milk and then are gradually weaned (put on to a different food by the breeder) from three or four weeks of age.

Some breeders purposely feed their pups a wide variety of different foods over the first few weeks to reduce the risk of them developing sensitive stomachs or becoming fussy eaters. However, most feed one food. Continue feeding the same puppy food and at the same times as the breeder when your puppy arrives home.

If you switch foods, do so gradually, as dogs' digestive systems cannot handle sudden changes of diet. (By the way, if you stick to the identical brand, you can change flavours in one go):

- ❧ Days 1-3 add 25% of the new food
- ❧ Days 4-6 add 50%
- ❧ Days 7-9 add 75%
- ❧ Day 10 feed 100% of the new food

Feed your puppy three or four times a day up to the age of 12-16 weeks. If at any time your puppy starts being sick, has loose stools or is constipated, slow the rate at which you are switching the food. Puppies soon dehydrate, so seek veterinary advice if vomiting or diarrhoea continues for more than a day.

 *If you live far away from the breeder, fill a large container with water from the breeder's house and mix it with your own water back home. Different types of water, e.g. moving from a soft to a hard water area or vice versa, can upset a sensitive pup's stomach.*

Bulldog puppies grow at an amazing rate, especially in the beginning. However, it is very important that they grow at a **controlled** rate. Giving your puppy more or less food will not affect adult size, it will only affect the rate of growth.

**FACT** 〉 *Puppies grow 20 times faster than adult dogs and so require a special diet while they are young. The average Golden Retriever, for example, grows from 14oz to over 65lb within one year, a 70-fold increase!*

Bulldog puppies also grow very quickly, but too much protein can strain their musculoskeletal systems, as their skeletons don't have time to catch up with the rest of their bodies. This can leave them vulnerable later in life to bone, joint, tendon and muscle problems. Too much protein can also cause kidney stones or obesity in Bulldogs.

There are three **Life Stages** to consider when feeding:

- ❧ Puppy

- ❧ Adult
- ❧ **Senior**, also called **Veteran**

Some manufacturers also produce a **Junior** feed for adolescent dogs. Each represents a different physical stage of life. If you decide on a commercially-prepared food, choose one approved either for **Puppies** or for **All Life Stages**. An **Adult** feed won't have enough protein, and the balance of calcium and other nutrients will not be right for a pup. Puppy food is very high in calories and nutritional supplements.

Some manufacturers offer foods specifically formulated for Bulldogs, as the breed has very specific dietary requirements. They may be worth considering, but read the label first, as some may be similar to general adult feeds.

# Feeding Puppies

Feeding a Bulldog puppy the right diet is important to help his young body and bones grow strong and healthy. Puppyhood is a time of rapid growth and development and puppies require different levels of nutrients to adult dogs.

For the first six weeks, puppies need milk about five to seven times a day, which they take from their mother. Generally, they make some sound if they want to feed. The frequency is then reduced.

Bulldog puppies should stay with their mothers and littermates until at least eight weeks old. During this time, the mother is still teaching her offspring some important rules about life.

For the first few days or weeks after that, continue feeding the same puppy food and at the same times as the breeder. You can then slowly change his food based on information from the breeder and your vet.

Because of their special nutritional needs, only give your puppy a food that is approved either for a **Puppy** or for **All Life Stages**. A feed marked **Adult** won't have enough protein, and the balance of calcium and other nutrients will not be right for a pup.

Switch to **Adult** food once he begins to approach maturity at 12 or 18 months old - check with your vet on the right time to switch. Some owners also feed a **Junior** food in between **Puppy** and **Adult**. Feeding puppy food too long can result in obesity and joint problems – and overweight puppies often grow into overweight adults.

DON'T:

- ❧ Feed table scraps. Your Bully will get used to begging and you'll end up with a 50lb mound of drooling dog next to you every time you eat. It will also affect a puppy's carefully balanced diet

- ❧ Give food that may be off. Puppies have sensitive stomachs

DO:

- ❧ Regularly check the weight of your growing puppy to make sure he is within normal limits for his age

- ❧ Take your puppy to the vet if he has diarrhoea or is vomiting for two days or more

- ❧ Remove food after it has been down for 15 to 20 minutes. Food available 24/7 encourages fussy eaters

Overfeeding large pups promotes too-rapid growth that puts stress on joints and can lead to problems such as hip dysplasia. You should not overfeed any Bulldog puppy; protein, calcium and phosphorus levels may be more critical than with some smaller breeds.

Most pet nutritionists recommend that fast growing puppies eat diets containing at least 30% protein and 9% fat (dry matter basis). The calcium content should be around 1.5% (or 3 grams per 1,000 kcal), check the labelling or ask your vet to recommend a feed - but be prepared, he or she may recommend an expensive option available only through them.

 *It's worth spending time to choose the right fuel to power healthy growth. It is a foundation stone towards future health. As a starting point, ask the breeder what she feeds her adults, or visit an online forum to ask what food other Bullies thrive on.*

Puppies should not have too much calcium, as it may cause the bones to grow too big too fast, resulting in joint problems later in life. Treats add calories to the overall diet and should not contain added calcium. Try getting your puppy used to slices of apple or carrot, **pictured,** as a healthy option.

## How Often?

Puppies have small stomachs but large appetites, so feed small amounts on a frequent basis. Establishing regular feeding times is a good idea, as this will also help with toilet training. Get him used to mealtimes at the same times daily and then let him outside to do his business as soon as he has finished. Puppies have fast metabolisms, so the results may be pretty quick!

Don't leave food out for the puppy so that he can eat it whenever he wants. You need to be there for the feeds because you want him and his body on a set schedule. Smaller meals are easier to digest, and energy levels don't peak and fall so much with frequent feeds.

- ❧ Up to the age of four months, feed your puppy four times a day

- ❧ Feed him three times a day until he is six months old

- ❧ Then twice a day for the rest of his life

Unless your Bulldog is particularly thin (which is very unusual), don't give in - no matter how much your cute pup pleads with those big, soulful eyes!

**Average Weight Table for Growing Bulldog Puppies**

One month old – 3kg (6.6lb)

Two months old – 5 kg (11lb)

Three months old – 7kg (15.4lb)

Four months old – 11kg (24.2lb)

Five months old – 15kg (33lb)

Six months old – 17kg (37.4lb)

Seven months old – 19kg (41.8lb)

Eight months old – 20kg (44lb)

Nine months old – 21kg (46.2lb)

Ten months old – 22kg (48.4lb)

Eleven months old - 22kg (48.4lb)

Twelve months old - 23kg (50.6lb)

As you will see, a Bulldog puppy puts most of his weight on during the first six months.

NOTE: The above weights are for normal-sized male Bulldogs, smaller ones and females weigh up to 20%-25% less.

.................................................................................................................................

# Feeding Options

The right food is a very important part of a healthy lifestyle for dogs as well as humans. Here are the main options explained:

**Dry dog food -** also called kibble, is a popular and relatively inexpensive way of providing a balanced diet. Millions of dogs thrive on kibble. It comes in a variety of flavours and with differing ingredients to suit the different stages of a dog's life, but cheap kibble is often false economy with Bulldogs.

Manufacturer Royal Canin has dried foods specially formulated for Bulldog puppies and adults. The company says of its adult Bulldog food:

*"Designed for Bulldogs from the age of 12 months, the special formulation helps to maintain the skin and coat of the Bulldog at its optimum condition."*

It claims that this food helps support healthy joints, has a special kibble to encourage chewing and reduces stool odour. There are also many other high quality manufactured foods popular with Bulldoggers.

**Canned food -** another popular choice – and it's often very popular with dogs too. They love the taste and it generally comes in a variety of flavours. These days there are hundreds of options, some are high quality, made from natural, organic ingredients with herbs and other beneficial ingredients.

As with dry food, read the label closely. Generally, you get what you pay for and the origins of cheap canned dog food are often somewhat dubious. Some Bulldogs can suffer from stomach upsets with too much tinned or soft food. Avoid fillers and preservatives, and brands with lots of grain or recalls.

**Semi-Moist** – this food typically has a water content of around 60%-65%, compared to 10% in dry food, making it easier to digest. It also has more sugar and salt, so is not suitable for some dogs. Semi-moist treats are shaped like pork chops, bacon *(pictured),* salamis, burgers, etc. They are the least nutritional of all dog foods, full of sugars, artificial flavourings and colourings, so avoid giving them regularly.

**Home-Cooked** - some owners want the ability to be in complete control of their dog's diet and to know exactly what their dog is eating. Feeding a home-cooked diet can be time-consuming and expensive. The difficult thing (as with the raw diet) is sticking to it once you have started out with the best of intentions, but your dog will love it and he won't be eating preservatives or fillers. Some high-end dog food companies now provide boxes of freshly-prepared meals with natural ingredients.

**Dehydrated** - this lightweight food is only minimally processed. It offers many of the benefits of raw feeding, including lots of nutrients, but with none of the mess or bacteria found in raw meats. Gentle heating slowly cooks proteins and helps start the digestive process, making it easier on the digestive tract of older Bulldogs, or those with sensitive stomachs. Owners just add water and let it stand for a minute or two to reconstitute the meal.

**Freeze-Dried** – this is usually raw, fresh food that has been freeze-dried by frozen food manufacturers. It's a more convenient, hygienic and less messy option than raw, and handy if you're going on a trip. It contains healthy enzymes but no preservatives. It is highly palatable and keeps for six months to a year. It says *"freeze-dried"* on the packet, but the process bumps up the cost and it is not available from every pet store – although it is widely available online. A good option for owners who can afford it.

## The Raw Diet

Opinions are divided on a raw diet. There is anecdotal evidence that some dogs thrive on it, particularly those with food intolerances or allergies, although scientific proof is lagging behind. Claims made by fans of the raw diet include:

- Reduced symptoms of - or less likelihood of - allergies, and less scratching
- Better skin and coats
- Easier weight management
- Improved digestion
- Less doggie odour and flatulence
- Higher energy levels
- Reduced risk of Bloat
- Helps fussy eaters
- Fresher breath and improved dental health
- Drier and less smelly stools, more like pellets
- Most dogs love a raw diet
- Overall improvement in general health and less disease

If your Bully is not doing well on a dry dog food, or has skin issues, lots of gas or allergies, you might consider a raw diet. Some commercial dog foods contain artificial preservatives, grains and excessive protein and fillers – causing a reaction in certain dogs. Dry, canned and other styles of processed food were mainly created as a means of convenience – for humans, not dogs!

Some nutritionists believe there are inherent beneficial enzymes, vitamins, minerals and other qualities in meats, fruits, vegetables and grains in their natural, uncooked state.

However, critics of a raw diet say that the risks of nutritional imbalance, intestinal problems and food-borne illnesses caused by handling and feeding raw meat outweigh any benefits.

It is true that owners must pay strict attention to hygiene when preparing a raw diet and it may not be a suitable option if you have children. The dog may also be more likely to ingest bacteria or parasites such as Salmonella, E. Coli and Ecchinococcus - although freeze-dried meals reduce the risk.

**FACT** 〉 *While some dogs do really well on a raw diet, it is not for every dog. It can cause loose stools, upset stomach and even vomiting in some, and there are other dogs that simply don't like the taste.*

There are two main types of raw diet, one involves feeding raw, meaty bones and the other is known as the BARF diet (*Biologically Appropriate Raw Food* or *Bones And Raw Food),* created by Dr Ian Billinghurst.

## Raw Meaty Bones

The diet is:

- 🐾 Raw meaty bones or carcasses form the bulk of the diet. **Cooked bones should NOT be fed, as they can splinter**

- 🐾 Table scraps both cooked and raw, such as vegetables

Australian veterinarian Dr Tom Lonsdale is a leading proponent of the raw meaty bones diet. He believes the following foods are suitable:

- 🐾 Chicken and turkey carcasses, after the meat has been removed for human consumption

- 🐾 Poultry by-products, including heads, feet, necks and wings

- 🐾 Whole fish and fish heads

- 🐾 Sheep, calf, goat, and deer carcasses sawn into large pieces of meat and bone

- 🐾 Other by-products, e.g. pigs' trotters, pigs' heads, sheep heads, brisket, tail and rib bones

- 🐾 A certain amount of offal can be included in the diet, e.g. liver, lungs, trachea, hearts, tripe

- 🐾 Table scraps and some fruit and vegetable peelings, but should not make up more than one-third of the diet

Low-fat game animals, fish and poultry are the best source of food. If you feed meat from farm animals (cattle, sheep and pigs), avoid excessive fat and bones too large to be eaten. It depends on price and what's available locally - start with your local butcher or farm shop.

**FACT** 〉 *Dogs are more likely to break their teeth eating large knuckle bones and bones sawn lengthwise than when eating meat and bone together.*

You'll also need to think about WHERE and WHEN you are going to feed. A dog takes some time to eat a raw bone and will push it around the floor, so the kitchen may not be the most hygienic place. Outside is one option, but what do you do when it's raining? Bulldogs are not known for their love of wet conditions! If you live in a hot climate, evening feeding may be best to avoid flies.

Establishing the right quantity to feed is based on your dog's activity levels, appetite and body condition. A very approximate guide of raw meaty bones for the average dog is:

**15%-20% of body weight per week, or 2%-3% a day.**

So, if your Bulldog weighs 45lb (20kg), he requires 6.75lb-9lb (3kg-4kg) of carcasses or raw meaty bones weekly. *These figures are only a rough guide for adult dogs.*

Dr Lonsdale says: "Wherever possible, feed the meat and bone ration in one large piece requiring much ripping, tearing and gnawing. This makes for contented pets with clean teeth." More information is available from www.rawmeatybones.com

NOTES: Pregnant or lactating females and growing puppies need more food. This diet may not be suitable for old dogs used to a processed diet or those with dental issues, or in households with children, due to the risk of bacterial infection from raw meat.

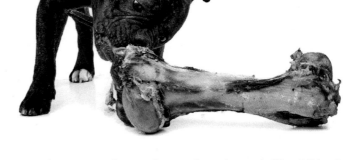

- ❧ Always monitor your Bulldog while he's eating

- ❧ Don't feed bones with sharp points, and remove any bone before it becomes small enough to swallow

- ❧ Raw meaty bones should be kept separate from human food and any surface the uncooked meat or bones have touched should be thoroughly cleaned afterwards

 *Puppies can and do eat diets of raw meaty bones, but consult your breeder or vet before embarking on this diet with a young dog.*

**The BARF diet -** A variation of the raw meaty bones diet is the BARF created by Dr Ian Billinghurst, who owns the registered trademark "Barf Diet."

A typical BARF diet is made up of 60%-75% of raw meaty bones - with about 50% meat, such as chicken neck, back and wings - and 25%-40% of fruit and vegetables, offal, meat, eggs or dairy foods. Bones must not be cooked or they can splinter inside the dog. There is lots of information on the BARF diet on the internet.

......................................................................................................................................................

## Reading Dog Food Labels

A NASA scientist would have a hard job understanding some manufacturers' labels, so it's no easy task for us lowly dog owners. Here are some things to look out for on the manufacturers' labels:

- ❧ **The ingredients are listed by weight and the top one should always be the main content,** such as chicken or lamb. Don't pick one where grain is the first ingredient; it is a poor-quality feed. If your Bulldog has a food allergy or intolerance to wheat (as many do) check whether a food is gluten free; all wheat contains gluten

- ❧ **Chicken meal (dehydrated chicken) has more protein than fresh chicken, which is 80% water.** The same goes for beef, fish and lamb. So, if any of these "meals" are No. 1 on the ingredient list, the food should contain enough protein

- ❧ Anything labelled *"human-grade"* is higher quality than normal dog food ingredients. E.g. Human-grade chicken includes the breast, thighs and other parts of the chicken suitable for human consumption. Human-grade chicken complies with United States Department of Agriculture (USDA) welfare standards

❧ A certain amount of flavourings can make a food more appetising for your dog. **Choose a food with a specific flavouring,** like *"beef flavouring"* rather than a general *"meat flavouring,"* where the origins are not so clear

❧ **Find a food suitable for the Bulldog breed and your dog's age and activity level.** Talk to your breeder or vet, or visit an online Bulldog forum to ask other owners' advice.

❧ **Natural is best.** Food labelled *"natural"* means that the ingredients have not been chemically altered, according to the FDA in the USA. However, there are no such guidelines governing foods labelled *'holistic'* – so check ingredients and how they have been prepared

❧ In the USA, dog food that meets American Feed Control Officials' (AAFCO) minimum nutrition requirements has a label that states: *"[food name] is formulated to meet the nutritional levels established by the AAFCO Dog Food Nutrient Profiles for [life stage(s)]"*

*If you live in the USA, we recommend looking for a food "as fed" to real pets in an AAFCO-defined feeding trial. The AAFCO label is the gold standard, and brands that do costly feeding trials indicate so on the package.*

Dog food labelled *"supplemental"* isn't complete and balanced. Unless you have a specific, vet-approved need for it, it's not something you want to feed your dog long term.

The *Guaranteed Analysis* listed on a sack or tin legally guarantees:

❧ **Minimum percentages of crude protein and crude fat, and**

❧ **Maximum percentages of crude fibre and moisture**

While it is a start, don't rely on it too much. One pet food manufacturer made a mock product with a guaranteed analysis of 10% protein, 6.5% fat, 2.4% fibre, and 68% moisture (similar to what's on some canned pet food labels) – the ingredients were old leather boots, used motor oil, crushed coal and water!

❧ **Protein** – found in meat and poultry, protein should be the first ingredient and is very important. It helps build muscle, repair tissue and contributes to healthy hair and skin. However, protein is packed with calories and too much can lead to weight gain and increased stress on the kidneys and liver

❧ **Fats** – these are a concentrated form of energy that give your dog more than twice the amount of energy that carbohydrates and proteins do. Common fats include chicken or pork fat, cottonseed oil, vegetable oil, soya bean oil, fish oil, safflower oil, and many more. They are highly digestible and are the first nutrients to be used by the body as energy.

❧ **Fibre** – found in vegetables and grains. It aids digestion and helps prevent anal glands from becoming impacted. The average dry dog food has 2.5%-4.5% crude fibre, but reduced-calorie feeds may be as high as 9%-10%

- **Carbohydrates** typically make up anywhere from 30%-70% of a dry dog food. They come mainly from plants and grains, and provide energy in the form of sugars
- **Vitamins and Minerals** — have a similar effect on dogs as humans. Glucosamine and chondroitin are good for joints
- **Omegas 3 and 6** — fatty acids that help give Bulldogs that sheen to their coat and a healthy skin; also good for inflammation control, arthritic pain, heart and kidneys

Well-formulated dog foods have the right balance of protein, fat, carbohydrates, vitamins, minerals and fatty acids. If you're still not sure what to choose for your Bulldog, check out these websites: www.dogfoodadvisor.com run by Mike Sagman in the USA and www.allaboutdogfood.co.uk run by UK canine nutritionist David Jackson.

## How Much Food?

This is another question that we are often asked on our website. The answer is … there is no easy answer! The correct amount of food for your dog depends on a number of factors:

- Breed
- Gender
- Age
- Energy levels
- Amount of daily exercise
- Health
- Environment
- Number of dogs in house
- Quality of the food

Some breeds have a higher metabolic rate than others. Bulldogs are generally regarded as dogs with fairly low activity levels, but energy levels vary from one Bulldog to the next. Young Bulldogs are usually full of energy.

Generally, smaller dogs have faster metabolisms so require a higher amount of food per pound of body weight. Female dogs are slightly more prone to putting on weight than male dogs. Some people say that dogs that have been spayed or neutered are more likely to put on weight, although this is disputed by others. Growing puppies and young dogs need more food than senior dogs with a slower lifestyle.

Every dog is different, you can have two Bulldogs with different temperaments and exercise requirements; the energetic dog will burn off more calories. Maintaining a healthy body weight for dogs — and humans — is all about balancing what you take in with how much you burn off. If your Bulldog is exercised twice a day and has play sessions with humans or other dogs, he will need more calories than a couch potato Bulldog.

Certain health conditions such as an underactive thyroid, diabetes, arthritis or heart disease can lead to dogs putting on weight, so their food has to be adjusted accordingly.

Just like us, a dog kept in a very cold environment will need more calories to keep warm than a dog in a warm climate. They burn extra calories in keeping themselves warm.

 **FACT** *A dog kept on his own is more likely to be overweight than a dog kept with other dogs, as he receives all of the food-based attention.*

Manufacturers of cheaper foods usually recommend feeding more to your dog, as much of the food is made up of cereals, which are not doing much except bulking up the weight of the food – and possibly triggering allergies in your Bulldog.

The daily recommended amount of food on the dog food sacks or tins are generally too high – after all, the more your dog eats, they more they sell! Because there are so many factors involved, there is no simple answer. However, below we have listed a broad guideline of the average number of **calories** a Bulldog with medium energy and activity levels needs.

Thanks to *"Better Food for Dogs - A Complete Cookbook and Nutrition Guide"* by D Bastin et al, published by Robert Rose, Inc for the following information and daily feeding guide: *"Target your dog at the highest acceptable weight of his breed class to begin with if he or she is overweight.*

*"On the other hand, if your dog is underweight, target your dog at the lowest acceptable weight of his breed class to begin with. Adjust the energy level gradually toward the middle of the range.*

*Note: if your dog's weight problems are caused by health problems, pregnancy or other conditions, consult your vet before implementing any weight management program as this must be supervised by your vet.*

**Disclaimer:** This chart is designed to give just a broad guideline on the amount of food to feed a dog every day based on size. Check your dog's ideal weight before embarking on a feeding regime. Consult your vet if your dog loses or gains considerable weight.

| IDEAL ADULT WEIGHT | ENERGY |
|---|---|
| 35lb / 15.8 Kg | 875 - 1050 Kcal |
| 40lb / 18.1 Kg | 965 - 1158 Kcal |
| 45lb / 20.4 Kg | 1056 - 1267 Kcal |
| 50lb / 22.6 Kg | 1143 - 1327 Kcal |

James Wellbeloved produce a dried hypoallergenic dog food, which we fed to a dog with allergies. Here are James Wellbeloved's recommended feeding amounts for dogs, listed in kilograms and grams (**28.3 grams=1 ounce. 1kg=2.2 pounds**).

The number on the left is the dog's **adult weight** in kilograms. An adult Bulldog should weigh somewhere between 40lb (18.14kg) and 55lb (25kg), depending on whether the dog is male or female.

The numbers on the right are the amount of daily food in grams that an average dog with average energy levels requires, measured in grams (divide this by 28.3 to get the amount in ounces). For example, a 3-month-old Bulldog puppy that will grow into a 20kg adult would require around 305 grams of food per day (10.75 ounces).

*NOTE: These are only very general guidelines, your dog may need more or less than this. Use the chart as a guideline only and if your dog appears to lose or gain weight, adjust his or her feeds accordingly.*

Puppy

| Size | Expected Adult Body Weight | Age of Puppy and daily Serving (grams) | | | | | |
|---|---|---|---|---|---|---|---|
| | | 2 mths | 3 mths | 4 mths | 5 mths | 6 mths | > 6 mths |
| Medium | 10kg | 155 | 190 | 195 | 190 | 190 | change to junior |
| Medium/Large | 20kg | 240 | 305 | 325 | 320 | 315 | change to junior /large breed junior |
| Large | 30kg | 300 | 400 | 435 | 435 | 430 | change to large breed junior |

Junior

| Size | Age of Puppy and daily Serving (g) | | | | | | | |
|---|---|---|---|---|---|---|---|---|
| | expected adult body weight (kg) | 6 mths | 7 mths | 8 mths | 10 mths | 12 mths | 14 mths | 16 mths |
| Medium | 10 | 200 | 195 | 185 | 175 | change to adult | | |
| Medium/Large* | 20 | 330 | 325 | 310 | 290 | 300 | change to adult/large breed adult | |
| Large* | 30 | 455 | 440 | 430 | 400 | 400 | | |

Adult

| Size | Body Weight (kg) | Daily Serving (g) |
|---|---|---|
| Toy | 2-5 | 55-115 |
| Small | 5-10 | 115-190 |
| Medium | 10-20 | 190-320 |
| Medium/Large | 20-30 | 320-430 |

# Top Tips for Feeding your Bulldog

1. If you choose a manufactured food, **don't pick one where meat or poultry content is NOT the first item listed on the bag.** Foods with lots of cheap cereals or sugar are not the best choice for many Bulldogs, particularly sensitive ones.

2. Some Bulldogs suffer from sensitive skin, "hot spots" or allergies. A cheap dog food, often bulked up with grain, will only make this worse. If this is the case, bite the bullet and **choose a high quality, usually more expensive, food.** You'll probably save money in vets' bills in the long run and your dog will be happier. A food may be described as *"hypoallergenic"* on the sack, this means *"less likely to cause allergies"* and is a good place to start with processed foods.

3. **Kibble, if you feed it, should be in small pieces.** Most Bulldogs suffer from too much gas, made worse by having a short muzzle and them gulping food. Feeding small kibble helps to slow them down, thereby reducing air intake.

4. **Avoid soya beans (soybeans), peas, beans, milk products and fatty or spicy foods.** They all increase flatulence (gas, farting, call it what you will, Bulldogs do a lot of it!).

5. **Feed your adult Bulldog twice a day**, rather than once. Two smaller feeds will reduce gas as well as the risk of gastric torsion, or Bloat (see **Chapter 11. Bulldog Health**).

6. **Establish a feeding regime and stick to it**. Dogs like routine. If you are feeding twice a day, feed once in the morning and then again at tea-time. Stick to the same times of day, which also helps your dog establish a toilet regime.

7. **Do not give the last feed too late,** or your dog's body will not have chance to process or burn off the food before sleeping. He will also need a walk or letting out in the garden or yard after his second feed to allow him to go to the toilet.

8. **Take away any uneaten food between meals.** Most Bullies LOVE their food, but any dog can become a fussy eater if it is available all day. Imagine if your dinner was left on the table for hours until you finished it. Returning to the table two or three hours later would not be such a tempting prospect, but coming back for a fresh meal would be far more appetising.

   Put the food bowl down twice a day and then take it up after 20 minutes – even if he has left some. If he is healthy and hungry, he will look forward to his next meal and should soon stop leaving food. If he does not eat anything for a couple of days, it could well be a sign that something is wrong with him.

9. **Try not to feed tidbits and treats between meals.** Bulldogs are often greedy and prone to obesity, which is a dangerous condition. Already a chunky breed, your Bully cannot afford to carry extra weight as it will place extra strain on his organs and joints, have a detrimental effect on his health and even his lifespan. Importantly, it also throws his balanced diet out of the window.

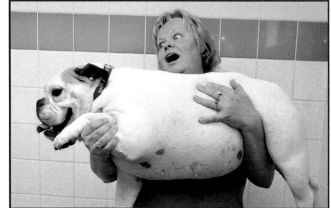

10. **Avoid feeding your dog from the table or your plate,** as this encourages drooling and attention-seeking behaviour.

11. **If you do feed leftovers, feed them INSTEAD of a balanced meal,** not as well as. High quality dog foods provide all the nutrients, vitamins, minerals and calories that your dog needs. Feeding tidbits or leftovers may be too rich for your dog in addition to his regular diet and cause him to scratch or have other problems, as well as put weight on.

12. **Start your puppy off with slices of raw carrots or apples** as a healthy low-calorie alternative to traditional dog treats.

13. **If you switch to a new food, do the transition gradually.** Unlike humans, dogs' digestive systems cannot handle sudden changes in diet. Do it over a week or so.

14. **NEVER feed the following items to your dog**: grapes, raisins, chocolate, onions, Macadamia nuts, any fruits with seeds or stones, tomatoes, avocados, rhubarb, tea, coffee or alcohol. ALL of these are poisonous to dogs.

15. **Check your dog's faeces** (aka stools, poo or poop!). If his diet is suitable, the food should be easily digested and produce dark brown, firm stools. If your dog produces soft or light stools, or has gas (even more than usual!) or diarrhoea, then the diet may not suit him, so consult your vet or breeder for advice.

16. **Check your dog's weight regularly.** Obesity in Bulldogs, as well as being generally unhealthy, can lead to the development of some serious health issues, such as diabetes. Although the weight will vary from one dog to another, a good rule of thumb is that an adult Bulldog's tummy should be higher than his rib cage. If his belly hangs down below it, he is overweight.

17. **Get him used to ice cubes or frozen yoghurt** while he is young, as these will help him to keep cool and avoid overheating. Most Bulldogs like ice cubes.

 *As well as plain water, you can also make beef or chicken broth from a stock cube - low sodium is best - and freeze it in ice cube trays. You can freeze vegetables and feed these as a treat. Ice cubes can also be a great help with teething Bulldogs.*

18. **Never give your dog cooked bones,** as these can splinter and cause him to choke or suffer intestinal problems, or rawhide. Bulldogs have a tendency to chew and then swallow rawhide, without first bothering to nibble it down into smaller pieces.

19. **Feed your dog in stainless steel dishes.** Plastic bowls don't last as long and, more importantly, a Bulldog has a sensitive face and plastic can trigger a reaction in some. Ceramic bowls are best for keeping water cold.

20. **If you have more than one dog, feed them separately**. Bulldogs generally get on well with other pets. But they are also greedy and feeding dogs together can lead to food aggression from one dog, either protecting his own food or trying to eat the food designated for another.

21. **Bulldogs are very loyal dogs** and they often form the strongest attachment with the person who feeds them. If your dog is not responding well to a particular family member, get that person to feed him every day. The way to a Bulldog's heart is often through his stomach!

22. And finally, **always make sure that your Bulldog has access to clean, fresh water.** Change the water and clean the bowl regularly — it gets slimy!

# Bulldogs and Food Allergies

Dog food allergies affect about one in 10 dogs. They are the third most common canine allergy after atopy (inhaled allergies) and flea bites. There is lots of evidence from owners that Bulldogs have a higher-than-normal incidence of food allergies and sensitivities.

Food allergies affect males and females, neutered and intact dogs in equal measures. They can start when your dog is five months or 10 years old - although the vast majority start between two and six years old. It is not uncommon for dogs with food allergies to have other types of allergies as well.

## Symptoms

If your Bulldog is not well, how do you know if the problem lies with his food or not? Here are some common symptoms of food allergies to look out for:

- Itchy skin (this is the most common). Your Bully may lick or chew his paws or legs and rub his face with his paws or on the furniture, carpet, etc.

- Excessive scratching

- Redness and inflammation on the chin and face

- Ear infections

- Hair loss

- Hot patches of skin

- Recurring skin infections

- Increased bowel movements (maybe twice as often as usual)

- Skin infections that clear up with antibiotics but recur when the antibiotics run out

There's a difference between dog food *allergies* and dog food *intolerance*:

### Typical reactions to allergies are skin problems and/or itching

### Typical reactions to intolerance are diarrhoea and/or vomiting

Allergies often cause a reaction in the skin. Dog food intolerance can be compared to people who get an upset stomach from eating spicy food. Both can be cured by a change to a diet specifically suited to your dog, although a food allergy may be harder to find the root cause of.

In the canine world generally, certain ingredients are more likely to cause allergies than others. In order of the most common triggers they are:

### Beef, dairy products, chicken, wheat, eggs, corn, soya (soy)

Unfortunately, these most common offenders are also the most common ingredients in dog foods!

**FACT** ▷ *A dog is allergic or sensitive to an ingredient, NOT to a particular brand, so it's important to read the food label. If your Bully has a reaction to beef, for example, he will react to any type of food containing beef, regardless of how much it costs or how well it has been prepared.*

AVOID corn, corn meal, corn gluten meal, artificial preservatives (including BHA, BHT, Propyl Gallate, Ethoxyquin, Sodium Nitrite/Nitrate and TBHQBHA), artificial colours, sugars and sweeteners, e.g. corn syrup, sucrose and ammoniated glycyrrhizin, powdered cellulose, propylene glycol.

## Bulldogs and Grain

**Although beef is the food most likely to cause allergies in the general dog population, there is evidence to suggest that the ingredient most likely to cause a problem in many Bulldogs is GRAIN. "Grain" is wheat or any other cultivated cereal crop.**

Many Bully breeds (such as all types of Bulldog, Boxers, Staffies, Pugs, Bull Terriers, Boston Terriers) are prone to a build-up of yeast in the digestive system. Foods that are high in grains and sugar can cause an increase in unhealthy bacteria and yeast in the stomach. This crowds out the good bacteria in the stomach and can cause toxins to occur that affect the immune system.

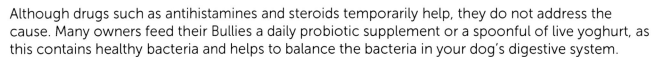

When the immune system is not functioning properly, the itchiness related to food allergies can cause secondary bacterial and yeast infections, which often show as ear infections, skin disorders, bladder infections and reddish or dark brown tear stains. Symptoms of a yeast infection also include:

* Itchiness

* A musty smell

* Skin lesions or redness on the underside of the neck, the belly or the feet, especially between the toes when they are called interdigital cysts

Although drugs such as antihistamines and steroids temporarily help, they do not address the cause. Many owners feed their Bullies a daily probiotic supplement or a spoonful of live yoghurt, as this contains healthy bacteria and helps to balance the bacteria in your dog's digestive system.

Switching to a grain-free diet may help to get rid of yeast and bad bacteria in the digestive system. However, avoid those based on soya beans and other legumes as they are not ideal for Bulldogs. Introduce the new food slowly and be patient, it may take a while for symptoms to subside – but you will definitely know if it has worked after 12 weeks.

It is worth noting that some of the symptoms of food allergies - particularly the scratching, licking, chewing and redness - can also be a sign of inhalant or contact (environmental) allergies, which are caused by a reaction to such triggers as pollen, grass or dust. Some dogs are also allergic to flea bites. See **Chapter 12. Bulldog Skin and Allergies** for more details.

If you suspect your Bully has a food allergy, the first port of call should be to the vet to discuss the best course of action.

Many vets' clinics promote specific brands of dog food, which may or may not be the best for your dog. Don't buy anything without first checking every ingredient on the label.

## Food Trials

The only way to completely cure a food allergy or intolerance is complete avoidance. This is not as easy as it sounds. First you have to determine your dog DOES have an allergy to food - and not pollen, grass, etc. - and then you have to discover WHICH food is causing the reaction.

Blood tests are nowadays not thought to be reliable. As far as I am aware, the only true way to determine exactly what your dog is allergic to, is to start a **food trial or exclusion diet.** This involves feeding one specific food for 12 weeks, something the dog has never eaten before.

Before you embark on one, you should know that food trials are a real pain-in-the-you-know-what. You have to be incredibly vigilant and determined, so only start one if you are prepared to see it through to the end, or you are wasting your time. The chosen food must be the **only thing** eaten during the trial. During the trial, your dog shouldn't roam freely, as you can't control what he is eating or drinking when out of sight. In reality, many owners soldier on with trial and error, trying to eliminate certain foods and add others until their Bulldog starts to improve.

If you do start a food trial, don't give:

- 🐾 Treats
- 🐾 Rawhide (not recommended anyway)
- 🐾 Pigs' ears
- 🐾 Cows' hooves
- 🐾 Flavoured medications (including heartworm treatments) or supplements
- 🐾 Flavoured toothpastes
- 🐾 Flavoured plastic toys

A more practical, less scientific approach is to eliminate ingredients one at a time by switching diets over a period of a week or so. If you switch to home-cooked or raw, you know exactly what your dog is eating; if you choose a commercial food, a *hypoallergenic* one is a good place to start. These feeds all have the word *"hypoallergenic"* in the name and do not include wheat protein or soya. They are often based around less common ingredients like venison, duck or fish.

## Feeding Seniors

Once your adolescent dog has switched to an adult diet he will be on this for several years. But, unlike most breeds that will have adult food for most of their life, Bulldogs mature slowly and have a relatively short lifespan – six to 10 years on average.

This means that a Bulldog may switch from **Puppy** to **Adult** food typically at one year old, and then start to slow down as early as five or six years of age, although this will vary from one dog to another. As a dog moves towards old age, his body has different requirements to those of a young dog. This is the time to consider switching to a **Senior** diet. Generally, a dog is considered to be "older" or "senior" if he is in the last third of his normal life expectancy.

Owners of large breeds and Bulldogs, with their relatively short lifespan, switch their dogs from an **Adult** to a **Senior** diet when they are only six or seven years old. Smaller breeds often have a longer life expectancy. They may remain relatively youthful for many more years and do not need a **Senior** diet until they are perhaps 10 or older. It all depends on the individual dog, energy levels and general health.

Look for signs of your dog slowing down or having joint problems. That may be the time to talk to your vet about moving to a **Senior** diet. You can describe any changes at your dog's annual vaccination appointment, rather than having the expense of a separate consultation.

As a dog grows older, his metabolism slows down, his joints may stiffen, his energy levels decrease and he needs less exercise, just like with humans. Bulldogs are prone to putting on weight, especially in middle or old age. The **Adult** diet he is on may be too rich and have too many calories, so it may be the time to consider switching.

Even though he is older, keep his weight in check as obesity only puts more strain on his body, especially joints and organs, and makes any health problems even worse. Because of lower activity levels, many older dogs will gain weight and getting an older dog to slim down can be very difficult.

It is much better not to let your dog get too chunky than to put him on a diet. This is one of the single most important things you can do to increase your Bulldog's quality and length of life.

Other changes are again similar to those in older humans and might include stiff joints or arthritis, moving more slowly and sleeping more. His hearing and vision may not be so sharp and organs don't all work as efficiently as they used to, his teeth may have become worn down or his underbite more pronounced.

When this starts to happen, it is time to feed your old friend a **Senior** diet, which will be lower in calories but help to create a feeling of fullness.

Older dogs are more prone to develop constipation, so senior diets are often higher in fibre - at around 3% to 5%. If your dog has poor kidney function, then a low phosphorus diet will help to lower the workload for the kidneys.

Aging dogs have special dietary needs, some of which can be supplied in the form of supplements, such as glucosamine and chondroitin, which help joints. If your dog is not eating a complete balanced diet, then a vitamin or mineral supplement may help to prevent any deficiencies. Some owners also feed extra antioxidants to an older dog – ask your vet's advice on your next visit. Antioxidants are also found naturally in fruit and vegetables.

While some older dogs suffer from obesity, others have the opposite problem – they lose weight and are disinterested in food. If your old Bulldog is getting thinner and not eating well, firstly get him checked out by the vet to rule out any possible disease problems. If he gets the all-clear, your next challenge is to tempt him to eat. He may be having trouble with his teeth.

*If he's on dry food, try smaller kibble or moistening it with water. Adding gravy or a small amount of canned food will make it even more appetising.*

Some dogs can tolerate a cooked egg added to their food; it can also be a good source of protein for dogs with sensitive stomachs. Home-made diets of boiled rice, fish, potatoes, vegetables and chicken or meat can also work well with older dogs.

## Bloat

Bloat occurs when there is too much gas in the stomach. It is known by several different names: **twisted stomach, gastric torsion** or **Gastric Dilatation-Volvulus (GDV)** and occurs mainly in deep chested breeds like the Bulldog and in dogs that gulp their food - again, like the Bulldog.

It is statistically more common in males than in females and in dogs over seven years old.

As the stomach swells with gas, it can rotate 90° to 360°. The twisting stomach traps air, food and water inside and the bloated organ stops blood flowing properly to veins in the abdomen, leading to low blood pressure, shock and even damage to internal organs.

**FACT** *Canine Bloat is a serious medical condition that requires urgent attention. Without it, the dog can die. In fact, it is one of the leading killers of dogs after cancer.*

The causes are not fully understood, but there are some well-known risk factors. One is the dog taking in a lot of air while eating - either because he is greedy and gulping the food too fast, or stressed. A dog that is fed once a day and gorges himself could be at higher risk, which is one reason why many owners feed twice a day.

Exercising straight after eating or after a big drink increases the risk - like colic in horses.

Another potential cause is diet. Fermentable foodstuffs that produce a lot of gas can cause problems for the stomach if the gas is not burped or passed into the intestines.

A dog may show one or more of the following symptoms:

- Swollen belly
- Standing uncomfortably or hunched
- Restlessness, pacing or looking for a place to hide
- Rapid panting or difficulty breathing
- Dry retching, or excessive saliva or foam
- White or colourless gums
- Excessive drinking
- Licking the air
- General weakness or collapse

**Tips to Avoid Canine Bloat:**

- Some owners buy a frame for food bowls so they are at chest height for the dog, other experts believe dogs should be fed from the floor – do whichever slows your Bully down
- Feed twice a day rather than once
- Avoid dog food with high fats or those using citric acid as a preservative
- Don't let your dog drink too much water just before, during or after eating
- Stress can possibly be a trigger, with nervous and aggressive dogs being more susceptible. Maintain a peaceful environment, particularly around his mealtimes
- Avoid vigorous exercise before or after eating, allow one hour either side of mealtimes before strenuous exercise

**FACT** ❯ *Bloat can kill a dog in less than one hour. If you suspect your Bulldog has Bloat, get him into the car and off to the vet IMMEDIATELY. Even with treatment, mortality rates range from 10% to 60%. With surgery, this drops to 15% to 33%.*

## Overweight Dogs

It is far easier to regulate your dog's weight and keep it at a healthy level than to try and slim down a voraciously hungry Bulldog when he becomes overweight. According to James Howie, Veterinary Advisor to Lintbells, overweight and obese dogs are susceptible to a range of illnesses, including:

**Joint disease** – excessive body weight may increase joint stress, which is a risk factor in joint degeneration (arthrosis), as is cruciate disease (knee ligament rupture). Joint disease tends to lead to a reduction in exercise that then increases the likelihood of weight gain, further reducing exercise. A vicious cycle is created. Overfeeding young, growing Bulldogs can lead to various problems.

**Heart and lung problems** – fatty deposits within the chest cavity and excessive circulating fat play important roles in the development of cardio-respiratory and cardiovascular disease.

**Diabetes** – resistance to insulin has been shown to occur in overweight dogs, leading to a greater risk of diabetes mellitus.

**Tumours** – obesity increases the risk of mammary tumours in female dogs.

**Liver disease** – fat degeneration may result in liver insufficiency.

**Exercise intolerance** – this is also a common finding with overweight dogs, which can compound an obesity problem as fewer calories are burned off and are therefore stored, leading to further weight gain.

**Reduced Lifespan** - one of the most serious proven findings in obesity studies is that obesity in both humans and dogs reduces lifespan.

Most Bulldogs are extremely loyal companions and very attached to their humans. They are a part of our family. However, beware of going too far.

*If you have to put your dog on a diet, be aware that a reduced amount of food will also mean reduced nutrients, so he may need a supplement during this time.*

The good news is that many of the problems associated with being overweight are reversible. Increasing exercise increases calories burned, which in turn reduces weight.

.......................................................................................................................

**To Recap:**

- ✓ Diet is VERY important for Bulldogs, but no one food is right for every dog; you must decide on the best for yours.

- ✓ Bulldog puppies are fast-growing and need the right diet and balance of minerals in the right quantities.

- ✓ The best test of a food is how well your dog is doing on it.

If your Bulldog is happy and healthy, interested in life, has lots of energy, is not too fat and not too thin, doesn't scratch a lot and has dark brown, firm stools, then...

**Congratulations,** you've got it right!

.......................................................................................................................

# 7. Crate and Housetraining

Used correctly, crates can help speed up housetraining (potty training). They also give you and your puppy short breaks from each other and keep the dog safe at night or when you are away from the house. Many adult dogs grow to love their crates. Breeders, trainers, behaviourists, and people who show, compete or train working dogs use them.

Countless numbers of dogs are happily crate-trained. However, there are two extra factors to consider if you decide to use a crate with your Bully.

The first is that Bulldogs can be very independent-minded and stubborn, so NEVER lock a Bulldog in a crate if he is showing signs of distress at being in there. Secondly, Bulldogs do not cope well with changes in temperature or hot conditions. They cannot pant enough to efficiently cool down, so they overheat - which can quickly become life-threatening.

................................................................................................................................

## Using A Crate

Many Bulldog owners decide NOT to use a crate. This section is for those who decide to give it a go. There is no doubt that, used correctly, it can help to speed up housetraining – which is to be welcomed, as some Bullies are notoriously slow to get the hang of it!

If you do decide to use one, start from a day or two after you bring your Bulldog home, so your new arrival gets used to the crate right from the beginning. Some breeders may have already started the process.

A crate should always be used in a humane manner. Spend time getting your puppy or adult dog used to a crate so he comes to regard it as his own safe haven, and not a punishment cell or prison. A crate should never be used as a means of confinement while you are out of the house for six or eight hours every day.

Crates may not be suitable for every Bulldog. They are social animals that thrive on interaction. Being caged for long periods is a miserable existence for any dog, but particularly for an independent spirit like the Bulldog.

**Tip** *If you buy a crate for daily use, get a heavy duty wire one that allows air to pass through, rather than a plastic one with holes in.*

Heavy-boned breeds like the Bulldog can suffer from joint problems if they are confined in a small space for too long. However, used properly and sparingly, a crate can become a great asset.

A couple of points to remember:

1. **Always remove your dog's collar before leaving him inside when you are not there. Sadly, dogs have been known to die after panicking when their collars got caught.**

2. If the door is closed, your Bulldog MUST have access to water while inside. Non-spill water bowls are available from pet shops and online, as are bowls to attach to the bars.

Crates are ideal for giving you or the puppy some down time, especially if your little Bully is chewing everything in sight, including the kids. You cannot watch a puppy 24/7 and a crate is a safe place for him while you get on with doing other things.

Young puppies need lots and lots of sleep – but they are easily distracted, so a crate is a quiet, safe place where they can get some of that sleep during the day.

 *It's very important to get him used to being in the crate before you start shutting him in for more than a few minutes. If you try to rush the process, it could backfire as he will avoid it like the Plague if he thinks it's a prison cell.*

A crate is also an excellent way of safely confining a puppy at night. Not every owner wishes to use a crate, but used correctly they:

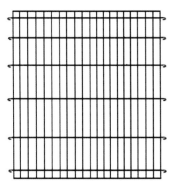

- ❧ Are a useful housetraining tool
- ❧ Create a canine den
- ❧ Give you a break
- ❧ Limit access to the rest of the house until potty trained
- ❧ Are a safe place for the dog to nap or sleep
- ❧ Provide a safe way to transport your dog in a car

## Which Crate and Where?

The crate should be large enough to allow your dog to stretch out flat on his side without being cramped, and he should be able to turn around easily and sit up without hitting his head on the top.

*While a small female might be fine in a 36" (91cm) crate, larger Bulldogs may need a 42" (107cm) one to be comfortable.*

The bigger the crate, the higher the cost, so most owners buy just the one and use crate dividers while the pup is growing. You can buy an inexpensive adjustable crate divider *(pictured, above)*, make one yourself, or put a box inside - preferably metal or hard wood. Blocking part of it off while he's small will help him to feel safe and secure, which he won't do if he's got the whole crate to roam around in.

 *If you cover the crate with an old blanket to create a den for your new puppy at night, only cover three sides - leave the front uncovered - and leave a gap of several inches at the bottom of all three sides to allow air to flow.*

Some breeders recommend putting the crate right next to the bed for the first night or two – even raised up next to the bed - to help the puppy settle in quicker. A few owners have even been known to sleep on the sofa or an air mattress next to the crate for the first one or two nights!

After that, you might put the crate in a place where the dog can hear or smell you during the night, e.g. the landing, or leave it in the same place downstairs all the time.

 *Most Bulldogs snore, wheeze, snuffle and fart while they sleep - so think very carefully about where to put the crate if you want a good night's sleep - the best place might well be out of earshot!*

During the day, place the crate in the kitchen or another room where there are people during the day, preferably one with a hard, easy-to-clean floor. Bulldog puppies are curious and like to see what is going on.

If you have children, strike the balance between putting the crate somewhere where the pup won't feel isolated, yet allowing him some peace and quiet.

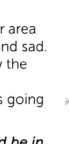

Don't put the crate in a closed utility room or area away from everybody, or he will feel lonely and sad. If you are using a room off the kitchen, allow the pup free run of the room and use a pet gate *(pictured)* or baby gate, so he can see what's going on.

 *The chosen location should be in the shade and free from draughts.*

You can buy or create a puppy playpen to use as well as - or instead of - a crate. See **Chapter 5. Bringing Puppy Home** for the options. If you have the space, put a pen around the crate to allow the puppy more freedom, or use a pet gate to block off the room where the puppy is.

Put the following items inside the crate:

❖ Bedding – Vet Bed or other bedding your puppy won't chew in a few days

❖ A towel or similar item that has been rubbed with the mother's scent

❖ A non-spill water bowl

❖ A healthy chew to stop him gnawing the crate and bedding

❖ A toy to keep him occupied

**At night, remove the water from the crate.**

Many Bulldog puppies are like sharks, so, at this stage, don't spend a lot of money on a fluffy floor covering for the crate, as it is likely to get destroyed.

The widely available "Vet Bed" is a good choice for bedding. Washable Vet Beds are widely used in vets' clinics to make dogs feel warm and secure. Made from double-strength polyester, they retain extra heat and allow air to flow though. They have drainage properties, so if your pup has an accident, he will stay dry.

Vet Beds are also a good option for older dogs, as the added heat is soothing for aging muscles and joints. You can buy "Vet Bedding" by the roll, which keeps the cost down.

*Consider putting a Snuggle Puppy in the crate with the new puppy. The Snuggle Puppy (pictured) is a safe soft toy with a heartbeat.*

One UK breeder adds: "In their new home, the puppies have the heartbeat sound like they had from laying on mum. We've had really good feedback from families about the Snuggle Puppies."

## Whining

If your puppy is whining or whimpering in the crate, make sure:

A. He doesn't need the toilet.

B. He is warm.

C. He is physically unharmed.

Then the reason he is whimpering is because he doesn't want to be alone. He has come from the warmth and security of his mother and litter, and the Brave New World can be a very daunting place for a two-month-old puppy all alone in a new home. He is not crying because he is in a cage. He would cry if he had the freedom of the room - he is crying because he is separated. Dogs are pack animals and being alone is not a natural state for a dog.

However, with patience and the right training, he will get used to being alone and being in the crate. Many adult Bulldogs choose the crate as their favourite resting place. Some owners make the crate their dog's only bed, so he feels comfortable and safe in there. Here are some other tips to help your puppy settle in his crate:

- Leave a ticking clock next to the crate
- Leave a radio on softly nearby
- Lightly spray DAP on a cloth or small towel and place in the crate

 *DAP, or Dog Appeasing Pheromone, is a synthetic form of the pheromone that nursing Bulldogs (and other breeds) give off after giving birth and then again after weaning to reassure their puppies that everything is fine.*

DAP has been found to help reduce fear in young puppies, as well as separation anxiety, phobias and aggression caused by anxiety in adult dogs. According to one French study: "DAP has no toxicities or side effects and is particularly beneficial for sick and geriatric dogs." Google *"Canadian Veterinary Journal Dog Appeasing Pheromone"* for more details of the study.

*NOTE: There is also an ADAPTIL collar with slow-release DAP, which is designed to reduce fear in anxious adult dogs. It gets good reports from many, not all, owners.*

Whether or not you decide to use a crate, the important thing to remember is that those first few days and weeks are a critical time for your puppy. Make him feel as safe and comfortable as you can. Bond with him, while at the same time gently and gradually giving him positive experiences with new places, humans and other animals.

## Travel Crates

You can use your everyday crate fastened with a seatbelt or buy a special travel crate. Choose a travel crate with holes or mesh in the side, to allow free movement of air rather than a solid one, in which a dog can soon overheat. *The travel crate pictured has holes in the side and a mesh top.*

Put the crate on the shady side of the interior and make sure it can't move around; put the seatbelt around it. If it's very sunny and the crate is wire mesh, cover the top so your dog has some shade, put the windows up and the air conditioning on.

Crate training applies to travel too. Remember to let the dog out to relieve himself before the journey.

Alternatively, you can buy a metal grille to keep your dog confined to the back of the car. You can also buy a Ventlock or similar, which keeps the car boot (trunk) slightly open, allowing air to flow.

Allowing your dog to roam freely inside the car is not a safe option, particularly if you - like me – are a bit of a "lead foot" on the brake and accelerator! Bulldogs are not the most agile of dogs and if you brake suddenly, they will fly forward.

Try to resist letting your Bulldog ride with his head out of the window - even if it does look macho! Wind pressure can cause ear infections and bits of dust, insects, etc. to fly into unprotected eyes.

Never leave your Bulldog unattended in a vehicle for more than a few minutes, especially if it's hot as he can overheat in a very short space of time - or be targeted by thieves.

........................................................................................................................................................

## Getting your Puppy Used to a Crate

Once you've got your crate, you'll need to learn how to use it properly so that it becomes a safe, comfortable den for your dog. Many breeders will have already started the process but, if not, here's a tried-and-tested method of getting your Bulldog firstly to accept a crate, and then to actually want to spend time in there.

Remember that Bulldogs are independent minded; they are not desperate to please you or follow your commands like Border Collies or German Shepherds! So, all training must be reward-based.

Shouting or being heavy-handed will have the opposite effect with a Bully; they will switch off.

These are the first steps:

1.  Drop a few puppy treats around and then inside the crate.

2.  Put your puppy's favourite toy in there.

3.  Keep the door open.

4.  Feed your puppy's meals inside the crate. Again, keep the door open.

 *Place a chew or treat INSIDE the crate and close the door while your puppy is OUTSIDE the crate. He will be desperate to get in there! Open the door, let him in and praise him for going in. Fasten a long-lasting chew inside the crate and leave the door open. Let your puppy wander inside to spend some time eating the chew.*

5.  **After a while, close the crate door and feed him some treats through the mesh.** At first just do it for a few seconds at a time, then gradually increase the time. If you do it too fast, he may become distressed.

6.  **Slowly build up the amount of time he is in the crate.** For the first few days, stay in the room, then gradually leave for a short time, first one minute, then three, then 10, 30 and so on.

### Next Steps

7.  Put your dog in his crate at regular intervals during the day - maximum two hours.

8.  If your pup is not yet housetrained, make sure he has relieved himself BEFORE you put him in the crate. Putting him in when he needs to eliminate will slow down training.

9. **Don't crate only when you are leaving the house.** Place the dog in the crate while you are home as well. Use it as a *"safe zone"* or *"quiet zone."* By using the crate both when you are home and while you are gone, your dog becomes comfortable there and not worried that you won't come back, or that you are leaving him alone. This helps to prevent separation anxiety.

10. **If you are leaving your dog unattended, give him a chew and remove his collar, tags and anything else that could become caught in an opening or between the bars.**

11. **Make it very clear to any children that the crate is NOT a playhouse for them,** but a *"special room"* for the dog.

12. **Although the crate is your dog's haven and safe place, it must not be off-limits to humans.** You should be able to reach inside at any time.

**The next points are important:**

13. **Try and wait until your dog is calm before putting him in the crate.** If he is behaving badly and you grab him and shove him in the crate, he will associate the crate with punishment. If you can't calm him down, try NOT to use the crate. A better option is to remove the privilege of your attention by either leaving the room or putting the dog in another room until he calms down.

14. The crate should ALWAYS be associated with a positive experience in your Bulldog's mind.

15. Don't let your dog out of the crate when he is barking or whining, or he'll think that this is the key to opening the door. Wait until it has stopped whining for at least 10 or 20 seconds before letting him out.

 **Reminder:**

❀ Consider keeping the pup right next to you for the first one or two nights

❀ During the day the crate door should not be closed until your pup is happy with being inside

❀ A young puppy should not be left in a crate for longer than an hour or two - and adult Bulldogs should only be crated for short periods up to three or four hours MAXIMUM during the day

❀ At night-time it is OK to close the door

❀ If you don't want to use a crate, use a pet gate, section off an area inside a room, or use a puppy pen to confine your pup at night

# Housetraining

Puppies naturally want to keep their space clean; it's genetic. From when he can first walk at the age of about three weeks, a pup will move away from his mother and sleeping area to eliminate.

The aim of housetraining it to teach the puppy exactly WHERE this space starts and finishes. When a puppy arrives at your home, he may think that a corner of the crate, the kitchen, or anywhere else in the house is an OK place for him to relieve himself.

*Through training and vigilance, you will teach him that the house is part of his and your "space" and therefore it's not OK for him to pee or poop indoors.*

Many good breeders will have already started the potty training process, so when you pick up your puppy, all you have to do is ensure that you carry on the good work! Although, in all honesty, Bulldogs are not noted for being the quickest breed to housetrain.

The speed of success varies greatly from one Bulldog to the next. Some can pick it up in a couple of weeks, while others seem to take months. A Bulldog will do something if:

a) He's going to get a reward – treat, praise, attention

b) It's in his own best interest

c) The commands and routine are repeated often

He will not do it simply to please you, like some other breeds.

 *It is worth taking time off work if you can to really get to grips with potty training. Vigilance during the early days really will speed things up. If you take your eye off the ball - or Bulldog in this case! - bad habits can start to become ingrained very quickly.*

How much time and effort are YOU prepared to put in at the beginning to speed up housetraining? Vigilance and being consistent with your routines and repetitions is the quickest way to get results. Clear your schedule for a week or so and make housetraining your No.1 priority.

I get complaints from some American readers when I say: "Book a week or two off work and housetrain your dog!" I know Americans get much shorter vacation time than almost anybody else, but truthfully, if you can take a few days off to focus on potty training, it will speed up the process no end!

If you're starting from scratch when you bring your puppy home, your new arrival thinks that the whole house is away from his sleeping quarters, and therefore a great place for a pee or a poop! And, if yours is a rescue Bulldog, he may well have picked up some bad habits before arriving at your home. In these cases, lots of time and patience are essential to teach your dog the new ways.

Bulldogs, like all dogs, are creatures of routine - not only do they like the same things happening at the same times every day, but establishing a regular routine with your dog also helps to speed up obedience and toilet training.

 *To keep things simple in a pup's mind, it's a good idea to have a designated area in your garden or yard that the pup can use as a toilet. Dogs are tactile creatures, so they pick a toilet area that feels good under their paws.*

Dogs often like to go on grass - but this will do nothing to improve your lawn, so think carefully about what area to encourage your puppy to use. You may want to consider a small patch of crushed gravel in your garden – but don't let the puppy eat it - or a particular corner of the garden or yard away from any attractive plants.

I would only advise using puppy pads, or "training pads," if you live in an apartment and it will be acceptable for your Bulldog to eliminate in a designated indoor area as an adult. Otherwise, puppy pads can actually slow down potty training. Because dogs are tactile and puppy pads are soft and comfy, dogs like going on them. When you remove the pads, the puppy may be tempted to find a similar surface - like a carpet or rug. Newspapers can also encourage a pup to soil inside the house. So, if you use them, only do so for a short space of time and reduce the area covered by them fairly quickly.

**A general rule of thumb is that puppies can last for one hour per month of age without urinating, sometimes a bit longer. So:**

- An eight-week pup can last for two hours
- A 12-week-old pup can last for three hours
- A 16-week pup can last for four hours
- A six-month-old can last for six hours

*NOTE: This only applies when the puppy is calm and relaxed.*

 *If a puppy is active or excited, he will urinate more often, and if he is excited to see you, he may urinate at will.*

To speed up the process even more, set your alarm clock to get up in the night to let the pup out to relieve himself for the first week. You might hate it, but it will shorten the overall time spent housetraining.

## Housetraining Tips

Follow these tips to speed up housetraining:

1. **Constant supervision** is essential for the first week or two if you are to housetrain your puppy quickly. If nobody is there, he will learn to pee or poop inside the house.

2. **Take your pup outside at the following times:**

- As soon as he wakes – every time
- Shortly after each feed
- After a drink
- When he gets excited
- After exercise or play
- Last thing at night
- Initially every hour or two - whether or not he looks like he wants to go

You may think that the above list is an exaggeration, but it isn't! Housetraining a pup is almost a full-time job in the beginning.

If you are serious about toilet training your puppy quickly, then clear your diary for a week or two and keep your eyes firmly glued on your pup...learn to spot that expression or circling motion just before he makes a mess on your floor.

3. Take your pup to **the same place** every time, you may need to use a lead (leash) in the beginning - or tempt him there with a treat. Some say it is better to only pick him up and dump him there in an emergency, as it is better if he learns to take himself to the chosen toilet spot. Dogs naturally develop a preference for going in the same place or on the same surface. Take or lead him to the same patch every time so he learns this is his toilet area.

4. **No pressure – be patient.** You must allow your distracted little darling time to wander around and have a good sniff before performing his duties – but do not leave him, stay around a short distance away. Unfortunately, puppies are not known for their powers of concentration, so it may take a while for him to select the perfect bathroom spot!

5. **Housetraining is reward-based.** Give praise and/or a treat IMMEDIATELY after he has performed his duties in the chosen spot. Bulldogs love praise, and reward-based training is the most successful method for quick results.

6. **Share the responsibility.** It doesn't have to be the same person who takes the dog outside all the time. In fact, it's easier if there are a couple of you, as this is a very time-demanding business. Just make sure you stick to the same principles, command and patch of ground.

7. **Stick to the same routine.** Dogs understand and like routine. Sticking to the same times for meals, short exercise sessions, playtime, sleeping and toilet breaks will help to housetrain him quicker, and help him settle into his new home.

8. **Use the same word** or command when telling your puppy to go to the toilet – or while he is in the act. He will gradually associate this phrase or word with toileting and you will even be able to get him to eliminate on command after some weeks.

9. **Use your voice if you catch him in the act indoors.** A short sharp negative sound is best - ACK! EH! It doesn't matter, as long as it is loud enough to make him stop. Then either pick him up or run enthusiastically towards your door, calling him to the chosen place and patiently wait until he has finished what he started indoors.

 *It is no good scolding your dog if you find a puddle or unwanted gift in the house but don't see him do it; he won't know why you are cross. And only use the negative sound if you actually CATCH HIM MID-ACT.*

10. **No punishment.** Accidents will happen at the beginning, do not punish your pup for them. He is a baby with a tiny bladder and bowels and little self-control. Housetraining takes time - it is perfectly natural to have accidents early on. Remain calm and clean up the mess with a strong-smelling cleaner to remove the odour, so he won't be tempted to use that spot again.

**FACT** ❯ *Bulldogs have a sense of smell dozens of times better than ours. Use a special spray from your vet or a hot solution of washing powder to completely eliminate the odour inside the house. Smacking or rubbing his nose in it can have the opposite effect - he will become afraid to do his business in your presence and may start going secretly behind the couch or under the bed, rather than outside.*

11. **Look for the signs.** These may be:

   a. Whining
   b. Sniffing the floor in a determined manner
   c. Circling and looking for a place to go
   d. Walking uncomfortably - particularly at the rear end!

   Take him outside straight away, and try not to pick him up all the time. He has to learn to walk to the door himself when he needs to go outside.

12. **Use a crate at night-time** and, for the first few nights, consider getting up four hours after you go to bed to take the pup outside, gradually increasing the time. By the age of four or five months a Bulldog pup should be able to last through a short night – provided you let him out last thing at night and first thing in the morning. Before then, you will have a lot of early mornings!

Don't let one or two little accidents derail your potty training - accidents WILL happen! Here is a list of some possible scenarios and action to take:

🐾 **Puppy peed when your back was turned** – Don't let him out of his crate or living space unless you are prepared to watch his every move

🐾 **Puppy peed or pooped in the crate** - Make sure the crate isn't too big. Also, make sure he is not left in the crate for too long

🐾 **Puppy pooped without warning** - Observe what he does immediately beforehand. That way, you'll be able to scoop the pup up and take him outside next time before an accident happens

🐾 **Puppy pees on the same indoor spot daily** - Make sure you clean up completely with a strong-smelling disinfectant, and don't give your puppy too much indoor freedom too soon

**Tip** *If your breeder has already started the housetraining process, ask if he or she uses a particular phrase, such as "Go toilet!" "Pee pee!" "Wee wee!" or "Go potty!"*

And finally, one British breeder added this piece of advice: "If you are getting a puppy, invest in a good dressing gown and an umbrella!"

## Apartment Living

If you live on the 21st floor of an apartment in downtown New York or Los Angeles - where the Bulldog is the most popular breed of dog - housetraining can be a little trickier, as you don't have easy access to the outdoors. One method is to indoor housetrain your puppy.

Most dogs can be indoor housetrained fairly easily, especially if you start early. Stick to the same principles already outlined, the only difference is that you will be placing your Bully on puppy pads or newspaper instead of taking him outdoors.

Start by blocking off a section of the apartment for your pup, you can use a baby gate or make your own barrier. Despite their strength, most Bulldogs will not usually attempt to breach a barrier, but make sure you choose a chew-proof material! You will be able to keep a better eye on him than if he has free run of the whole place. It will also be easier to monitor his "accidents."

Select a corner away from his eating and sleeping area that will become his permanent bathroom area – a carpeted area is to be avoided if at all possible. At first, cover a larger area than is actually needed - about 3x3 or 4x4 feet - with puppy pads or newspapers and gradually reduce the area as training progresses. Take your puppy there as indicated in the **Housetraining Tips** section.

Praise him enthusiastically when he eliminates on the puppy pad or newspaper. If you catch him doing his business out of the toilet area, pick him up and take him back there. Correct with a firm voice - never a hand. With positive reinforcement and a strict schedule, he should soon be walking to the area on his own.

Owners attempting indoor housetraining should be aware that it does generally take longer than outdoor training. Some dogs will resist. Also, once a dog learns to go indoors, it can be difficult to train them to go outdoors on their walks.

If you don't monitor your puppy carefully enough in the beginning, indoor housetraining will be a longer and more difficult process. The first week or two is crucial to your puppy learning what is expected of him.

# Bell Training

Bell Training is a method that works well with some dogs. There are different types of bells, the simplest are inexpensive and widely available.

They consist of a series of adjustable bells that hang on a nylon strap from the door handle *(pictured)*. This type is more suitable for the Bulldog as some of the bells are near the floor, so he doesn't have to jump up.

Another option is a small metal bell attached to a metal hanger that fixes low down on the wall next to the door with two screws *(pictured, overleaf)*.

As with all puppy training, do it in short bursts of five to 10 minutes or your easily-distracted little student will switch off! The technique is quite simple:

1. Show your dog the bell, either on the floor, before it is fixed anywhere or by holding it up. Point to it and give the command *"Touch," "Ring,"* or whatever word you decide.

2. Every time he touches it with his nose, reward with praise.

3. When he rings the bell with his nose, give him a treat. You can rub something tasty on the bell, like peanut butter, to make it more interesting.

4. Take the bell away between practice sessions.

5. Once he rings the bell every time you show it to him, move on to the next step.

6. Take the bell to the door you use for housetraining. Place a treat just outside the door while he is watching. Then close the door, point to the bell and give the command.

7. When he rings the bell, open the door and let him get the treat outside.

8. When he rings the bell as soon as you place a treat outside, fix the bell to the door or wall.

9. The next time you think he needs to relieve himself, walk to the door, point to the bell and give the command. Give him a treat or praise if he rings it, let him out immediately and reward him again with enthusiastic praise when he performs his duty.

 *In between training sessions, ring the bell yourself EVERY time you open the door to let him outside.*

Some dogs can get carried away by their own success and will ring the bell any time they want a treat, your attention or fancy a wander outdoors!

Make sure that you ring the bell every time he goes out through the door to potty, but DON'T ring the bell if he is going out to play. And if he starts playing or dawdling around the garden or yard, bring him in!

# 8. Bulldog Behavior

Just as with humans, a dog's personality is made up of a combination of temperament and character. While every Bulldog is an individual, there are also shared character traits. Understanding your dog, what makes him or her tick and why they behave like that will give you a greater understanding of - and ultimately a deeper bond with - your dog.

**FACT** Temperament is the nature – or inherited characteristics - a dog is born with; a predisposition to act or react in a certain way. Character varies from one dog to the next. It develops through the dog's life and is formed by a combination of temperament and environment - or NURTURE AND NATURE.

Getting your puppy from a good breeder is important. Their dogs should be physically healthy AND have good temperaments.

Then, how you treat your dog will have a huge effect on her personality and behaviour. Starting off on the right foot with good routines is very important; so, treat your dog well and spend lots of time with her.

Bulldogs spend a good deal of time indoors with people and it's a good idea to get yours used to being left alone for short periods while young to avoid Separation Anxiety.

Also, make time for socialisation with other dogs and short walks away from the home - different environments, scents and experiences keep dogs stimulated, well-balanced and relaxed, rather than fearful or aggressive, in new situations.

Originally a fighting dog, the aggression has largely been bred out since the late 19th century and these days the Bulldog is first and foremost a companion dog. Some Bulldoggers would say that the breed is a companion without equal.

## Typical Bulldog Traits

Every dog is different, of course, but there are also shared traits. Here are some typical characteristics - some of them also apply to other breeds, but put them all together and you have a blueprint for the Bulldog, a dog which has perhaps the most unique personality in the canine world.

1.  Bulldogs are companion dogs.

2. Adult Bulldogs generally have calm, laid-back temperaments.

3. They make great family dogs and are known for being excellent with children – some are almost besotted by youngsters - but never leave a small child alone with any dog; either can be unpredictable.

4. They are chunky love machines and have a quiet dignity.

5. They are playful and enjoy games. With their powerful jaws, you will never win a tug-o-war against them.

6. Some Bulldogs never "grow up." Living with a Bulldog can be like living with a furry, stubborn toddler that naps a lot!

7. Bulldog puppies are notorious chewers – some go through their *"shark"* period where they bite and chew almost everything, including fingers and toes.

8. Bulldog puppies are lively, often having bursts of energy before they crash.

9. Sometimes Bulldogs have a mad couple of minutes charging around the room barging into things – stand clear and let them burn off steam unless you want to get steamrollered!

10. Bulldogs are strong-willed and often stubborn.

11. Unlike working breeds, the Bulldog is not desperate to follow your commands.

12. Don't be fooled into thinking they are not intelligent because they don't immediately jump to your command. Bulldogs are cleverer than many people think and, if you don't establish your authority (in a positive way), they can end up ruling you!

13. They can be sensitive and intuitive, picking up on a person's mood. They do not like shouting, arguments or rough training methods.

14. With training and potty training, they require *lots of repetition* of commands, praise, rewards and routine.

15. ...then they will decide if they want to obey you or not!

16. They have *"selective deafness"* when you try and get them to do something they don't want to do, e.g. get down from the sofa or go for a walk in the rain.

17. Bulldogs love to be the centre of attention.

18. They sulk! If you have done something to offend them, they will sit and stare at the wall or floor – try not to pander to their moods. They will get over it... eventually.

19. They have a delicately balanced body and need extra care from their owners, such as regular wrinkle cleaning. If yours has a screw tail, you may also have to regularly clean the less appealing end of your Bully.

20. Their shortened muzzle means that many do not breathe easily and sadly, Bulldogs have many health problems. According to the UK Kennel Club, the average lifespan is six to 10 years, although some live longer.

21. Allergies and/or skin conditions are not uncommon.

22. They overheat easily, so should not be walked when temperatures are high. They may also need air conditioning at home if they live in a hot climate.

23. Bulldogs can fart for the whole of America and Europe combined! Many have delicate digestive systems and do not do well with grain and certain other foodstuffs.

24. They are messy eaters and drinkers. They also drool and beg for food, if allowed near the table when you're eating.

25. They are greedy and often possessive with food – so feed them away from other animals and children. They can also be protective of toys.

26. They put on weight easily.

27. They have a memory like an elephant.

28. Although some Bulldogs have more energy, most have a low tolerance to exercise.

29. They do, however, have a high tolerance to pain, so it's up to the owner to keep a close eye on them for signs that something is amiss.

30. They like to lie on their backs and have their tummies tickled.

31. Bulldogs can talk! They make all sorts of funny noises, as well as snoring, belching, snuffling and growling. A growl does not always mean aggression; listen to your Bulldog and learn her language.

32. They generally get on well with other dogs and animals. However, if not well socialised, some Bulldogs can show aggression towards other dogs, especially males.

33. A Bulldog will not seek a fight, but if threatened, will not back down from one either, which is to be avoided at all costs. Fortunately, it usually takes a lot to provoke these placid dogs.

34. Pound for pound, the Bulldog is one of the strongest of all breeds.

35. Most adults generally do not bark much.

36. They are usually not aggressive with strangers, but can be protective of their family.

37. Most Bulldogs swim like stones so, if yours is near or on water, get him a doggie lifejacket.

38. The good news is that the short, sleek coat is easy to care for, although they do shed quite a bit. Regular grooming reduces shedding.

39. There's no doubt that Bulldogs have unique mannerisms and habits and yours will definitely make you laugh.

........................................................................................................................................

## Understanding Canine Emotions

As pet lovers, we are all too keen to ascribe human characteristics to our dogs; this is called **anthropomorphism** – "the attribution of human characteristics to anything other than a human being." Most of us dog lovers are guilty of that, as we come to regard our pets as members of the family - and it's especially hard not to do this with Bulldogs, who often seem like little people.

An example of anthropomorphism might be that the owner of a male dog might not want to have him neutered because he will "miss sex," as a human might if he or she were no longer able to have sex. This is simply not true.

**FACT ❯** *A male dog's impulse to mate is entirely governed by his hormones, not emotions. If he gets the scent of a female on heat, his hormones (which are just body chemicals) tell him he has to mate with her.*

He does not stop to consider how attractive she is or whether she is "the one" to produce his puppies. No, his reaction is entirely physical, he just wants to dive in there and get on with it!

It's the same with females. When they are on heat, a chemical impulse is triggered in their brain

making them want to mate – with any male, they aren't at all fussy. So, don't expect your little princess to be all coy when she is on heat, she is not waiting for Prince Charming to come along - the tramp down the road or any other scruffy pooch will do! It is entirely physical, not emotional.

Food is another example. A dog will not stop to count the calories of that lovely treat; you have to do that. No, she is driven by food and just thinks about getting the food or the treat. Most non-fussy eaters will eat far too much, given the opportunity.

Bulldogs are not only uniquely handsome dogs, they are also extremely loving and eager to please you, not to mention quirky. If yours doesn't make you laugh from time to time, you must have had a humour by-pass! All of this adds up to one thing: a hugely engaging and affectionate family member that it's all too easy to reward - or spoil.

It's fine to treat your dog like a member of the family - as long as you keep in mind that she is a dog and not a human. Understand her mind, patiently train her to adjust to her place in the household and that there are household rules she needs to learn – like not barging into the kids or Grandma - and you will be rewarded with a companion who is second to none and fits in beautifully with your family and lifestyle.

Dr Stanley Coren is a psychologist well known for his work on canine psychology and behaviour. He and other researchers believe that in many ways a dog's emotional development is equivalent to that of a young child. Dr Coren says: "Researchers have now come to believe that the mind of a dog is roughly equivalent to that of a human who is two to two-and-a-half years old. This conclusion holds for most mental abilities as well as emotions."

Anyone who has ever owned a Bulldog will recognise the truth of these words.

Dr Coren adds: "Thus, we can look to human research to see what we might expect of our dogs. Just like a two-year-old child, our dogs clearly have emotions, but many fewer kinds of emotions than found in adult humans. At birth, a human infant only has an emotion that we might call excitement. This indicates how excited he is, ranging from very calm up to a state of frenzy. Within the first weeks of life the excitement state comes to take on a varying positive or a negative flavour, so we can now detect the general emotions of contentment and distress.

"In the next couple of months, disgust, fear, and anger become detectable in the infant. Joy often does not appear until the infant is nearly six months of age and it is followed by the emergence of shyness or suspicion. True affection, the sort that it makes sense to use the label "love" for, does not fully emerge until nine or ten months of age."

So, our Bulldogs truly love us – but we knew that already!

## Simplified Range

According to Dr Coren, dogs can't feel shame, so if you are housetraining your puppy, don't expect her to be ashamed if she makes a mess in the house, she can't; she simply isn't capable of feeling shame. But she will not like it when you ignore her when she's behaving badly, and she will love it when you praise her for eliminating outdoors. She is simply responding to your reaction with her simplified range of emotions.

Dr Coren also believes that dogs cannot experience guilt, contempt or pride. I'm not a psychology expert, but I'm not sure I agree. Take a Bulldog to a local dog show, obedience class or agility competition, watch him perform and maybe win a rosette and applause - is the dog's delight something akin to pride?

Bulldogs can certainly experience joy. They love your attention and praise; is there a more joyful sight for you both than when your Bulldog runs towards you, tail wagging like crazy, with those big, loving eyes that say you're the best person in the world?

If you want to see a happy dog, watch a Bulldog snuggle up on the sofa with her favourite human. Bulldogs are quite intuitive and can certainly show empathy - "the ability to understand and share the feelings of another." They can pick up people's moods and emotions.

One emotion that all dogs can experience is jealousy. It may display itself by possessive or aggressive behaviour over food, a toy or a person, for example.

An interesting article was published in the PLOS (Public Library of Science) Journal following an experiment into whether dogs get jealous. Building on research that shows that six-month old infants display jealousy, the scientists studied 36 dogs in their homes and videoed their actions when their owners displayed affection to a realistic-looking stuffed canine *(pictured).*

Over 75% of the dogs were likely to push or touch the owner when they interacted with the decoy! The envious mutts were more than three times as likely to do this for interactions with the stuffed dog, compared to when their owners gave their attention to other objects, including a book. Around a third tried to get between the owner and the plush toy, while a quarter of the put-upon pooches snapped at the dummy dog!

The researchers think that the dogs believed that the stuffed dog was real. They cite the fact that 86% of the dogs sniffed the toy's rear end during and after the experiment!

Professor Christine Harris from University of California in San Diego said: "Our study suggests not only that dogs do engage in what appear to be jealous behaviours, but also that they were seeking to break up the connection between the owner and a seeming rival. We can't really speak of the dogs' subjective experiences, of course, but it looks as though they were motivated to protect an important social relationship.

"Many people have assumed that jealousy is a social construction of human beings - or that it's an emotion specifically tied to sexual and romantic relationships. Our results challenge these ideas, showing that animals besides ourselves display strong distress whenever a rival usurps a loved one's affection."

## Cause and Effect

As you've read, Bulldogs make superb canine companions. But any dog can develop behaviour problems given a certain set of circumstances.

Every Bulldog is an individual with his or her own temperament and environment, both of which influence the way the dog interacts with the world. Poor behaviour can result from a number of factors, including:

- Poor breeding
- Boredom, due to lack of exercise or mental challenges
- Lack of socialisation
- Being badly treated
- Being left alone too long
- A change in living conditions
- Anxiety or insecurity
- Fear
- Being spoiled

Bad behaviour may show itself in different ways:

- Constantly demanding attention
- Chewing or destructive behaviour
- Nipping or biting
- Growling
- Jumping up or barging
- Excessive barking
- Soiling or urinating inside the house
- Aggression towards other dogs

# 10 Ways to Avoid Bad Behaviour

Different dogs have different reasons for exhibiting bad behaviour; there is no single cure for everything. The best chance of ensuring your dog is well-adjusted and well-behaved is to start out on the right foot by following these simple guidelines:

1.  **Buy from a good breeder** who uses her expertise to match suitable breeding pairs, taking into account good temperament, health, appearance and being "fit for function."

2.  **Start socialisation right away.** We now realise the vital role that early socialisation plays in developing a well-rounded adult dog. Lack of socialisation is one of the major causes of unwanted behaviour, timidity or aggression. Some male Bulldogs can be aggressive towards other males, but early socialisation should prevent that. It is essential to expose your puppy to other dogs, people, places, and experiences as soon as possible; it will go a long way towards helping her become a stable, happy and trustworthy companion.

**FACT** > *Dogs are social creatures that thrive on sniffing, seeing, hearing and even licking. While the foundation for good behaviour is laid down during the first few months, dogs behave better when socialisation and training continues throughout their life.*

Bulldogs like to be involved and be the centre of attention and it is important they learn that they are not the centre of the universe! Socialisation helps them to learn their place in that universe and to become comfortable with it.

3.  **Start training early** - you can't start too soon. Like babies, puppies have enquiring minds that absorb a lot of new information quickly. Start teaching your puppy to learn her own name as well as some simple commands a couple of days after bringing her home.

4.  **Basic training should cover several areas:** housetraining, chew prevention, puppy biting, simple commands like "sit," "come" or "here," "stay" and familiarising her with a collar or harness and lead. Adopt a gentle approach and keep training sessions short. Start with five or 10 minutes a day and build up. Puppy classes or adult dog obedience classes are a great way to start, but follow up at home afterwards. Spend a few minutes each day reinforcing what you have both learned in class - owners need training as well as Bulldogs!

5.  **Reward your dog for good behaviour.** All Bulldog behaviour training should be based on positive reinforcement. So, praise and reward your dog when she does something good. Bulldogs love treats and praise. The main aim of training is to build a good understanding between you and your dog and to establish your authority in the household.

6.  **Ignore bad behaviour,** no matter how hard this may be. If, for example, your dog is chewing her way through your shoes, the couch or toilet rolls or eating things she shouldn't, remove her from the situation and then ignore her. For some dogs even negative attention is some attention. Remove yourself from the room so she learns that you give attention when YOU want to give it, NOT when she demands it. The more time you spend praising and rewarding

good behaviour, while ignoring bad behaviour, the more likely she is to respond. If your pup is a chewer – and nearly all Bullies are - make sure she has durable toys and chews.

7. **Take the time to learn what sort of temperament your dog has.** Is she by nature confident or timid? What was she like as a puppy, did she rush forward or hang back? Does she fight to get upright when on her back or is she happy to lie there? Is she a couch potato or a ball of fire? Your puppy's temperament affects her behaviour and how she responds to the world. A timid Bulldog will not respond well to a loud approach on your part, whereas a stubborn, strong-willed one will require more repetition and patience.

8. **Exercise and stimulation.** A lack of either is another major reason for dogs behaving badly. Regular daily exercise as well as indoor or outdoor games and toys are all ways of stopping your dog from becoming bored or frustrated.

9. **Learn to leave your dog.** Just as leaving your dog alone for too long can lead to problems, so can being with her all the time. Bulldogs love being with their humans, but also need to learn that being alone for short periods is fine too, and not a cause for anxiety. When a dog becomes over-reliant on you, she gets stressed when you leave; this is called *separation anxiety*. Start a few days after she arrives home by leaving her for a few minutes and gradually extend the time so that you can eventually leave her for up to four hours.

10. **Love your Bulldog – but don't spoil her,** however difficult that might be. Resist the urge to pick her up all the time or to give too much attention or too many treats. Don't constantly respond to her demands for attention or allow her to behave as she wants inside the house.

# Separation Anxiety

When a dog leaves the litter, her owners become her new family or pack, and separation anxiety is an exaggerated fear response to being separated. It's not just dogs that experience it, people do too. About 7% of adults and 4% of children suffer from it. Typical symptoms for humans are:

❧ Distress at being separated from a loved one

❧ Fear of being alone

**FACT** ❯ *Some 10%-15% of dogs suffer from separation anxiety. It is on the increase and recognised as the most common form of stress in dogs.*

## Tell-Tale Signs

Does your Bulldog do any of the following?

❧ Tear paper, or chew furniture or other objects?

❧ Dig, chew, or scratch at the carpet, doors or windows trying to join you?

❧ Soil or urinate inside the house, even though she is housetrained? (This only occurs when left alone)

❧ Greet you ecstatically when you come home – even if you've only been out to the garage?

- ❧ Get anxious or stressed when you're getting ready to leave the house?
- ❧ Howl, whine or bark when you leave?
- ❧ Exhibit restlessness - such as licking her coat excessively, pacing or circling?
- ❧ Wait by the window or door until you return?
- ❧ Dislike spending time alone in the garden or yard?
- ❧ Refuses to eat or drink if you leave her?
- ❧ Cry when one person leaves - even though others are still in the room or car?

If so, she may suffer from separation anxiety. Fortunately, in many cases this can be cured.

 *Following you around the house is not necessarily a sign of separation anxiety - unless she gets visibly distressed when you leave. However, if they even want to follow you into the toilet, this CAN be a sign that separation anxiety is developing.*

## Causes

Dogs are pack animals and being alone is not a natural state for them. A puppy will emotionally latch on to her new owner, who has taken the place of mother and siblings. Puppies should be patiently taught in a structured way to get used to short periods of isolation if they are to be comfortable with it. It is also important for them to have a den where they feel safe - this may be a crate or dog bed where they can sleep in peace and quiet.

One thing that surprises some first-time owners, is just how much love they feel for their Bulldog - and this is reciprocated by the dog! Dogs are truly life-enhancing.

In the beginning you are setting patterns for the future and it is all too easy to give a lovable Bulldog pup a huge amount of attention and cuddles, pick them up a lot, and not leave them alone for any length of time.

As the dog reaches adolescence, this can lead to behaviour issues, as the dog thinks she has the upper hand or becomes anxious about you not being there – or both. It may lead to issues such as attention-seeking behaviour, excessive barking, fussiness with food or separation anxiety.

There are different causes of separation anxiety:

- ❧ Not being left alone for short periods when young
- ❧ Being left for too long by owners who are out of the house for most of the day
- ❧ Lack of encounters with other dogs and people, resulting in too much focus and dependence on the owner
- ❧ Boredom - Bulldogs need mental as well as physical exercise
- ❧ Leaving a dog too long in a crate or confined space
- ❧ Being over-indulgent with your dog; giving her too much attention
- ❧ Making too much of a fuss when you go out and then return to the house

- ❧ Mistreatment in the past; a dog from a rescue centre may have insecurities and feel anxious when left alone
- ❧ Wilful behaviour due to a lack of training and not knowing the boundaries

Separation anxiety can also develop in older dogs. As they age, their hearing, sense of smell and sight often deteriorate. When this happens, a dog can become more dependent on its owners and anxious when separated from them.

 **FACT** ⟩ It may be very flattering and cute that your dog wants to be with you all of the time, but insecurity and separation anxiety are distressing for the dog.

If your dog starts showing the first signs, help her become more self-reliant and confident; she will be happier and more relaxed. Every dog is different, but here are some techniques that have proved effective in helping some dogs with separation anxiety:

## Tips to Combat Separation Anxiety

1. After the first few days, leave your new puppy or adult dog for short periods, starting with literally a minute or two and gradually lengthening the time you are out of sight.

2. Tire your dog out before leaving her. Take her for a walk or play a game and, if you can, leave her with a view of the outside world, e.g. in a room with a patio door or low window.

3. Keep arrivals and departures low key and don't make a big fuss. Don't say hello or goodbye – either in words or body language, and don't sneak in and out of the house either.

4. Leave your dog a *"security blanket,"* such as an old piece of clothing you have recently worn that still has your scent on it, or leave a radio on - not too loud - in the room with the dog. Avoid a heavy rock station! If it will be dark when you return, leave a lamp on a timer. One breeder leaves a TV on low, on the same channel, so her dogs become familiar with the same programmes. This also cuts out any background noise such as traffic, people and barking dogs.

5. Associate your departure with something good. As you leave, give a rubber toy, like a Kong filled with a tasty treat, or a frozen treat, or spread her favourite treat over a Lickimat. This may take her mind off your departure – although some dogs may refuse to touch the treat until you return home! Give her the treat when you are at home as well, so she doesn't just associate it with being left.

6. If your dog is used to a crate, try crating her when you go out. Many dogs feel safe there, and being in a crate can also help to reduce destructiveness. Always take the collar off first. Pretend to leave the house, but listen for a few minutes. NEVER leave a dog in a crate with the door closed all day; two or three hours are long enough during the day. **Warning:** if your dog starts to show major signs of distress, remove her from the crate immediately as she may injure herself.

7. Structure and routine can help to reduce anxiety in your dog. Carry out regular activities, such as feeding and exercising, at the same time every day. Dogs read body language very well; many Bulldogs are intuitive. They may start to fret when they think you are going to leave them. Some dogs show anxiety in new places; get her better socialised and used to different environments, dogs and people.

*One technique is to mimic your departure routine when you have no intention of leaving. So, put your coat on, grab your keys, go out of the door and return a few seconds later. Do this randomly and regularly and it may help to reduce your dog's stress levels when you do it for real.*

8. However lovable your Bulldog is, if she is showing early signs of anxiety when separating from you, do not shower her with attention all the time when you are there. She will become overly dependent on you.

9. If you have to leave the house for a few hours at a time, ask a neighbour or friend to call in - or drop the dog off with them. Bulldogs thrive on interaction with humans and get very sad when left alone for long periods.

10. Getting another dog to keep the first one company can help, but only if you have the time and money for two or more dogs. Can you afford double the vet and food bills?

## Sit-Stay-Down

Another technique for helping to reduce separation anxiety is to practise the common **"Sit-Stay"** or **"Down-Stay"** exercises using positive reinforcement. The goal is to be able to move briefly out of your dog's sight while she is in the **Stay** position.

Through this your dog learns that she can remain calmly and happily in one place while you go about your normal daily life. You have to progress slowly with this! Get her to sit and stay and then walk away for five seconds, then 10, 20, a minute and so on. Reward her with a treat or toy every time she stays calm.

Then move out of sight or out of the room for a few seconds, return and give her the treat if she is calm, gradually lengthen the time you are out of sight. If you're watching TV with your Bulldog snuggled up at your side and you get up for a snack, say "stay" and leave the room. When you come back, give her a treat or praise her quietly. It is a good idea to practise these techniques after exercise or when your dog is a little sleepy (but not exhausted), as she is likely to be more relaxed.

 *Canine separation anxiety is NOT the result of disobedience or lack of training. It's a psychological condition; your dog feels anxious and insecure.*

**NEVER** punish your dog for showing signs of separation anxiety – even if she has chewed your best shoes or entire kitchen. This will only make her worse.

**NEVER** leave your dog unattended in a crate for long periods or if she is frantic to get out, it can cause physical or mental harm. If you're thinking of leaving an animal all day in a crate while you are out of the house, consider a rabbit or a hamster - not a Bulldog.

## Excessive Barking

Bulldogs are not known for barking a lot, but like any dog, they can get into the habit of barking too much if you don't put a stop to it. Dogs, especially youngsters and adolescents, sometimes behave in ways you might not want them to, until they learn:

a)  that this type of unwanted behaviour doesn't earn them any rewards, and

b)  to respect your authority

Some puppies start off by being noisy from the outset, while others hardly bark at all until they reach adolescence or adulthood. Some may be triggered by other, noisier dogs in the household. Our website hears from owners worried that their young dogs are not barking enough. However, we get far more posts from owners whose dogs are barking too much!

We had one dog that hardly barked at all until he was two years old. We needn't have worried, by the time he got to four or five, he loved the sound of his own voice! We have been in contact with several owners in a similar position; their dog hardly barked when young and now barks too much. If that's the case, then try the **Speak and Shush** technique outlined later in this chapter.

Some Bulldogs will bark if someone comes to the door – and then welcome them like best friends - while others remain quiet. There can be a number of reasons a dog barks too much. A dog may be:

* 🐾 Anxious or Fearful
* 🐾 Lonely
* 🐾 Bored
* 🐾 Attention-Seeking
* 🐾 Possessive
* 🐾 Over-Protective/Territorial
* 🐾 Copying Other Dogs

 *Excessive, habitual barking often develops during adolescence or early adulthood (before the age of two years), as your dog becomes more confident.*

If your barking dog is young, she may still be teething, so get a good selection of hardy toys, healthy chews and frozen treats to keep her occupied and gnawing - give her these when she is *quiet,* not when she is barking.

 *Your behaviour can also encourage excessive barking. If your dog barks non-stop for several seconds or minutes and then you give her a treat to quieten her, she associates barking with getting a nice treat.*

A better way to deal with it is to say in a firm voice: *"Quiet"* after she has made a few barks. Don't use her name when she is doing something you don't like; only use her name in a positive, encouraging manner. When she stops, praise her and she will get the idea that what you want her to do is stop. The trick is to stop the bad behaviour straight away before it becomes ingrained.

If she's barking to get your attention, ignore her. If that doesn't work, leave the room and don't allow her to follow you, so you deprive her of your attention. Do this as well if her barking and attention-seeking turns to nipping. Tell her to *"Stop"* in a firm voice - not shouting - remove your hand or leg and, if necessary, leave the room.

As humans, we can use our voice in many different ways: to express happiness or anger, to scold, to shout a warning, and so on. Dogs are the same; different barks and noises give out different messages.

 *Listen to the tone of the bark, a high-pitched bark is usually a sign of fear or nervousness. Ears flattened back on the head are another sign of nerves or fear. Learn to recognise the difference between an alert bark, an excited bark, a demanding bark, a high pitched bark, an aggressive bark or a plain "I'm barking 'coz I can bark" bark!*

If your dog is barking at other dogs, arm yourselves with lots of treats and spend time calming her down. This may be aggression or a fear response – especially if they are on a leash, as they know they cannot escape so are trying to make themselves look and sound fierce to the other dog.

When she starts to bark wildly at another dog while on the lead, distract her by letting her sniff a treat in your hand. Make her sit and give a treat. Talk in a gentle manner and keep showing and giving her a treat for remaining calm and not barking. Get her to focus her attention and gaze on you and the treat, not the other dog. There are several videos on YouTube that show how to deal with this problem in the manner described here.

## Speak and Shush!

Many Bulldogs are not good guard dogs, they couldn't care less if somebody breaks in and walks off with the family silver – they are more likely to greet the burglar with a wagging backside and approach for a treat or a pat as the villains make off with your prize possessions!

But if you do have a problem with excessive barking when visitors arrive, the Speak and Shush technique is one way of getting a dog to quieten down. If your Bulldog doesn't bark and you want her to, a slight variation of this method can also be used to get her to bark as a way of alerting you that someone is at the door. We have used this method very successfully.

When your dog barks at an arrival at your house, gently praise her after the first few barks. If she persists, gently tell her that that is enough. Like humans, some dogs can get carried away with the sound of their own voice, so try and discourage too much barking from the outset. The Speak and Shush technique teaches your dog or puppy to bark and be quiet on command.

Get a friend to stand outside your front door and say "Speak" - or "Woof" or "Alert." This is the cue for your accomplice to knock or ring the bell – don't worry if you both feel like idiots, it will be worth the embarrassment!

When your dog barks, praise her profusely. You can even bark yourself in encouragement! After a few good barks, say "Shush" and then dangle a tasty treat in front of her nose. She will stop barking as soon as she sniffs the treat, because it is physically impossible for a dog to sniff and woof at the same time.

Praise your dog again as she sniffs quietly and then give her the treat. Repeat this routine a few times a day and your Bulldog will quickly learn to bark whenever the doorbell rings and you ask her to speak.

Eventually your dog will bark AFTER your request but BEFORE the doorbell rings, meaning she has learned to bark on command. Even better, she will learn to anticipate the likelihood of getting a treat following your "Shush" request and will also be quiet on command.

With Speak and Shush training, progressively increase the length of required shush time before offering a treat - at first just a couple of seconds, then three, five, 10, 20, and so on. By alternating

"Yes, I live on the third floor ... but I have never heard any howling sounds."

instructions to speak and shush, the dog is praised and rewarded for barking on request and also for stopping barking on request.

If you want your dog to be more vocal, you need to have some treats at the ready, waiting for that rare bark. Wait until she barks - for whatever reason - then say "Speak" or whatever word you want to use, praise her and give her a treat.

At this stage, she won't know why she is receiving the treat. Keep praising her every time she barks and give her a treat. After you've done this for several days, hold a treat in your hand in front of her face and say "Speak."

Your dog will probably still not know what to do, but will eventually get so frustrated at not getting the treat that she will bark. At which point, praise her and give her the treat.

We trained a Labrador to do this in a week or so and he barked his head off when anybody came to the door or whenever we give him the command: "Speak" – a Bulldog may take a little longer.

 *Always use your 'encouraging teacher voice' when training; speak softly when instructing your dog to Shush, and reinforce the Shush with whisper-praise. The softer you speak, the more your dog will be likely to pay attention. Bulldogs respond very well to training when it is fun, short and reward-based.*

## Dealing with Aggression

Some Bullies are more prone to aggression than others, so if yours is a little love machine with other dogs and people, feel free to skip this section.

Given certain situations, any dog can growl, bark or even bite. Sometimes a dog learns unwanted behaviour from another dog or dogs, but often it is because the dog feels insecure or has become too territorial or protective of her food, toys or owner. Aggression towards other dogs is more often seen in male Bulldogs.

NOTE: Puppy biting is not aggression; all puppies bite; they explore the world with their noses and mouths. It is, however, important to train your cute little pup not to bite, as he or she may cause injury to someone if the biting continues when the dog weights 40lb to 50lb and has jaws like a hammerhead shark.

Any dog can bite when under stress and so can Bulldogs. Here are some different types of aggressive behaviour:

- 🐾 Snarling or lunging at other dogs
- 🐾 Growling or biting if you or another animal goes near her food
- 🐾 Being possessive with toys
- 🐾 Growling at you or other people
- 🐾 Growling if you pet or show attention to another animal
- 🐾 Marking territory by urinating inside the house
- 🐾 Growling and chasing other small animals
- 🐾 Growling and chasing cars, joggers or strangers

- Standing in your way or charging through you
- Pulling and growling on the lead

> **Tip** *As well as snarling, lunging, barking or biting, look out for other physical signs, such as raised hackles, top lip curled back to bare the teeth, ears up and tail raised.*

One reason for aggression can be that the dog has not been fully socialised, and so feels threatened or challenged. Rather than being comfortable with new situations, other dogs or intrusions, he responds using *"the best form of defence is attack"* philosophy and displays aggressive behaviour to anything or anyone he is unsure of.

If the aggression is rooted in fear, it may stem from a bad experience the dog has suffered. I know a number of naturally non-aggressive dogs that have started to growl and snarl at other dogs in later life, after they have been the victim of an attack by another dog or dogs, often when they were young.

An owner's treatment of a dog can be a further reason. An owner that shouts, uses physical violence or reprimands the dog too often can cause snapping or other unwanted behaviour from the dog. Aggression breeds aggression. Dogs can also become aggressive or depressed if they are consistently left alone, cooped up, under-fed or under-exercised.

Many dogs are more combative on the leash. This is because they cannot run away; *fight or flight.* They know they can't escape, and so make themselves as frightening as possible and bark or growl to warn off the other dog or person.

Train your dog from an early age to be comfortable walking on the lead. And socialisation is, of course, vital – the first four to five months of a puppy's life is the critical time.

If your dog suddenly shows a change of behaviour and becomes aggressive, have him checked out by a vet to rule out any underlying medical reason for the crankiness, such as earache or toothache. Raging hormones can be another reason for aggression or a change in behaviour.

A further reason is they have been spoiled by their owners and have come to believe that the world revolves around them. Not spoiling your Bulldog and teaching him what is acceptable behaviour in the first place is the best preventative measure.

Early training, especially during puppyhood and adolescence - before he develops unwanted habits - can save a lot of trouble in the future.

Professional dog trainers employ a variety of techniques with a dog that has become aggressive. Firstly, they will look at the causes and good trainers use reward-based methods to try and cure aggressive or fearful dogs. *Counter conditioning* is a positive training technique used by many professionals to help change a dog's aggressive behaviour towards other dogs.

A typical example would be a dog that snarls, barks and lunges at other dogs while on the lead. It is the presence of other dogs that is triggering the dog to act in a fearful or anxious manner. Every time the dog sees another dog, he is given a tasty treat to counter the aggression. With enough steady repetition, the dog starts to associate the presence of other dogs with a tasty treat.

Properly and patiently done, the final result is a dog that calmly looks to the owner for the treat whenever she sees another dog while on the lead. Whenever you encounter a potentially aggressive situation, divert your Bulldog's attention by turning his head away from the other dog and towards you, so that he cannot make eye contact with the other dog.

## Aggression Towards People

**Desensitisation** is the most common method of treating aggression. It starts by breaking down the triggers for the behaviour one small step at a time. The aim is to get the dog to associate pleasant things with the trigger, i.e. people or a specific person whom he previously feared or regarded as a threat.

This is done through using positive reinforcement, such as praise or treats. Successful desensitisation takes time, patience and knowledge. If your dog is starting to growl at people, there are a couple of techniques you can try to break him of this bad habit before it develops into full-blown biting.

One method is to arrange for some friends to come around, one at a time. When they arrive at your house, get them to scatter kibble on the floor in front of them so that your dog associates the arrival of people with tasty treats.

 As they move into the house, and your dog eats the kibble, praise him for being a good boy. Manage your dog's environment. Don't over-face him.

Most Bulldogs love children, but if yours is at all anxious around them, separate them or carefully supervise their time together in the beginning. Children typically react enthusiastically to dogs and some dogs may regard this as frightening or an invasion of their space.

Some dogs, particularly spoiled ones, may show aggression towards people other than the owner. Several people have written to our website on this topic and it usually involves a partner or husband. Often the dog is jealous of the attention the owner is giving to the other person, or it could be that the dog feels threatened by him.

If it happens with your Bulldog, the key is for the partner to gradually gain the trust of the dog. He or she should show that they are not a threat by speaking gently to the dog and giving treats for good behaviour. Avoid eye contact, as the dog may see this as a challenge. If the subject of the aggression lives in the house, then let this person give the dog his daily feeds.

A crate is also a useful tool for removing an aggressive dog from the situation for short periods of time, allowing him out gradually and praising good behaviour. In extreme cases, when a dog exhibits persistent bad behaviour that the owner is unable to correct, a canine professional may be the answer. This can be expensive if your Bulldog needs a lot of sessions, so it's far better to spend time training and socialising your dog as soon as you get him.

## Coprophagia (Eating Faeces)

It is hard for us to understand why a dog would want to eat his or any other animal's faeces (stools, poop or poo, call it what you will), but it does happen - some dogs love the stuff!

Nobody fully understands why; it may simply be an unpleasant behaviour trait, or there could be an underlying reason. It is thought that the inhumane and useless potty-training technique of *"sticking the dog's nose in it"* when she has eliminated inside the house can also encourage it.

If your dog eats poop from the cat litter tray, place the litter tray somewhere your dog can't get to it – but the cat can. Perhaps on a shelf, or put a guard around it, small enough for the cat to get through, but not your dog.

Our dog sometimes eats cow or horse poop on walks in the countryside. He usually stops when we tell him to and hasn't suffered any after effects – so far. But the offending material sticks to the fur around his mouth and has to be cleaned off - sometimes he allows himself the treat of rolling in the stuff and then has to be hosed down. You may find that your Bulldog will roll in fox poop to cover the fox's scent.

 *Try and avoid areas you know are frequented by foxes if you can, as their faeces can transmit several diseases, including Canine Parvovirus or worms. Neither of these should pose a serious health risk if your dog is up to date with vaccinations and worming treatments.*

Vets have found that canine diets with low levels of fibre and high levels of starch increase the likelihood of coprophagia. If your dog is exhibiting this behaviour, first check that the diet you are feeding is nutritionally complete. Look at the first ingredient on the dog food packet or tin – is it corn or meat? Does he look underweight? Check that you are feeding the right amount.

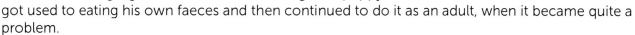

If there is no underlying medical reason, you will have to try and modify your dog's behaviour. Remove cat litter trays, clean up after your dog and do not allow him to eat his own faeces. If it's not there, he can't eat it.

One breeder told us of a dog that developed the habit after being allowed to soil his crate as a pup, caused by the owners not being vigilant in their housetraining. The puppy got used to eating his own faeces and then continued to do it as an adult, when it became quite a problem.

Don't reprimand the dog for eating faeces. A better technique is to cause a distraction while he is in the act and then remove the offending material.

 *Coprophagia is sometimes seen in pups six months to a year old and often disappears after this age.*

This chapter provides just a general overview of canine behaviour. If your Bulldog exhibits persistent problems, particularly if he or she is aggressive towards people or other dogs, consider seeking help from a reputable canine behaviourist, such as those listed by the Association of Professional Dog Trainers, at: http://www.apdt.co.uk (UK) or https://apdt.com (USA).

Check they use positive reinforcement techniques - the old Alpha-dominance theories of forcefully imposing your will on a dog have largely been discredited. Even if they hadn't, Bulldogs do not respond well to this type of treatment.

# 9. Training a Bulldog

Training a young dog is not unlike bringing up a child. Put lots of time in early on to work towards a better mutual understanding and you'll be rewarded with a well-adjusted individual who is a joy to live with and who gets on well with others.

Bulldogs are not clones, some are more strong-willed and independent than others, and being the proud owner of a handsome, well-behaved Bully isn't something that happens magically overnight. You have to make time for training. Bulldogs are family dogs and companions second to none, but let yours behave exactly how he or she wants and you could finish up with a stubborn adult who rules your house!

..................................................................................................................................

Too many dogs end up in rescue shelters because they didn't turn out how their owners expected. Often, it's not the dog's fault; lack of training usually plays a part in why a dog develops unwanted behaviour traits. How can your Bulldog behave as you want if he has not learned what you expect of him?

If you want a Bulldog who will be a perfect companion and not a pain in the you-know-what, make time to teach him good manners and a few rules. The last thing you want on your hands is a self-centred Bully that barges into you, is aggressive with food and bites the kids.

Bulldogs are placid by nature, but underneath that mellow and often comical exterior lies a streak of single-mindedness. You are not going to click your fingers and have your Bully jump to attention every time. Nope.

He might or he might not, but he will want to weigh everything up first before he decides **IF** he is going to do what you ask. Some of this may be down to his nature, some of it may be that he can't be bothered and some is due to the inherent nature of the breed itself.

Bulldogs are highly motivated by food — but they also love attention and praise, which is good for training. The secret of good training can be summed up in four words:

- ❧ Consistency
- ❧ Reward
- ❧ Praise
- ❧ PATIENCE

 *Police and other service dogs are trained to a very high level with only a ball for reward. Don't always use treats; praise or play time is often enough reward. Try getting your Bully used to a small piece of carrot or apple as a healthy low-calorie alternative to traditional dog treats.*

Many owners say that their Bulldog is surprisingly sensitive and has empathy (the ability to pick up on the feelings of others). They respond well to your encouragement and a positive atmosphere; they do not respond well to shouting or heavy-handed training methods.

## The Intelligence of Dogs

Psychologist and canine expert Dr Stanley Coren has written a book called *"The Intelligence of Dogs"* in which he ranks 138 breeds of dog. He used "understanding of new commands" and "obey first command" as his standards of intelligence, surveying dog trainers to compile the list. He says there are three types of dog intelligence:

- ❧ Adaptive Intelligence (learning and problem-solving ability). This is specific to the individual animal and is measured by canine IQ tests

- ❧ Instinctive Intelligence. This is specific to the individual animal and is measured by canine IQ tests

- ❧ Working/Obedience Intelligence. This is breed-dependent

Bulldoggers will be horrified to hear that their beloved breed was listed 136th out of 138 breeds, with only the Basenji and Afghan Hound lower down the list. They were all in the section headed *"Lowest Degree of Working/Obedience Intelligence:"*

- ❧ Understanding of new commands: 80 to 100 repetitions or more

- ❧ Obey first command: 25% of the time or worse

So, you may have your work cut out!

**FACT** > *The Bulldog is not unintelligent - Bulldogs can be empathetic, picking up on your mood. The list does not take account of genetic intelligence, which can be measured by ingenuity and a dog's understanding of a common situation.*

The drawback of this rating scale, by the author's own admission, is that it is heavily weighted towards obedience-related behavioural traits, found in working or protection dogs, rather than understanding or creativity, which is found in hunting dogs.

As a result, some breeds appear lower on the list due to their stubborn or independent nature, but this nature does not make them unintelligent or impossible to train. And the Bulldog falls firmly into this category. Incidentally, the top dogs were, in order, Border Collie, Poodle and German Shepherd.

OK, so we all know that the Bulldog is not a Border Collie, nor would we want him to be, so how do we go about training him?

## Five Golden Rules

1. Training must be reward-based, not punishment based.
2. Keep sessions short or your Bulldog will get bored.
3. Never train when you are in a rush or a bad mood.
4. Never train when your Bully is too tired to concentrate.
5. Keep sessions fun; *give your Bulldog a chance to shine!*

 *If you have a stubborn Bulldog, you have to use your brain to think of ways to make training fun and to persuade him that what YOU want him to do is actually what HE wants to do!*

Then he will come to realise that when he does what you ask of him, something good happens – treats, praise, pats, play time, etc. You have to be firm and patient with a strong-willed or stubborn dog, but all training should still be carried out using positive techniques.

 *Establishing the natural order of things is not something forced on a dog through shouting or violence; it is brought about by mutual consent and good training.*

If you have adopted an adult Bulldog, you can still train him, but it will take a little longer to get rid of bad habits and instil good manners. Patience and persistence are the keys here.

Socialisation is a very important aspect of training. Young pups can absorb a great deal of information, but they are also vulnerable to bad experiences.

They need exposing – in a positive manner - to different people, other animals and situations. If not, they can find them very frightening when they do finally encounter them later. Depending on their personality, they may react by being aggressive, barking, cowering or urinating.

If they have a lot of good experiences with other people, places, noises, situations and animals before four or five months old, they are less likely to either be timid or nervous or try to establish dominance later.

 *Even though Bulldogs don't need a lot of exercise, don't just leave your dog at home in the early days, take him out and about with you on short trips, get him used to new people, places and noises. Dogs that miss out on being socialised can pay the price in terms of personality later.*

All Bulldog pups are chewers. If you are not vigilant, some young pups and adolescents will chew through anything – wires, phone chargers, remote controls, bedding, rugs, etc. Young dogs are not infrequent visitors to veterinary clinics to have *"foreign objects"* removed from their stomachs.

Train your young pup only to chew the things you give – so don't give him your old slippers, an old piece of carpet or anything that resembles something you don't want him to chew, he won't know the difference between the old and the new. Buy purpose-made long-lasting chew toys.

Barging is another common issue with Bulldogs. You don't want your 45lb Bully to barge through Granny on his charge to the food bowl. While still small, teach your dog some manners – SIT and STAY are a good start!

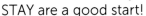

A puppy class is one of the best ways of getting a pup used to being socialised and trained. This should be backed up by short sessions of a few minutes of training a day back home.

Anybody prepared to put in a fair bit of time can train a Bulldog. But if you do need some professional one-on-one tuition (for you and the dog), choose a trainer registered with the Association of Professional Dog Trainers (APDT) or other positive reward-based training school, as the old Alpha-dominance theories have gone out the window.

When you train your dog, it should never be a battle of wills; it should be a positive learning experience for you both. Bawling at the top of your voice or smacking should play NO part in training any dog, but especially one as sensitive and loving as the Bulldog.

# Top Training Tips

1. **Start training and socialising straight away**. Like babies, puppies learn quickly and it's this learned behaviour that stays with them through adult life. Puppy training should start with just a few minutes a day a couple of days after arriving home.

2. **Your voice is a very important training tool.** Your dog has to learn to understand your language and you have to understand him. Commands should be issued in a calm, authoritative voice - not shouted. Praise should be given in a happy, encouraging voice, accompanied by stroking or patting. If your dog has done something wrong, use a stern voice, not a harsh shriek. This applies even if your Bulldog is unresponsive at the beginning.

3. **Avoid giving your dog commands you know you can't enforce.** Every time you give a command you don't enforce, he learns that commands are optional. One command equals one response. Give your dog only one command - twice maximum - then gently enforce it.

   Repeating commands will make him tune out, and teach him that the first few commands are a bluff. Telling your dog to *"SIT, SIT, SIT, SIT!!!"* is neither efficient nor effective. Say a single *"SIT,"* gently place him in the Sit position and praise him.

4. **Train your dog gently and humanely.** Bulldogs are sensitive by nature and do not respond well to being shouted at or hit. Keep training sessions short and upbeat so the whole experience is enjoyable for you and for him. If obedience training is a bit of a bore, pep things up a bit by *"play training"* by using constructive, non-adversarial games.

5. **Do not try to dominate your dog.** Training should be mutual, i.e. your dog should do something because he WANTS to do it and he knows that you want him to do it.

6. **Begin training at home around the house and garden/yard**. How well your dog responds at home affects his behaviour away from the home as well. If he doesn't respond well at home, he certainly won't respond any better out and about where there are 101 distractions, e.g. interesting people, food scraps, scents, other dogs and small animals or birds.

7. **Mealtimes are a good time to start training.** Teach Sit and Stay at breakfast and dinner, rather than just putting the dish down and letting him dash over immediately. At first, he won't know what you mean, so gently place him into the sit position while you say *"Sit."* Place a hand on his chest during the Stay command - gradually letting go — and then give him the command to eat, followed by encouraging praise - he'll soon get the idea.

8. **Use his name often and in a positive manner** so he gets used to the sound of it. He won't know what it means at first, but it won't take long before he realises you're talking to him.

9. **DON'T use his name when reprimanding, warning or punishing.** He should trust that when he hears his name, good things happen. He should always respond to his name with

enthusiasm, never hesitancy or fear. Use words such as *"No," "Ack!"* or *"Bad Boy/Girl"* in a stern (not shouted) voice instead. When a puppy is corrected by his mother, e.g. – if he bites her – she growls to warn him not to do it again. Using a short sharp sound like *"Ack!"* can work surprisingly well; it does for us.

NOTE: Some parents prefer not to use "No" with their dog, as they use it so often around the kids that it can confuse the pup!

10. **Don't give your dog lots of attention (even negative attention) when he misbehaves.** Bulldogs love attention and if yours gets lots when he jumps up on you, you are inadvertently reinforcing bad behaviour. If he jumps up demanding your attention, push him away, use the command *"No"* or *"Down"* and then ignore him. If necessary, leave the room so he learns that when he has displeased you, he is deprived of your presence.

11. **Timing is critical.** When your puppy does something right, praise him immediately. If you wait a while, he will have no idea what he has done right. Similarly, when he does something wrong, correct him straight away.

12. **If he has an "accident" in the house, don't shout and definitely don't rub his nose in it.** This will only make things worse and encourage your dog to fear you. He may even start hiding and peeing or pooping behind the couch or other inappropriate places. If you catch him in the act, use your *"No!"* or *"Ack!"* sound and immediately carry him out of the house. Then use your toilet command and praise or give a treat when he performs. If your pup is constantly eliminating indoors, you are probably not keeping a close enough eye on him or not picking up on the signs.

13. **In the beginning, give your dog attention when YOU want to – not when he wants it.** When you are training, give your puppy lots of positive attention when he is good. But if he starts jumping up, nudging you constantly or barking to demand your attention, ignore him. Don't give in to the demands. Wait a while and pat him when you are ready and AFTER he has stopped demanding your attention.

14. **You can give a Bulldog TOO MUCH attention in the beginning.** This may create a rod for your own back when they grow into needy adults that are over-reliant on you. They may even develop Separation Anxiety, which is stressful for both dog AND owner.

15. **Start as you mean to go on.** In terms of training, treat your cute little pup as though he were fully-grown. Introduce the rules you want him to live by as an adult. If you don't want your dog to take over your couch or bed or jump up at people when he is an adult, train him not to do it while still young. You can't have one set of rules for a pup and one set for a fully-grown dog; he won't understand.

16. **Enrol your puppy in a local puppy training class,** it's a great way for your pup or adolescent to train while socialising with his peers.

17. **THE GOLDEN RULE: Training should always be a positive experience** based on rewards, not punishment. It is not a battle of wills between you and your dog. Bulldogs can be sensitive critters, and bawling at the top of your voice or smacking should play no part in training.

 *Everybody in the household should stick to the same set of rules. If the kids let him jump on the couch and you don't, your dog won't know what is allowed and what isn't.*

Dogs are pack animals and are happy when they know their place in the pack - and it should be somewhere below you! This is not forced on a dog through shouting and hitting, it is the natural order of things brought about by mutual consent through good training and bonding.

Bulldogs may push the boundaries, especially as lively puppies or adolescents. Stick to your guns and establish your authority and the household rules in a positive manner and things will run much smoother. Again, this is done with positive techniques, not threats. Being aggressive will either frighten your Bully, or cause him to be aggressive back or to switch off.

Bulldogs are not fierce by nature. The vast majority do not show aggression towards other dogs or humans or bark incessantly. If they do, then you need to nip it in the bud with repetitive training. The first few months are a very important time for the development of his character and behaviour.

# Teaching Basic Commands

## The Three Ds

The three Ds – **Distance, Duration** and **Distraction** – are the cornerstone of a good training technique.

**Duration** is the length of time your dog remains in the command.

**Distance** is how far you can walk away without your dog breaking the command.

**Distraction** is the number of external stimuli - such as noise, scents, people, other animals, etc. - your dog can tolerate before breaking the command.

**Only increase one of the Three Ds at a time.** For example, if your new pup has just learned to sit on command, gradually increase the time by a second or two as you go along. Moving away from the dog or letting the kids or the cat into the room would increase the Distance or Distraction level and make the command too difficult for your pup to hold.

If you are teaching the Stay, gradually increase EITHER the distance OR the time he is in the Stay position; don't increase both at once.

Start off by training your dog in your home before moving into the garden or yard where there are more distractions - even if it is quiet and you are alone, outdoor scents and sights will be a big distraction for a young dog. Once you have mastered the commands in a home environment, progress to the park.

*Don't expect too much too soon. The key to successful training is to implement the Three Ds progressively and slowly. Remember that Bulldogs may need 100 repetitions before they consistently perform the command. Work within your dog's capabilities, move forward one tiny step at a time and set your Bulldog up to consistently succeed, not fail.*

## The Sit

Teaching the Sit command to your Bulldog is relatively easy. Teaching a young pup to sit still for any length of time is a bit more difficult! If your little protégé is very distracted or lively, it may be easier to put him on a leash (lead) to hold his attention in the beginning. Stand facing each other and hold a treat between your thumb and fingers just an inch or so above his head and let him sniff it.

Don't let your fingers and the treat get much further away or you might have trouble getting him to move his body into a sitting position. In fact, if your dog jumps up when you try to guide him into the Sit, you're probably holding your hand too far away from his nose. If your dog backs up, you can practise with a wall behind him.

As he reaches up to sniff it, move the treat upwards and back over the dog towards his tail at the same time as saying *"Sit."* Most dogs will track the treat with their eyes and follow it with their noses, causing their snouts to point straight up.

As his head moves up toward the treat, his rear end should automatically go down towards the floor. TaDa! (drum roll!).

The second he sits, say "**Yes!**" Give him the treat and tell your dog he's a good boy/girl. Stroke and praise him for as long as he stays in the sitting position. If he jumps up on his back legs and paws you while you are moving the treat, be patient and start all over again. At this stage, don't expect your bouncy little pupil to sit for more than a nanosecond!

**NOTE:** For positive reinforcement, use the words *Yes!, Good Boy!* or *Good Girl!*

Another method is to put one hand on his chest and with your other hand, gently push down on his rear end until he is sitting, while saying *"Sit."* Give him a treat and praise; even though you have made him do it, he will eventually associate the position with the word "sit."

Once your dog catches on, leave the treat in your pocket (or have it in your other hand). Repeat the sequence, but this time your dog will just follow your empty hand. Say *"Sit"* and bring your empty hand in front of your dog's nose, holding your fingers as if you had a treat. Move your hand exactly as you did when you held the treat. When your dog sits, say *"Yes!"* and then give him a treat from your other hand or your pocket.

Gradually lessen the amount of movement with your hand. First, say *"Sit"* then hold your hand eight to 10 inches above your dog's face and wait a moment. Most likely, he will sit. If he doesn't, help him by moving your hand back over his head, like you did before, but make a smaller movement this time. Then try again. Your goal is to eventually just say *"Sit"* without having to move or extend your hand at all.

Once your dog reliably sits on cue, you can ask him to sit whenever you meet and talk to people (it may not work straight away, but it might help to calm him down a bit). The key is anticipation. Give your dog the cue before he gets too excited to hear you and before he starts jumping up on the person just arrived. Generously reward him the instant he sits. Say *"Yes"* and give treats/praise every few seconds while he holds the Sit.

Whenever possible, ask the person you're greeting to help you out by walking away if your dog gets up from the sit and lunges or jumps towards them. With many consistent repetitions of this exercise, your dog will learn that lunging or jumping makes people go away, and polite sitting makes them stay and give attention. You may need to have him on a leash to begin with.

*You can practise training a boisterous Bulldog not to jump up by arranging for a friend to visit, then for him or her to come in and out of the house several times. Each time, show the treat, give the "Sit" command (initially, don't ask your dog to hold the sit for any length of time), and then allow him to greet your friend. Ask your friend to reach down to pat your dog, rather than standing straight and encouraging the dog to jump up for a greeting.*

If your dog is still jumping up, you can use a harness and leash inside the house to physically prevent him from jumping up at people, while still training him to sit when someone arrives. Treats and praise are the key. You can also use the *"Off"* command - and reward with praise or a treat for success - when you want your dog NOT to jump up at a person, or not to jump up on furniture.

*"Sit"* is a useful command and can be used in a number of different situations. For example, when you are putting his leash on, while you are preparing his food, when he returns the ball you have just thrown, when he is jumping up, demanding attention or getting over-excited.

## The Stay

This is a very useful command, but it's not so easy to teach a lively and distracted Bulldog pup to stay still for any length of time. Here is a simple method to get your dog to stay; if you are training a young dog, don't ask him to stay for more than a few seconds at the beginning.

**This requires concentration from your dog, so pick a time when he's relaxed or just after a game or mealtimes - but not too exhausted to concentrate.**

1. Tell your dog to sit or lie down, but instead of giving a treat as soon as he hits the floor, hold off for one second. Then say *"Yes!"* in an enthusiastic voice and give him a treat. If your dog bounces up again instantly, have two treats ready. Feed one right away, before he has time to move; then say *"Yes!"* and feed the second treat.

2. You need a release word or phrase. It might be *"Free!"* or *"Here!"* or a word that you only use to release your dog from this command. Once you've given the treat, immediately give your release cue and encourage your dog to get up. Then repeat the exercise, perhaps up to a dozen times in one training session, gradually wait a tiny bit longer before releasing the treat. (You can delay the first treat for a moment if your dog bounces up).

3. A common mistake is to hold the treat high and then give the reward slowly. As your dog doesn't know the command yet, he sees the treat coming and gets up to meet the food. Instead, bring the treat toward your dog quickly - the best place to deliver it is right between his front paws. If you're working on a Sit-Stay, give the treat at chest height.

4. When your dog can stay for several seconds, start to add a little distance. At first, you'll walk backwards, because your dog is more likely to get up to follow you if you turn away from him. Take one single step away, then step back towards your dog and say *"Yes!"* and give the treat. Give him the signal to get up immediately, even if five seconds haven't passed. The stay gets harder for your dog depending on how long it is, how far away you are, and what else is going on around him.

5. Remember **DISTANCE, DURATION, DISTRACTION.** For best success in teaching a Stay, work on one factor at a time. Whenever you make one factor more difficult, such as distance, ease up on the others at first, then build them back up. So, when you take that first step back from your dog, adding distance, you should cut the duration of the stay.

6. Once he's mastered the Stay with you alone, move the training on so that he learns to do the same with distractions. Have someone walk into the room, or squeak a toy or bounce a ball once. A rock-solid stay is mostly a matter of working slowly and patiently to start with. Don't go too fast.

If he does get up, take a breather and then give him a short refresher, starting at a point easier than whatever you were working on when he cracked.

 *If you think he's tired or had enough, leave it for the day and come back later – just finish off on a positive note by giving one very easy command you know he will obey, followed by a reward.*

Don't use the Stay command in situations where it is unpleasant for your dog. For instance, avoid telling him to stay as you close the door behind you on your way to work or if he feels threatened by another dog.

........................................................................................................................................

## Down

There are a number of different ways to teach this command, which here means for the dog to lie down. If you are teaching this command, then use the *"Off"* command to teach your dog not to jump up.

This does not come naturally to a young pup, so it may take a little while to master the Down command. Don't make it a battle of wills and, although you may gently push him down, don't physically force him down against his will. This will be seen as you asserting dominance in an aggressive manner and your Bulldog will not like it.

1. Give the Sit command.

2. When your dog sits, don't give him the treat immediately, but keep it in your closed hand. Slowly move your hand straight down toward the floor, between his front legs. As your dog's nose follows the treat, just like a magnet, his head will bend all the way down to the floor.

3. When the treat is on the floor between your dog's paws, start to move it away from him, like you're drawing a line along the floor. (The entire luring motion forms an L-shape).

4. At the same time say *"Down"* in a firm manner.

5. To continue to follow the treat, your dog will probably ease himself into the Down position. The instant his elbows touch the floor, say *"Yes!"* and immediately let him eat the treat. If

your dog doesn't automatically stand up after eating the treat, just move a step or two away to encourage him to move out of the Down position. Then repeat the sequence above several times. Aim for two short sessions of five minutes per day.

If your dog's back end pops up when you try to lure him into a Down, quickly snatch the treat away. Then immediately ask your dog to sit and try again. It may help to let your dog nibble on the treat as you move it toward the floor.

If you've tried to lure your dog into a Down, but he still seems confused or reluctant, try this trick:

1. Sit down on the floor with your legs straight out in front of you. Your dog should be at your side. Keeping your legs together and your feet on the floor, bend your knees to make a 'tent' shape.

2. Hold a treat right in front of your dog's nose. As he licks and sniffs the treat, slowly move it down to the floor and then underneath your legs. Continue to lure him until he has to crouch down to keep following the treat.

3. The instant his belly touches the floor, say *"Yes!"* and let him eat the treat. If your dog seems nervous about following the treat under your legs, make a trail of treats for him to eat along the way.

Some dogs find it easier to follow a treat into the Down from a standing position.

🐾 Hold the treat right in front of your dog's nose, and then slowly move it straight down to the floor, right between his front paws. His nose will follow the treat

🐾 If you let him lick the treat as you continue to hold it still on the floor, your dog will probably plop into the Down position

🐾 The moment he does, say *"Yes!"* and let him eat the treat (some dogs are reluctant to lie on a cold, hard surface. It may be easier to teach yours to lie down on a carpet). The next step is to introduce a hand signal. You'll still reward him with treats, though, so keep them nearby or hidden behind your back

1. Start with your dog in a Sit.

2. Say *"Down."*

3. Without a treat in your fingers, use the same hand motion you did before.

4. As soon as your dog's elbows touch the floor, say *"Yes!"* and immediately get a treat to give him. Important: Even though you're not using a treat to lure your dog into position, you must still give him a reward when he lies down. You want your dog to learn that he doesn't have to see a treat to get one.

5. Clap your hands or take a few steps away to encourage him to stand up. Then repeat the sequence from the beginning several times for a week or two. When your dog readily lies down as soon as you say the cue and then use your new hand signal, you're ready for the next step. You probably don't want to keep bending all the way down to the floor to make your Bulldog lie down. To make things more convenient, you can gradually shrink the signal so that it becomes a smaller movement. To make sure your dog continues to understand what you want him to do, you'll need to progress slowly.

6. Repeat the hand signal, but instead of guiding your dog into the Down by moving your hand all the way to the floor, move it almost all the way down. Stop moving your hand when it's an inch or two above the floor. Practise the Down exercise for a day or two, using this slightly smaller hand signal. Then you can make your movement an inch or two smaller, stopping your hand three or four inches above the floor.

7. After practising for another couple of days, you can shrink the signal again. As you continue to gradually stop your hand signal farther and farther from the floor, you'll bend over less and less. Eventually, you won't have to bend over at all. You'll be able to stand up straight, say *"Down,"* and then just point to the floor.

Your next job is a bit harder - it's to practise your dog's new skill in many different situations and locations so that he can lie down whenever and wherever you ask him to. Practise in calm places at first, like different rooms in your house or in your garden/yard when there's no one else around. Then increase the distractions; so, do some sessions at home when family members are moving around, on walks and then at friends' houses, too.

..................................................................................................................................

## The Recall

This basic command is perhaps the most important command of all and one that you can teach right from the beginning. If your dog won't come back, you are limiting both your lives. A Bulldog who consistently responds can enjoy freedoms that other dogs cannot. Although you might spend more time teaching this command than any other, the benefits make it well worth the investment.

 *Whether you're teaching a young puppy or an older Bulldog, the first step is always to establish that coming to you is the BEST thing he can do. Any time your dog comes to you whether you've called him or not, acknowledge that you appreciate it. You can do this with praise, affection, play or treats. This consistent reinforcement ensures that your dog will continue to "check in" with you frequently.*

1. Start off a short distance away from your dog.

2. Say your dog's name followed by the command *"Come!"* in an enthusiastic voice. You might be more successful if you walk or run away from him while you call. Some dogs find it hard to resist chasing after a running person, especially their owner.

3. He should run towards you.

4. Often, especially outdoors, a young dog will start running towards you but then get distracted and head off in another direction. Pre-empt this situation by praising your puppy and cheering him on when he starts to come to you and **before** he has a chance to get distracted. Your praise will keep him focused so that he'll be more likely to come all the way to you.

   If he stops or turns away, you can give him feedback by saying *"Oh-oh!"* or *"Hey!"* in a different tone of voice (displeased or unpleasantly surprised). When he looks at you again, smile, call him and praise him as he approaches you.

5. When your puppy comes to you, give him the treat BEFORE he sits down or he may think that the treat was earned for sitting, not coming to you.

6. Another method is to use two people. You hold the treats and let your dog sniff them while the accomplice holds on to the dog by his harness. When you are about 10 or 15 yards away, get your helper to let the dog go, and once he is running towards you, say *"COME!"* loudly and enthusiastically. When he reaches you, stop,

bend down and make a fuss of him before giving a treat. Do this several times. The next step is to give the Come command just BEFORE getting your helper to release the dog, and by doing this repetitively, the dog begins to associate the command with the action.

*"Come" or a similar word is better than "Here" if you intend using the "Heel" command, as "Here" and "Heel" sound too similar.*

Progress your dog's training in baby steps. With Bulldogs, it's a case of REPETITION, REPETITION, REPETITION.

If he's learned to come when called in your kitchen, you can't expect him to be able to do it straight away at the park, in the woods or on the beach when surrounded by distractions. When you first use the recall outdoors, make sure there's no one around to distract your dog. It's a good idea to consider using a long training leash - or to do the training within a safe, fenced area. Only when your dog has mastered the recall in a number of locations and in the face of various distractions can you expect him to come to you regularly.

## Hot to Stop Puppy Biting and Chewing

All puppies spend a great deal of time chewing, playing, and investigating objects. And it's natural for them to explore the world with their mouths and needle-sharp teeth. When puppies play with people, they often bite, chew, nip and mouthe on people's hands, limbs and clothing.

Play biting is normal for puppies; they do it all the time with their littermates. They also bite moving targets with their sharp teeth; it's a great game.

**FACT** *Some Bulldog puppies are extremely mouthy – they go through what is known as their "shark" phase where they bite anything and everything.*

When your little Bully arrives home, he has to learn that human skin is sensitive and body parts are not suitable biting material. Biting is NOT acceptable, not even from a puppy, and can be a real problem initially with some Bulldogs, especially if you have children.

When your puppy bites you or the kids, he is playing and investigating; he is not being aggressive. Even though the Bulldog has a reputation for being non-aggressive, young pups can easily get carried away with energy and excitement.

**FACT** *Another reason for too much biting is that, like babies, puppies go through a teething phase when their gums are sore and irritated.*

By the time your Bully is six months old, all his puppy teeth should have fallen out and he should be through the teething stage - but that doesn't stop all of them chewing and nipping.

Every Bulldog is different. Some are very quickly through the chew stage, while others would eat the whole house - and nibble the kids to pieces, given half a chance.

You have more chance of a Bulldog coming out of the phase earlier if you deal with puppy biting right from the beginning.

*If not dealt with, puppy biting can go on for a couple of years with some Bullies - and in extreme cases it even becomes a decision between keeping the kids or the dog. Needless to say, it's the Bulldog that ends up in rescue.*

If things are getting out of control, here are some tried and tested methods to deal with a baby Hammerhead.

## REDIRECTION

Every time you have a play session, have a soft toy nearby and when he starts to chew your hands or feet, clench your fingers (or toes, Bulldogs love biting feet!) to make it more difficult and distract him with a soft toy in your other hand. Keep the game interesting by moving the toy around or rolling it around in front of him. He may continue to chew you, but should eventually realise that the toy is far more interesting and livelier than your boring hand.

## IGNORE

If he becomes over-excited and too aggressive, if he growls a lot, stop playing and walk away. When you walk away, don't say anything or make eye or physical contact with your puppy. **Simply ignore him,** this is often extremely effective.

If your pup is more persistent and tries to bite your legs as you walk away, thinking this is another fantastic game, stand still and ignore him. If he still persists, say *"No!"* or *"No Bite!"* in a very stern voice, then praise him when he lets go. If you have to physically remove him from your trouser leg or shoe, leave him alone in the room and ignore demands for your attention if he starts barking.

## OUCH!

Bulldogs are people-loving dogs and another method is to make a sharp cry of "OUCH!" when your pup bites your hand – even when it doesn't hurt.

This has worked very well for us. Many pups will jump back in amazement, surprised to have hurt you. Divert your attention from your puppy to your hand. He will probably try to get your attention or lick you as a way of saying sorry.

Praise him for stopping biting and continue with the game. If he bites you again, repeat the process. A sensitive dog should soon stop biting you.

## OTHER METHODS

Put a couple of *coins in a tin can* and the next time your pup bites you or the kids, rattle the can and make a lot of noise. Generally, Bulldogs don't like loud noises. A lot of Bully owners have had success with this method.

Spray **bitter apple, pictured,** on your fingers, toes, furniture or anywhere else that your Bully is biting - as well as using the other methods. Most dogs hate the taste - although a few persistent Bullies will chew right through the stuff.

*A water spray* can be very effective. Fill an empty plastic spray bottle with water and spray your Bulldog with it when he bites and AFTER he has ignored your commands to stop.

*Frozen chew toys or ice cubes* are a great way to redirect your biting Bully. This method can be doubly effective, as the ice soothes and numbs irritated gums when teething.

*Avoid immediately putting your pup in a crate when he is being naughty, or he will associate the crate with punishment. Remove yourself or the pup from the room for a short while and ignore his pleas - or put him in a pen. Wait until he has calmed down before you put him in his crate.*

Here are some general tips to discourage puppy biting:

- ❧ Puppies growl and bite more when they are excited. Don't allow things to escalate, so remove your pup from the situation BEFORE he gets too excited by putting him in a crate or pen for some time-out

- ❧ Don't put your hand or finger into your pup's mouth to nibble on; this promotes puppy biting

- ❧ Limit your children's play time with pup - and always supervise the sessions in the beginning. Teach them to gently play with and stroke your puppy, not to wind him up

- ❧ Don't let the kids (or adults) run around the house with the puppy chasing – this is an open invitation to nip the ankles

- ❧ If your puppy does bite, remove him from the situation and people – never smack him

If puppy chewing is a problem it is because your pup is chewing on something you don't want him to. So, the trick is to keep him, his mouth and sharp little teeth occupied with something he CAN chew on, such as a durable toy – see **Chapter 5. Bringing Puppy Home** for more information on suitable toys and chews.

You might also consider freezing peanut butter and/or a liquid inside a Kong toy. Put the Kong into a mug, plug the small end with peanut butter and fill it with gravy before putting it into the freezer. (Check the peanut butter doesn't contain the sweetener xylitol as this can be harmful to dogs). Don't leave the Kong and your Bulldog on your precious Oriental rug!

This should keep your pup occupied for quite a long time. It is also worth considering giving the dog a frozen Kong or Lickimat when you leave the house if your dog suffers from separation anxiety. There are lots of doggie recipes for Kongs and other treats online.

# Clicker Training

Clicker training is a method of training that uses a sound - a click - to tell an animal when he does something right. The clicker is a tiny plastic box held in the palm of your hand, with a metal tongue that you push quickly to make the sound. The clicker creates an efficient language between a human trainer and a trainee.

First, a trainer teaches a dog that every time he hears the clicking sound, he gets a treat. Once the dog understands this, the click becomes a powerful reward. When this happens, the trainer can use the click to mark the instant the dog performs the right behaviour.

For example, if a trainer wants to teach a dog to sit, he or she will click the instant the dog's rump hits the floor and then deliver a tasty treat. With repetition, the dog learns that sitting earns rewards.

So, the *Click* takes on huge meaning. To the animal it means: "What I was doing the moment my trainer clicked, that's what he wants me to do." The clicker in animal training is like the winning buzzer on a game show that tells a contestant he's just won the money! Through the clicker, the trainer communicates precisely with the dog, and that speeds up training.

Although the clicker is ideal because it makes a unique, consistent sound, you do need a spare hand to hold it. For that reason, some trainers prefer to keep both hands free and instead use a one-syllable word like *"Yes!"* or *"Good!"* to mark the desired behaviour. In the steps below, you can substitute the word in place of the click to teach your pup what the sound means.

It's easy to introduce the clicker to your Bulldog. Spend half an hour or so teaching him that the sound of the click means *"Treat!"* Here's how:

1. Sit and watch TV or read a book with your dog in the room. Have a container of (healthy) treats within reach.

2. Place one treat in your hand and the clicker in the other. (If your dog smells the treat and tries to get it by pawing, sniffing, mouthing or barking at you, just close your hand around the treat and wait until he gives up and leaves you alone).

3. Click once and immediately open your hand to give your dog the treat. Put another treat in your closed hand and resume watching TV or reading. Ignore your dog.

4. Several minutes later, click again and offer another treat.

5. Continue to repeat the click-and-treat combination at varying intervals, sometimes after one minute, sometimes after five minutes. Make sure you vary the time so that your dog doesn't know exactly when the next click is coming. Eventually, he'll start to turn toward you and look expectantly when he hears the click - which means he understands that the sound of the clicker means a treat is coming his way.

If your dog runs away when he hears the click, you can make the sound softer by putting it in your pocket or wrapping a towel around your hand that's holding the clicker. You can also try using a different sound, like the click of a retractable pen or the word *"Yes!"*

Once your dog understands the connection between the click and the treat, you're ready to start:

1. Click just once, right when your pup does what you want him to do. Think of it like pressing the shutter of a camera to take a picture of the behaviour.

2. Remember to follow every click with a treat. After you click, deliver the treat to your puppy's mouth as quickly as possible.

3. It's fine to switch between practising two or three behaviours within a session, but work on one command at a time. For example, say you're teaching your dog to sit, lie down and raise his paw. You can do 10 repetitions of sit and take a quick play break. Then do 10 repetitions of down and take another quick break. Then do 10 repetitions of stay, and so on. Keep training sessions short and stop before you or your dog gets tired of the game.

 *Always set your dog up to succeed, not fail. If he has been struggling with a new command, end training sessions on a good note with something he CAN do.*

# Collar, Harness and Leash (Lead) Training

You have to train your dog to get used to a collar or harness and leash and then to walk nicely beside you. Teaching these manners can be challenging because Bulldogs don't usually want to walk at the same pace as you! Bulldogs are extremely strong and, if not leash-trained, will pull you where THEY want to go, not where YOU want to go. They might even pull you off your feet.

Most dogs will pull on a leash initially. It's not because they want to show you who's boss, it's usually because they are excited to be out and are forging ahead. However, a few Bullies are just the opposite - they slump to the ground and refuse to move!

Harnesses work very well with Bulldogs, they take the pressure away from the dog's sensitive neck area and distribute it more evenly around the body, which is a good thing, given the breed's breathing issues.

If you decide to use a harness but still want your Bully to have a collar - spiked, diamante or whatever takes your fancy – that's fine. Attach the ID tag to it, but not the leash; attach the leash to the harness. One with a chest ring for the leash can be effective for training. When your dog pulls, the harness turns him around.

Another option is to start your dog on a small lightweight collar and then change to a harness once he has learned some leash etiquette. Some dogs don't mind collars, some will try to fight them, while others will drop to the floor!

Be patient and calm and proceed at a pace comfortable to your dog; don't fight him and don't force the collar on.

1. If you start your puppy off with a collar, you need a small, lightweight one - not a heavy, spiked one. You can buy one with clips to start with, *pictured,* rather than fiddling with buckles, which can be scary when he's wearing a collar for the first time. Stick to positive reward-based training and give a treat or praise once the collar is on, not after you have taken it off. Then gradually increase the length of time you leave the collar on.

*We don't recommend choke collars with Bulldogs; if they pull, it's too much pressure on the sensitive neck area. And if you leave your dog in a crate or alone in the house, take the collar off as it may get caught on something, causing panic or injury.*

2. Put the collar on when there are other things that will occupy him, like when he is going outside to be with you, or in the home when you are interacting with him. Or put it on at mealtimes or when you are doing some basic training. Don't put the collar on too tight, you want him to forget it's there; **you should be able to get two fingers underneath.**

Some pups may react as if you've hung a two-ton weight around their necks, while others will be more compliant. If yours scratches the collar, get his attention by encouraging him to follow you or play with a toy to forget the irritation.

3. Once your puppy is happy wearing the collar, introduce the leash. Many owners prefer an extending or retractable leash for their Bulldog, but consider a fixed-length one to start training him to walk close to you. Begin around the house, garden or yard; don't go out and about without practising first.

 *Think of the leash as a safety device to stop him running off, not something to drag him around with. You want a Bulldog that doesn't pull, so don't start by pulling him around; you don't want to get into a tug-of-war contest with a Bulldog.*

4. Attach the leash and give him a treat while you put it on. Use the treats (instead of pulling on the leash) to lure him beside you, so that he gets used to walking with the collar and leash on. You can also make good use of toys to do exactly the same thing - especially if your dog has a favourite. Walk around the house with the leash on and lure him forwards.

It might feel a bit odd but it's a good way for your pup to develop a positive relationship with the collar and leash with the minimum of fuss. Act as though it's the most natural thing in the world for you to walk around the house with your dog on a leash – and just hope the neighbours aren't watching!

Some dogs react the moment you attach the leash and they feel some tension on it – a bit like when a horse is being broken in for the first time.

Drop the leash and allow him to run around the house or yard, dragging it behind, just be careful he doesn't get tangled and hurt himself.

Try to make him forget about it by playing or starting a short fun training routine with treats. Treats are a huge distraction. While he is concentrating on the new task, occasionally pick up the leash and call him to you. Do it gently and in an encouraging tone.

5. **The most important thing is not to yank on the leash.** If it gets tight, just lure him back beside you with a treat or a toy while walking. All you're doing is getting him to move around beside you. Remember to keep your hand down (the one holding the treat or toy) so your dog doesn't get the habit of jumping up at you. If you feel he is getting stressed when walking outside on a leash, try putting treats along the route you'll be taking to turn this into a rewarding game: good times are ahead... That way he learns to focus on what's ahead of him with curiosity and not fear.

 *Take collar and leash training slowly. Let him gain confidence in you, the leash and himself. Some dogs sit and decide not to move! If this happens, walk a few steps away, go down on one knee and encourage him to come to you, then walk off again.*

Some dogs are perfectly happy to walk alongside you off-leash, but behave differently when they have one on. Proceed in tiny steps if that is what your puppy is happy with, don't over face him, but stick at it if you are met with resistance. With training and patience, your puppy will learn to walk nicely on a leash.

## Walking on a Leash

There are different methods, but we have found the following one to be successful for quick results. Initially, the leash should be kept fairly loose. Have a treat in your hand as you walk, it will encourage your dog to sniff the treat as he walks alongside. He should not pull ahead as he will want to remain near the treat.

Give the command *"Walk"* or *"Heel"* and then proceed with the treat in your hand, keep giving him a treat every few steps initially, then gradually extend the time between treats. Eventually, you should be able to walk with your hand comfortably at your side, periodically (every minute or so) reaching into your pocket to grab a treat to reward your dog.

If your dog starts pulling ahead, first give him a warning, by saying *"No"* or *"Steady"* or a similar command. If he slows down, give him a treat. But if he continues to pull ahead so that your arm becomes fully extended, stop walking and ignore your dog. Wait for him to stop pulling and to look up at you. At this point reward him for good behaviour before carrying on your walk.

If your dog refuses to budge, DON'T drag him. This will ultimately achieve nothing as he will learn to resent the leash. Also, many Bulldogs have a low tolerance to exercise.

Coax him along with praise and, if necessary, treats so that when he moves forward with you, it is because HE wants to and not because he has been dragged by somebody several times bigger.

Be sure to quickly reward your dog any time he doesn't pull and walks with you with the leash slack. If you have a lively young pup who is dashing all over the place on the leash, try starting training when he is already a little tired, after a play or exercise session – but not exhausted.

Another method is what dog trainer Victoria Stillwell describes as the *"Reverse Direction Technique."* When your dog pulls, say *"Let's Go!"* in an encouraging manner, then turn away from him and walk off in the other direction, without jerking on the leash. When he is following you and the leash is slack, turn back and continue on your original way.

It may take a few repetitions, but your words and body language will make it clear that pulling will not get your dog anywhere, whereas walking calmly by your side - or even slightly in front of you - on a loose leash will get him where he wants to go.

There is an excellent video (in front of her beautiful house!) which shows Victoria demonstrating this technique and highlights just how easy it is – if your dog is eager to please (and not all Bulldogs are). It only lasts three minutes: 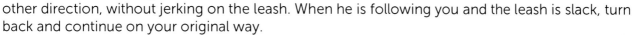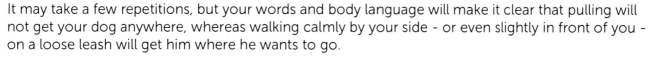https://positively.com/dog-behavior/basic-cues/loose-leash-walking

....................................................................................................................................................

## Harnesses

These are very popular with owners of Bulldogs as they do not put any strain on the neck. You may start off with a puppy harness, such as the Ruffwear, and then move on to a more heavy-duty or no-pull harness, such as a large Julius K9 or Chai's Choice. There are several different options:

❧ **Front-clip or training harness -** this has a leash attachment in front of the harness at the centre of your dog's chest. Dog trainers often choose this type as it helps to discourage your dog from pulling on the leash by turning him around

- **Back-clip** – this is generally the easiest for most dogs to get used to and useful for dogs with delicate throats that are easily irritated by collars. This type is for calm dogs or ones that have already been trained not to pull on the leash

- **Comfort wrap or step-in harness** - lay the harness on the ground, have your dog step in, pull the harness up and around his shoulders and then clip him in; simple!

- **Soft or vest harness** - typically made of mesh and comes in a range of colours and patterns. Some slip over the head and some can be stepped into

- **No-pull harness** - similar to a training harness, designed to help discourage your dog from pulling. The leash attachment ring is at the centre of the dog's chest and the harness tightens pressure if the dog pulls, encouraging him to stay closer to you. Some styles also tighten around the dog's legs

- **Auto or car harness** - these are designed for car travel and have an attachment that hooks into a seat belt

When choosing a harness, decide what its primary purpose will be – is it instead of or in addition to a collar? Do you need one that will help to train your dog, or will a back-clip harness do the job? You want to make sure that it is a snug fit, and if it's a front clip, that it hangs high on your dog's chest. If it dangles too low, it can't help control forward momentum.

Make sure the harness isn't too tight or too difficult to get on. It shouldn't rub under your dog's armpits or anywhere else. If possible, take your dog to try on a few options before buying one for the first time.

**Tip** *If you've never used a harness before, it's easy to get tangled up while your pup is jumping around, excited at the prospect of a walk. It's a good idea to have a few "dry runs" without the dog!*

Lay the harness on the floor and familiarise yourself with it. Learn which bits the legs go through, which parts fit where and how it clicks together once the dog is in.

*We strongly recommend that all new owners book their new Bulldog, whether puppy or adult, on to a training course. As well as learning basic obedience, he or she will learn how to socialise with other dogs. It is also the best, least expensive way for owners to learn how to train their dog properly. Many local veterinary clinics now run puppy training classes.*

*GENERAL NOTE:* If your puppy is in a hyperactive mood or extremely tired, he is not likely to be very receptive to training.

**CREDIT:** Thanks to the American Society for the Prevention of Cruelty to Animals for assistance with parts of this chapter. The ASPCA has a lot of good advice and training tips at: www.aspca.org

# 10. Exercise

Bulldogs have, somewhat unfairly, got themselves a reputation as couch potatoes. Many people have confused the placid temperament and the Bulldog's love of being indoors alongside his family as meaning he doesn't want or need any exercise.

This is far from the truth. All dogs require exercise – even Bulldogs, particularly as the breed is prone to put on weight.

But let's be realistic, most Bulldogs are not athletic and are quite happy sitting at home, snoozing in a comfortable chair surrounded by their human family.

Although young Bullies are often playful and full of energy, most slow down as they mature and are regarded as a breed which does well indoors with medium to low exercise requirements. Indeed, this may have been a major reason why you chose one.

The Bulldog is primarily a companion dog. If you have an active lifestyle and are looking for a canine jogging or cycling partner, then the Bulldog will not be suitable. You should choose a more athletic breed with more stamina.

Don't expect your Bully to go swimming with you either - or plunge into lakes and the ocean to retrieve that ball or stick. Some Bulldogs are OK around water, but most swim like stones and drowning is a major cause of death within the breed. If you regularly visit water, buy a lifejacket for your dog. Neither is the Bulldog suited to very hot or very cold conditions, so if you live in a warm climate, exercise him in the cool of the morning or evening.

This chapter will outline why daily exercise – even in small doses – is good for your dog and then what a good exercise regime is for a Bulldog.

One thing all dogs – including every Bulldog ever born - have in common is that they need daily exercise, and the best way to give them this is by regular walks. Daily exercise away from the home helps to keep you and your dog healthy, happy and free from disease.

Start early so your dog gets used to a routine. **Dogs love routine.** Exercise:

- Strengthens respiratory and circulatory systems
- Helps keep a healthy heart
- Wards off obesity
- Helps get oxygen to tissue cells
- Keeps muscles toned and joints flexible
- Aids digestion
- Releases endorphins that trigger positive feelings
- Helps to keep dogs mentally stimulated and socialised

Bulldogs can be susceptible to heart problems and one way of staving off heart disease is a daily walk or two to keep the heart muscles exercised.

 *Bulldogs are not known for their longevity, but regular exercise that raises the heartbeat can help to prolong your Bully's life.*

Whether you live in an apartment or on a farm, start regular exercise and feeding patterns early so the dog gets used and adapts to his and your daily routine. **Dogs love routine.** When you are out on a walk, keep your Bulldog within sight. The breed tends to want to suit itself, not you, and may wander off with a stranger.

## How Much Exercise?

Bulldogs are regarded as having low to medium exercise requirements. However, some Bullies enjoy lots of daily exercise. There is no one-rule-fits-all solution, the amount of exercise that each individual dog needs varies tremendously. It depends on a number of issues, including:

- 🐾 Temperament
- 🐾 Natural energy levels
- 🐾 Bloodline
- 🐾 Your living conditions
- 🐾 Whether your dog is kept with other dogs
- 🐾 What he gets used to

Some of your dog's natural temperament and energy level will depend on the bloodline - ask the breeder how much exercise he or she recommends.

**FACT** *Vets advise that you take your Bulldog out for at least one walk every day, even if you have a large garden or yard – two is even better. For some Bulldogs 20 minutes is enough, while others enjoy longer daily walks more often.*

Boredom is one of the main causes of poor behaviour – and chewing - in dogs. A walk is a stimulating experience for a dog. As well as the physical exercise, there are new scents, people, places, sounds, dogs and experiences, all of which help to keep him mentally stimulated and socialised.

Despite originally being a very athletic breed, since bull-baiting was banned some 180 years ago, the Bulldog has been bred to accentuate certain features. The knock-on effect is that the flat face and short neck mean that the Bulldog's air passages are very small for its size, restricting the flow of oxygen. Over-strenuous exercise, or exercising in heat, can lead to serious respiratory problems and even death - see the section on **Overheating** in **Chapter 11. Bulldog Health** for the signs your Bully is overdoing it.

A fenced garden or yard is an advantage, but should not be seen as a replacement for daily walks. You shouldn't think about getting a Bulldog - or any other type of dog - if you can't commit to at least one walk every day.

It's good practice to establish an exercise regime early in your dog's life. Dogs like routine, but remember there are strict guidelines to stick to with puppies.

## Establish a Routine

Get your dog used to exercise at the same time every day at a time that fits in with your daily routine - and stick to it. If you begin by taking your Bully out once or twice a day and then suddenly stop, he may start chewing, become attention-seeking or simply switch off because he has been used to having more exercise. Conversely, don't expect a Bulldog used to very little exercise to suddenly go on long walks, he will struggle.

Test your dog's temperament, show him his leash and see how he reacts. Is he excited at the prospect of leaving the home and going for a walk or would he rather snooze on the sofa? Adjust the level of exercise to suit your dog — but one short daily walk should be the minimum.

If your Bulldog's behaviour deteriorates or he suddenly starts chewing things he's not supposed to, the first question you should ask yourself is: *"Is he getting enough exercise?"*

Boredom through lack of exercise or mental stimulation - such as being alone or staring at four walls all day - leads to bad behaviour and it's why some Bullies end up in rescue centres through no fault of their own. On the other hand, a Bulldog at the heart of the family getting daily exercise and playtime is a happy dog and a wonderful companion.

Don't think that as your dog gets older, he won't need exercising. Old dogs need gentle exercise to keep their bodies, organs, joints and systems functioning properly. They need a less strenuous regime, but still enough to keep them alert, healthy and interested in life.

Bulldogs are known for being perpetual toddlers; they love games and your attention. To keep yours exercised mentally as well as physically, do a few minutes of reward-based training a day, have plenty of "indestructible" toys and factor in some regular play time with your dog — even gentle playtime for old Bullies.

.........................................................................................................................................................

## Exercising Puppies

There are strict guidelines to stick to with Bulldog puppies. They grow at a phenomenal rate for the first six months of life and their bones have to catch up to the rest of their body. During this time, bones and joints are still soft and cannot tolerate a lot of stress or too much exercise on hard surfaces. High-impact activities are to be avoided, as they can cause permanent damage.

Playing Fetch or Frisbee for hours on end with your lovely new puppy is definitely not a good plan, nor is allowing the pup to freely run up and down stairs in your home. You'll end up with an injured dog and a pile of vet's bills.

Just like babies, puppies have different temperaments and energy levels; some will need more exercise than others. Start slowly and build it up. The worst combination is over-exercise and overweight. Don't take your pup out of the yard or garden until the all-clear after the vaccinations - unless you carry him around to start the socialisation process. Puppies have enquiring minds; get yours used to being outside the home and experiencing new situations as soon as possible.

The general guideline for exercising puppies is:

Five minutes of on-leash exercise per month of age

So, a total of 15 minutes when three months (13 weeks)

30 minutes when six months (26 weeks) old, etc.

This applies until around one year to 18 months old, when most of their growing has finished. Slowly increase the time as he gets used to being exercised and this will gradually build up muscles and stamina.

**FACT** ❯ *It is OK for your young pup to have free run of your garden or yard, provided it has grass or another soft surface. This does not count towards the five minutes per month rule.*

It is also fine for your pup to run freely around the house to burn off energy - although not up and down stairs or jumping on and off furniture. If the yard is stone or concrete, limit the time your dog runs around on it, as the hard surface will impact joints.

A pup will take things at his own pace and stop to sniff, look at things or rest. If you have other dogs, restrict the time pup is allowed to play with them, as he won't know when he's had enough. When older, your dog can go out for much longer walks.

One breeder added: "Whilst the puppy's bones are soft and developing, it's best not to over-exert and put strain on the joints. Daily gentle walking is great, just not constant fast and hard running/chasing in the puppy stage, as too much is a big strain."

And when your little pup has grown into a beautiful adult Bulldog with a skeleton capable of carrying him through a happy and healthy life, it will have been worth all the effort:

**A long, healthy life is best started slowly**

# Exercise Tips

- 🐾 All dogs benefit from regular walks away from the home

- 🐾 Vary your exercise route – it will be more interesting for both of you

- 🐾 Always have a treat or two in your pocket on walks - just in case your Bulldog sits down and decides he's not going one step further!

- 🐾 Try and do some exercise or game which raises your Bulldog's heart rate without over-exerting him

- 🐾 Some Bulldogs have a stubborn streak. If your Bulldog puppy stares at you and tries to pull or lead you in another direction, ignore him. Do not return his stare as he is challenging you. Just continue along the way YOU want to go, with coaxing and rewards. Avoid pulling on his neck.

- Never exercise your dog on a full stomach as this can cause Bloat, which is very dangerous. Strenuous exercise, such as running round with other dogs, should be avoided within an hour before or after eating. **Chapter 6. Feeding a Bulldog** for more information

- Do not throw a ball or toy repeatedly for a puppy. He may get over-tired, damage his joints, pull a muscle, strain his heart or otherwise damage himself

- Bulldogs overheat easily, avoid exercise in hot or humid conditions – wait until it's cooler

- On hot days, always carry water on your walks

- Most Bulldogs don't have a lot of stamina – don't over-exert your dog. Keep play sessions and walks within his limits

- Be vigilant near water

- If your Bulldog seems to be panting excessively, foaming or struggling for breath, stop the exercise immediately and help him to cool down. See **Chapter 11. Bulldog Health** for details on how

- Exercise old dogs more gently - especially in cold weather when it is harder to get their bodies moving. Have a cool-down period after exercise to reduce stiffness and soreness; it helps to remove lactic acids from the dog's body

- Bulldogs of all ages love a body massage. If he's a bit stiff after exercise, go on, treat him!

Daily exercise helps you to bond with your dog, it helps keep both of you fit and healthy, you'll experience new scenery and socialise with other companions – both canine and human. It will enhance both your lives.

..................................................................................................................................

# Socialisation

Socialisation actually begins from the moment the puppy is born and the importance of picking a good breeder cannot be over-emphasised.

Not only will he or she breed for good temperament and health, but the canine mother will be well-balanced, friendly and unstressed and the pup will learn a lot in this positive environment.

**FACT ❯** *Scientists now realise the importance that socialisation plays in a dog's life. There is a fairly small window regarded as the optimum time for socialisation - and this is up to the age of four to five months.*

## Learning When Young Is Easiest

Most young animals, including dogs, are naturally able to get used to their everyday environment until they reach a certain age. When they reach this age, they become much more suspicious of things they haven't yet experienced. This is why it often takes longer to train an older dog.

When you think about it, humans are not so different. Babies and children have a tremendous capacity to learn, we call this early period our *"formative years."* As we age, we can still learn, but not at the speed we absorbed things when very young. Also, as we get older we are often less receptive to new ideas or new ways of doing things.

This age-specific natural development allows a puppy to get comfortable with the normal sights, sounds, people and animals that will be a part of his life. It ensures that he doesn't spend his life jumping in fright, snapping, or growling at every blowing leaf. The suspicion that dogs develop later also ensures that they react with a healthy dose of caution to new things that could really be dangerous - Mother Nature is clever!

Socialisation means *"learning to be part of society,"* or *"integration."* This means helping dogs become comfortable within a human society by getting them used to different people, environments, buildings, traffic, sights, noises, smells, animals, other dogs, etc.

It is essential that your dog's introductions to new things are all **positive**. Negative experiences lead to a dog becoming fearful and untrusting.

Your dog may already have a wonderful temperament, but he still needs socialising to avoid him thinking that the world is tiny and it revolves around him. Bulldogs can be demanding enough of your attention without developing a *"Little Emperor"* complex as well!

Good socialisation helps puppies – whether bold or timid - learn their place in society and become more relaxed and integrated adults. It gives your dog confidence and the ultimate goal of socialisation is to have a happy, well-adjusted dog that you can take anywhere.

Ever seen a therapy dog in action and noticed how incredibly well-adjusted to life they are? This is no coincidence. These dogs have been extensively socialised and are ready and able to deal in a calm manner with whatever situation they encounter. They are relaxed and comfortable in their own skin - just like you want your dog to be.

Start socialising your puppy as soon as you bring him home; start around the house and garden and, if it is safe, carry him out of the home environment. Regular socialisation should continue until your dog is around 18 months of age.

After that, don't just forget about it; socialisation isn't only for puppies, it should continue throughout life. As with any skill, if it is not practised, your dog will become less proficient at interacting with other people, animals, loud or unexpected noises and new situations.

## Developing the Well-Rounded Adult Dog

Dogs that have not been properly integrated are more likely to react with fear or aggression to unfamiliar people, animals and experiences.

Bulldogs who are relaxed around strangers, other dogs, honking horns, cats, farm animals, cyclists, veterinary examinations, traffic, crowds and noise are easier to live with than dogs who find these situations challenging or frightening. And if you are planning on taking part in showing or canine competitions, get yours used to the buzz of these events early on.

 *Well-socialised dogs live more relaxed, peaceful and happy lives than dogs that are constantly stressed by their environment.*

Socialisation isn't an *"all or nothing"* project. You can socialise a puppy a bit, a lot, or a whole lot. The wider the range of positive experiences you expose him to when young, the better his chances are of becoming a more relaxed adult. Don't over-face your little puppy.

Socialisation should never be forced, but approached systematically and in a manner that builds confidence and curious interaction. If your pup finds a new experience frightening, take a step back, introduce him to the scary situation much more gradually, and make a big effort to do something he loves during the situation or right afterwards.

For example, if your puppy seems to be frightened by noise and vehicles at a busy road, a good method would be to go to a quiet road, sit with the dog away from - but within sight of - the traffic. Every time he looks towards the traffic say *"YES!"* and reward him with a treat.

If he is still stressed, you need to move further away. When your dog takes the food in a calm manner, he is becoming more relaxed and getting used to traffic sounds, so you can edge a bit nearer - but still just for short periods until he becomes totally relaxed. Keep each session short and *POSITIVE.*

## Meeting Other Dogs

When you take your gorgeous and vulnerable little pup out with other dogs for the first few times, you are bound to be a bit apprehensive. To begin with, introduce your puppy to just one other dog – one that you know to be friendly, rather than taking him straight to the park where there are lots of dogs of all sizes racing around, which might frighten the life out of your timid little darling.

On the other hand, your puppy might be full of confidence right from the off, but you still need to approach things slowly. If your puppy is too cocksure, he may get a warning bite from an older dog, which could make him more anxious when approaching new dogs in the future.

*Always make initial introductions on neutral ground, so as not to trigger territorial behaviour. You want your Bulldog to approach other dogs with friendliness, not fear.*

From the first meeting, help both dogs experience good things when they're in each other's presence. Let them sniff each other briefly, which is normal canine greeting behaviour. As they do, talk to them in a happy, friendly tone of voice; never use a threatening tone.

Don't allow them to sniff each other for too long as this may escalate to an aggressive response.

After a short time, get the attention of both dogs and give each a treat in return for obeying a simple command, e.g. *"Sit"* or *"Stay."* Continue with the *"happy talk"* and rewards.

Lying on his back with his paws in the air, *as in this photo,* is a submissive gesture, as is submissive urination. It shows the other dog that he poses no threat and is normal behaviour for a puppy.

Learn to spot the difference between normal rough and tumble play and interaction that may develop into fear or aggression. Here are some signs of fear to look out for when your dog interacts with other canines:

- Running away or freezing on the spot
- Licking the lips or lips pulled back
- Trembling or panting, which can be a sign of stress or pain
- Frantic/nervous behaviour, e.g. excessive sniffing, drinking or playing frenetically with a toy
- A lowered body stance or crouching

- Lowering of the head or turning the head away, when you may see the whites of the eyes as the dog tries to keep eyes on the perceived threat
- Growling and/or hair raised on her back (raised hackles)
- Tail (if he has one) lifted high in the air or ears high on the head

Some of these responses are normal. But if the situation looks like escalating, calmly distract the dogs or remove your puppy – don't shout or shriek. Dogs will pick up on your fear and this in itself could trigger an unpleasant situation.

 *Try not to be over-protective; your puppy has to learn to interact with other dogs. Don't be too quick to rush in and pick him up, as he will sense your anxiety. The same is true when walking your dog on a leash – don't be nervous every time you seen another dog – your Bulldog will pick up on it and react.*

Always follow up a socialisation experience with praise, patting, a game or treat. One positive sign from a dog is the *"play bow" (pictured),* when he goes down on to his front elbows but keeps his backside up in the air.

This is a sign that he's feeling friendly towards the other dog and wants to play. Relaxed ear and body position and wagging tail or backside are other positive signs.

**FACT ❯** *One sign to look out for is eyeballing. In the canine world, staring a dog in the eyes is a challenge and may cause an aggressive response.*

This is more relevant to adult dogs, as a young pup will soon be put in his place by bigger or older dogs; it is how they learn. The rule of thumb with puppy socialisation is to keep a close eye on your pup's reaction to whatever you expose him to, so you can tone things down if he seems at all frightened.

Although Bulldogs are not naturally aggressive dogs, aggression is often grounded in fear, and a dog that mixes easily is less likely to be combative. Similarly, without frequent and new experiences, occasionally Bulldogs can become nervous and noisy.

Take your new dog out a lot. You want him to feel relaxed and calm in any situation, even noisy and crowded ones. Take treats with you and praise him when he reacts calmly to new situations.

Once he's settled into your home, introduce him to your friends and teach him not to jump up, nip their fingers and toes or charge through them. If you have young children, it is not only the dog that needs socialising! Youngsters also need training on how to act around dogs, so both parties learn to respect the other.

An excellent way of getting your new puppy to meet other dogs in a safe environment is at a puppy class. We highly recommend this for all puppies. Ask around locally if any classes are being run. Some vets and dog trainers run classes for very junior pups who have had all their vaccinations.

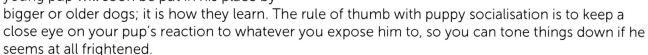

# 11. Bulldog Health

Health has a major impact on an animal's quality of life and should always be a consideration when choosing and raising a dog. The first step is to select a puppy from a breeder who produces Bulldogs that are sound in both body and temperament – and this involves health screening - and secondly, to play your part in keeping your Bully healthy throughout his or her life.

The Bulldog has many wonderful qualities, but being a naturally healthy breed is sadly not one of them. While some owners enjoy a decade of happiness with their wonderful Bulldog and would not consider any other breed, many others have to deal with expensive veterinary bills or a shortened lifespan for their beloved pet.

NOTE: This chapter is intended to be used as a medical encyclopaedia to help you to identify potential health issues and act promptly in the best interests of your dog. Please don't read it thinking your Bulldog will get lots of these ailments – he or she WILL NOT!

.......................................................................................................................................

## The Importance of Health Testing

It is becoming increasingly evident that genetics can have a huge influence on a person's health and life expectancy – which is why so much time and money is currently being devoted to genetic research. A human is more likely to suffer from a hereditary illness if the gene - or genes - for that disorder is passed on from parents or grandparents. That person is said to have a "predisposition" to the ailment if the gene(s) is in the family's bloodline. Well, the same is true of dogs.

There is not a single breed without the potential for some genetic weakness. For example, Bulldog Dogs are more prone to hip problems than many other breeds, and 30% of Dalmatians have problems with their hearing. If you get a Bulldog or a Dalmatian, your dog will not automatically suffer from these issues, but if he comes from unscreened parents, the dog will statistically be more likely to have them than a dog from a breed with no history of the complaint.

**FACT** › *Faulty genes carrying genetic illnesses can be inherited along with all the good genes that you love, like those for a big head, wrinkled face, placid temperament and coat colour. Just because a puppy's parents are registered with the Kennel Club in the UK or AKC in the USA and have pedigree certificates does NOT mean that they have passed any health tests.*

 *When choosing a puppy, base your decision on what's going on INSIDE the puppy as well as external appearance - do this by asking to see health certificates for the puppy's parents.*

A pedigree certificate's only guarantee is that the puppy's parents can be traced back several generations and the ancestors were all purebred Bulldogs. Many breeding dogs have indeed passed health tests, but prospective buyers should always find out *exactly* what screening the parents have undergone. Ask to see original certificates - and what, if any, health guarantees the breeder is offering with the puppy.

**FACT** *"Vet Checked" does NOT mean health tested. It means that a vet has given the puppy a fairly brief once-over and everything seems to be fine. Health tests are scientific DNA tests that breeding dogs undergo to prove they do not have hereditary diseases.*

There is so much money to be made breeding Bulldogs, that many breeders have sprung up who:

A. **Are unscrupulous and doing it primarily for the cash, or are**

B. **Breeding their pets from home, usually for appearance or colour, and who are not experts in the breed nor its complex genetics.**

The Bulldog Club of America (BCA) has this advice for breeders: "Testing your dog for certain genetic diseases greatly affects your chances of not reproducing those issues in future generations.

"While there are no guarantees, the knowledge that your individual dogs are tested free of certain conditions gives you a tremendous advantage as a breeder and gives your puppy buyers a sense of your dedication to the welfare of not only your own breeding program, but to the breed as well. The tests for issues that affect Bulldogs are easily attained, and for the most part, fairly inexpensive."

> **NOTE:** The UK's Bulldog Breed Council awards Bronze, Silver and Gold Health Scheme Certificates to dogs that have passed health tests. These literally are the *"gold standard."* The Bronze certificate requires the dog to pass examinations for heart, eyes, spine and temperament.
>
> In the US, The BCA Bulldog Ambassador for Health Program awards five levels of recognition, starting with Bronze for dogs and going up to Diamond for dogs that have had all eligible tests. When the program launched in 2007, there were five health tests: cardiac, patella, thyroid, elbows, and hips. Three additional tests have been added since then: tracheal hypoplasia, hyperuricosuria and cystinuria.

## Concerns About Bulldog Health

The Bulldog was one of the breeds highlighted in the 2008 BBC documentary *Pedigree Dogs Exposed*, which investigated health and welfare issues caused by the breeding of some purebred dogs, and caused a stir around the world.

Three separate health reports were then commissioned and they all concluded that some breeding practices were detrimental to the welfare of pedigree dogs. Bulldogs were noted in all three reports as a breed in need of intervention.

In November 2011, the New York Times Magazine ran a feature entitled *"Can the Bulldog be Saved?"* in which it claimed that the Bulldog had more health issues than any other breed.

The UK Kennel Club has revised the Bulldog Breed Standard in an effort to make Bulldogs sleeker and healthier. The new UK Breed Standard calls for a "relatively" short face, a slightly smaller head and less-pronounced facial wrinkling.

The Bulldog Club of America (BCA), which owns the copyright to the American Breed Standard, says it has no plans to follow suit and still calls for a "massive, short-faced head," a "heavy, thick-set, low-swung body," a "very short" face and muzzle, and a "massive" and "undershot" jaw.

The UK Kennel Club has a health monitoring system, called **Breed Watch** with three Categories:

1. Breeds with no current points of concern reported
2. Breeds with Breed Watch points of concern
3. Breeds where some dogs have visible conditions or exaggerations that can cause pain or discomfort

Unfortunately, the Bulldog is in Category 3, and these are the main Points of Concern:

* Dogs showing respiratory distress including difficulty in breathing or laboured breathing
* Excessive amounts of loose facial skin with conformational defects of the upper and/or lower eyelids so that the eyelid margins are not in normal contact with the eye when the dog is in its natural pose (e.g. they turn in, or out, or both abnormalities are present).
* Hair loss or scarring from previous dermatitis
* Heavy overnose wrinkle (roll)
* Inverted tail
* Lack of tail
* Pinched nostrils
* Significantly overweight
* Sore eyes due to damage or poor eyelid conformation
* Tight tail
* Unsound movement

When we read about "designer dogs," we usually think of crossbreeds such as Cockapoos, Labradoodles or Maltipoos. However, the Bulldog can be considered the original designer dog, as it has been specifically bred over many decades to look a certain way in order to appeal to humans, rather than for any other purpose.

The original Bulldogs of centuries ago were extremely athletic dogs bred for sport. Those trademark features of huge head, powerful jaws, muscular chest, shortish tail and wrinkled face all served a purpose in making the dog more effective in fighting the bull. Humans have taken those features, exaggerated them and, while they have sculptured a stunning looking animal, they have also created a dog which is riddled with health problems due to its physical conformation.

A modern Bulldog looks very different from a Bulldog of even 50 years ago. He has a larger head, shorter nose, shorter legs, heavier body and more wrinkled skin.

Bulldogs, along with other breeds, including Boxers, Boston Terriers, Cavalier King Charles Spaniels, Pekingese, Chinese Pugs, Lhasa Apsos, Shih Tzus and Bull Mastiffs, are all "**brachycephalic**" breeds. "Brachy" means shortened and "cephalic" means head.

Over the years, successive breeding has led to the skull bones of brachycephalic dogs being shortened to create a flat face and nose. Although this looks very appealing, it also causes some major health issues as there is still the same amount of flesh crammed inside, but far less room for air to flow within and around the soft tissue.

The oversized shortened head, coupled with short legs, have led to breathing, skin, eye, mating and birthing problems and an intolerance to heat.

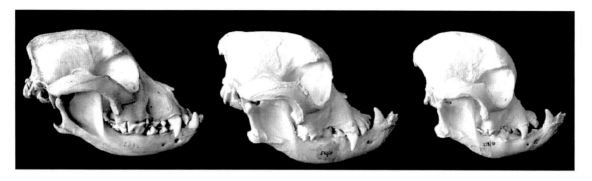

*The change in the skull shape of the (British) Bulldog over the last 50 years, left to right. Image courtesy of Natural History Museum, Bern.*

James Serpell, director of the Center for the Interaction of Animals and Society at the University of Pennsylvania said that those physical handicaps can be easily masked by an outgoing, playful personality. He said: "Bulldog breeders will insist that their dogs are happy and have a very good life.

"A dog can love its owner and be happy at times, but that doesn't mean his life isn't needlessly compromised. In many ways, dogs are their own worst enemy. They don't complain. They just kind of plod along, trying to make the best of things. That's how I see many bulldogs. They are severely handicapped because of what we have done to them, but they still have these amazing personalities that shine through despite it all."

On a positive note, when bull-baiting was outlawed in England back in 1835, the Bulldog was a vicious killing machine. Over the decades, breeders have worked to successfully eliminate this trait until today, when Bulldogs are regarded as one of the most gentle and loving breeds around.

Let's hope good breeders continue to use their skills and genetic knowledge to improve the general health of today's Bulldogs and for decades to come.

Some Bulldog owners argue that to change the look of the Bulldog even a little would mean that the dog is no longer a Bulldog. All this book is recommending is that, if the Bulldog is definitely the dog for you, that you choose one bred from healthy stock and then do your level best to keep your beloved Bulldog healthy for the rest of his or her life.

········································································································································································

## Bulldog Insurance

Insurance is another point to consider for a new puppy or adult dog. The best time to get pet insurance is definitely BEFORE you bring your Bulldog home and before any health issues develop. Don't wait until you need to seek veterinary help - bite the bullet and take out annual insurance.

A survey carried out by a large pet insurance company revealed that Bulldogs were one of the five dog breeds in the list of the 10 most expensive pets. The others were French Bulldog, Bernese Mountain Dog, Great Dane and Rottweiler - the rest were cats.

**FACT** 〉 *Almost ALL Bulldogs require veterinary attention at some point during their lives. If you take out insurance right from the beginning, there are no underlying health conditions, so everything is claimable.*

If you can afford it, take out life cover. This may be more expensive, but will cover your dog throughout his or her lifetime - including for chronic (recurring or long term) ailments, such as eye, heart, breathing or joint problems, ear infections and cancer.

Insuring a healthy puppy or adult dog is the only sure-fire way to ensure vets' bills are covered before anything unforeseen happens - and you'd be a rare owner if you didn't use your policy at least once during your dog's lifetime.

According to the UK's Bought By Many, monthly cover for a healthy nine-week-old Bulldog puppy varies from around £35 to £55, depending on where you live, how much excess you are willing to pay and the amount of total vets' bills covered per year. In the UK, Bought By Many offers policies from insurers More Than.

They get groups of single breed owners together, so you have to join the Bulldog Group, but it claims you'll get a 10% saving on normal insurance. We are not on commission - just trying to save you some money! There are numerous companies out there offering pet insurance. Read the small print and the amount of excess; a cheap policy may not always be the best long-term decision.

I ran a few examples for US pet insurance on a nine-week-old Bulldog pup and came back with quotes from $35 to $65, depending on location, amount of coverage in dollars and deductible. With advances in veterinary science, there is so much more vets can do to help an ailing dog - but at a cost. Surgical procedures can rack up bills of thousands of pounds or dollars.

According to https://englishbulldoginsurance.com these are some treatment costs: Breathing problems $1,500-$5,500, Cherry Eye $300-$1,000 per eye, Elbow Dysplasia $3,000 per elbow, Hip Dysplasia $4,000 per hip, Testing for Head Tremors $3,000-$5,000, Interdigital Cysts (Furunculosis) $150-$1,500, Tail Infections $600-$1,400. ($1.25 = approximately £1 at the time of writing).

PetInsuranceQuotes rates insurance companies based on coverage, cost, customer satisfaction and the company itself and came up with the top eight: 1.Healthy Paws, 2.Embrace, 3.Trupanion, 4.ASPCA, 5.Petplan, 6.Nationwide, 7.PetsBest, 8.Figo.

 *Factor in the cost of health insurance when you get your Bulldog. It's expensive, but you'll have peace of mind if your beloved Bully falls ill. Make sure the policy covers theft.* Although nothing can ever replace your favourite companion, good insurance will ensure you are not out of pocket.

Dogs are at increasing risk of theft by criminals, including organised gangs. With the purchase price of puppies rising, dognapping has shot up. More than 1,900 dogs were stolen in the UK in 2019. Some 49% of dogs are snatched from owners' gardens and 13% from people's homes.

........................................................................................................................

## Three Health Tips

1. **Buy a well-bred puppy** - A responsible breeder selects their stock based on:

   - General health and DNA testing of the parents
   - Conformation (physical structure)
   - Temperament

Although well-bred puppies are not cheap, believe it or not, committed Bulldog breeders are not doing it for the money, often incurring high bills for health screening, stud fees, veterinary costs, supplements, C-sections, etc. The main concern of a good breeder is to produce healthy, handsome puppies with good temperaments that are *"fit for function."*

**Chapter 4. Finding Your Puppy** has detailed information on how to find a good breeder and the questions to ask.

- ❧ **Get pet insurance as soon as you get your dog -** Don't wait until your dog has a health issue and needs to see a vet as most insurers exclude all pre-existing conditions on their policies. When choosing insurance, check the small print to make sure that all conditions are covered and that if the problem is recurring, it will continue to be covered year after year. Some breeders provide free insurance for the first 30 days in their Puppy Pack - ask yours if this is the case.

- ❧ **Find a good vet who knows Bulldogs -** Ask around your pet-owning friends, rather than just going to the first one you find. A vet who understands the special needs of flat-faced breeds and who then gets to know your dog from puppy vaccinations right through his or her life is more likely to understand your dog and diagnose quickly and correctly when something is wrong. If you visit a big veterinary clinic, ask for the vet by name when you make an appointment.

We all want our dogs to be healthy - so how can you tell if yours is? Well, here are some positive things to look for in a healthy Bulldog:

# Signs of a Healthy Bulldog

1. **Breathing** – most Bulldogs snore, but they should not pant excessively, nor should their breathing be excessively noisy or laboured when excited or exercising. Regular, quiet breathing is an excellent sign.

2. **Eyes** – a healthy Bulldog's eyes are shiny and bright with no yellowish tint. The area around the eyeball (the conjunctiva) should be a healthy pink; paleness could be a sign of underlying problems. A red swelling in the corner of one or both eyes could by a sign of Cherry Eye. There should be no thick green or yellow discharge from the eyes. A cloudy eye could be a sign of cataracts.

3. **Coats** – these are easy-to-monitor indicators of a healthy dog. A Bulldog has a short, smooth coat which should be glossy. It sheds a little right throughout the year. A dull, lifeless coat, a discoloured one or a coat that loses excessive hair can be a sign that something is amiss.

4. **Skin** – this should be smooth without redness. (Normal skin pigment can vary according to the colour of the Bulldog). Some Bulldogs are prone to skin conditions, such as hot spots and inter-digital cysts between the toes. If your dog is scratching, licking or biting himself a lot, he may have a problem that needs addressing before he makes it worse. Signs of fleas, ticks and other external parasites should be treated immediately. Pimples on the muzzle is canine acne.

5. **Ears** – ear infections can affect many breeds, including Bulldogs. The warm place under the ear flap is an ideal breeding ground for mites and infections. The ears should smell normal and not be hot. A bad smell, a hot ear or one full of brown wax is often a sign of infection, so get him to the vet for early treatment.

Ear problems may be caused by a number of factors, including bacteria, ear mites, allergies, hypothyroidism, the shape of the ear or even excessive cleaning. Your dog's ears should be clean with no dark or bloody discharge, redness, swelling or unpleasant odours. The key to healthy ears is to keep them clean and dry, checking them regularly.

6.   **Mouth** – Gums should be a healthy pink or pigmented with black. A change in colour can be an indicator of a health issue. Paleness or whiteness can be a sign of anaemia or lack of oxygen due to heart or breathing problems. Blue gums or tongue are a sign that your Bulldog is not breathing properly. Red, inflamed gums can be a sign of gingivitis or other tooth disease. Again, your Bulldog's breath should smell OK. Young dogs have sparkling white teeth, whereas older dogs have darker, yellowy teeth.

7.   **Weight** – Bulldogs are known for their sturdy bodies, and should tip the scales at around 40lb to 55lb, with males heavier than females. Bulldogs are greedy and prone to putting on weight. Dogs may be overweight due to factors such as diet, lack of exercise, allergies, diabetes, thyroid or other problems. A Bulldog has a deep chest and a general rule of thumb is that your Bulldog's stomach should be above or, at worse, in a line with his rib cage when standing. If his stomach hangs below, he is overweight or he may have a pot belly, which can also be a symptom of other conditions.

8.   **Nose** – All Bulldog puppies are born with pink noses, but these should turn to jet black. The Kennel Clubs state that a Bulldog's nose must be black for showing, but in reality some have mottled pink and black noses. The nose should normally be moist and cold to the touch, and free from clear, watery secretions. Any yellow, green or foul smelling discharge is not normal - in younger dogs this can be a sign of canine distemper.

9.   **Tail –** If these are too short, too screwed or inverted, they can cause problems as bacteria get trapped. To prevent infection, the area has to be cleaned regularly - by the owner, as the Bulldog cannot reach.

10.   **Attitude –** a generally positive attitude is a sign of good health. Symptoms of illness may be not eating food, a general lack of interest in his or her surroundings, lethargy and sleeping a lot – although these last two traits are fairly typical of many Bulldogs! The important thing is to look out for any behaviour which is out of the ordinary for your dog.

11.   **Energy** – The Bulldog is generally regarded as a dog with low to medium energy levels, although puppies and adolescents are livelier. Your dog should have good energy levels with fluid and pain-free movements. Lethargy or lack of energy – if it is not the dog's normal character – could be a sign of an underlying problem.

12.   **Stools –** poop, poo, business, faeces – call it what you will! - it's the stuff that comes out of the less appealing end of your dog on a daily basis! It should be firm, not runny, with no signs of worms or parasites. Watery stools or a dog not pooping regularly are both signs of an upset stomach or other ailments. If it continues for a day or two, consult your veterinarian. If puppies have runny poop they need checking out much quicker as they can quickly dehydrate.

13.   **Smell –** your Bulldog should have a pleasant "doggie" smell. If there is a musty, "off" or generally unpleasant odour coming from his body, it could be a sign of yeast infection. There can be a number of reasons for this, such as his facial wrinkles not being cleaned properly or an allergy to a certain type of food. You need to get to the root of the problem.

## Four Signs of Illness

There are many different symptoms that can indicate that your beloved canine companion isn't feeling great. If you don't know your Bully, then we recommend you spend some time getting to do so.

What are his normal character and temperament? Lively or sedate, playful or serious, happy to be alone or loves to be with people, a keen appetite or a fussy eater? How often does he empty his bowels, does he ever vomit? (Dogs will often eat grass to make themselves sick, this is perfectly normal and a canine's natural way of cleansing his digestive system).

*You may think your Bulldog can't talk, but he can! If you really know your dog, then he CAN tell you when he's not well. He does this by changing his patterns of behaviour.*

Some symptoms are physical, some emotional and others are behavioural. It's important to be able to recognise these changes as soon as possible. Early treatment can be the key to keeping a simple problem from snowballing into a serious illness.

If you think your Bulldog is unwell, it is useful to keep an accurate and detailed account of his symptoms to give to the vet. This will help him or her correctly diagnose and effectively treat your dog. Most canine illnesses are detected through a combination of signs and symptoms.

1. **Heart Rate -** You can feel your Bulldog heartbeat by placing your hand on his lower ribcage – just behind the elbow. Don't be alarmed if the heartbeat seems irregular compared to that of a human; it IS often irregular in dogs. Your dog will probably love the attention, so it should be quite easy to check his heartbeat. Just lay him on his side and bend his left front leg at the elbow, bring the elbow in to his chest and place your fingers on this area and count the beats. The larger the dog, the slower the heartbeat.

   * Big dogs have a normal rate of 70 to 120 beats per minute

   * Medium-sized dogs have a normal rate of 80 to 120 beats per minute

   * Small dogs have a normal rate of 90 to 140 beats per minute

   * A young puppy has a heartbeat of around 220 beats per minute

   * An older dog has a slower heartbeat

2. **Temperature -** A new-born puppy has a temperature of 94-97°F. This reaches the normal adult body temperature of around 101°F at four weeks old. A vet takes a dog's temperature reading via the rectum. If you do this, only do it with a special digital rectal thermometer (not glass), get someone to hold the dog

and be very careful. Ear thermometers *(pictured)* are now widely available for home use. There are also digital forehead thermometers - for humans and dogs.

 *Exercise or excitement can cause temperature to rise by 2°F to 3°F when your dog is actually in good health, so wait until he is relaxed before taking his temperature. If it is above or below the norms and the dog seems under par, give your vet a call.*

3. **Respiratory Rate** - Another symptom of illness is a change in breathing patterns. This varies a lot depending on the size and weight of the dog. An adult dog will have a respiratory rate of 15-25 breaths per minute when resting. You can easily check this by counting your dog's breaths for a minute with a stopwatch handy. Don't do this if he is panting; it doesn't count.

4. **Behaviour Changes** - Classic symptoms of illness are any inexplicable behaviour changes. If there has NOT been a change in the household atmosphere, such as another new pet, a new baby, moving home, the absence of a family member or the loss of another dog, then the following symptoms may well be a sign that all is not well:

   - Depression or lethargy
   - Anxiety and/or trembling
   - Falling or stumbling
   - Loss of appetite
   - Walking in circles
   - Being more vocal - grunting, whining or whimpering
   - Aggression
   - Tiredness - sleeping more than normal or not wanting to exercise
   - Abnormal posture

If any of them appear for the first time or worse than usual, you need to keep him under close watch for a few hours or even days. Quite often he will return to normal of his own accord. Like humans, dogs have off-days too.

If he is showing any of the above symptoms, then don't over-exercise him, and avoid stressful situations and hot or cold places.

Make sure he has access to clean water. There are many other signals of ill health, but these are four of the most important. Keep a record for your vet, if your dog does need professional medical attention, most vets will want to know:

**WHEN** the symptoms first appeared in your dog

**WHETHER** they are getting better or worse, and

**HOW FREQUENT** the symptoms are - intermittent, continuous or increasing?

# Bulldogs and Anaesthetic

It is always a concern for owners if their beloved Bully needs to be anaesthetised for a surgical procedure – and it's also a factor to be considered when deciding whether to have them spayed or neutered.

The problem with all brachycephalic dogs is that there is simply too much soft, pink tissue in their heads. While successive breeding has led to the skulls and necks becoming much shorter to create a particularly appealing look, the size of everything inside – such as the tongue, windpipe and palate - has remained the same.

In practical terms what this means is that brachycephalic breeds may have difficulty breathing, or at least have smaller airways than other types of dog. Dogs that cope perfectly well on a daily basis may have difficulty with anaesthetic when all their muscles are at rest and the narrow airways effectively become blocked.

 *Make sure that your chosen vet is familiar with Bulldogs - or at least brachycephalic breeds, as they react differently to other dogs under anaesthetic. If surgery is required, ask your vet to outline the extra care he or she will be taking with your Bulldog.*

Keep your dog's weight in check, obesity increases the risk of breathing problems. Here are some points to be familiar with before agreeing to surgery.

- The vet should have a special anaesthetic procedure or protocol for brachycephalic dogs
- He or she should provide oxygen before anaesthesia to help saturate the dog's lungs with extra oxygen
- The protocol should take into account anti-vomiting, anti-inflammatory, anti-anxiety measures and pain management to reduce common complications
- Bulldogs should not be masked; they can become anxious and experience breathing difficulties
- The dog should have an endotracheal tube (ET) in his or her windpipe to keep the airway open at all times.
- The tube should be kept in place as long as possible and until the dog is fully awake

The French Bulldog Rescue Network has an Anesthesia Protocol developed by Dr Lori Hunt, DVM and Dr Dawn Ruben, DVM. The same advice applies to Bulldogs. They recommend AGAINST the use of the following drugs:

- Acepromazine
- Phenobarbital (injectable anaesthetic)
- Xylazine (sedative)
- Halothane (gas anaesthetic)

Follow this link to see the full Anesthesia Protocol: www.frenchbulldogrescue.org/adoption-info/faq/anesthesia-policy

A critical time is the recovery phase after the surgical procedure - and this is where YOU come in. Here are some tips to help your Bully towards a full and speedy recovery:

- Keep your dog within sight for 12 to 24 hours after surgery
- Monitor the colour of your dog's tongue – pink is good, blue is bad

- 🐾 Keep your Bulldog well ventilated. If your dog is panting excessively, check his temperature (with a canine thermometer). If it is above 100°F, switch a fan on and turn it towards him
- 🐾 Keep your dog in a quiet, stress-free place, and try and keep him relaxed

# Brachycephalic Airway Obstruction Syndrome (BAOS)

Although the Bulldog head has been getting flatter over time, the amount of soft tissue inside it has remained the same. This includes the soft palate, the cartilage inside the nose and the tongue, which are all now crammed into a small space. There is also a lack of nasal bone which causes the nostrils to become very narrow, like small slits instead of open holes.

BAOS is the term used to describe the range of abnormalities which result from this and includes an *elongated soft palate, stenotic nares, a hypoplastic trachea and everted laryngeal saccules.* A dog with this syndrome may have one or a combination of these conditions, with variable effects on respiration.

*An elongated soft palate* (the soft part of the roof of the mouth) is too long for the short mouth and so partially blocks the entrance to the trachea, or windpipe, at the back of the throat.

Dogs with *stenotic nares* have nostrils that are too narrow, restricting the amount of air that can be inhaled.

*A hypoplastic trachea* means that the windpipe is narrower than normal.

The knock-on effect of a dog struggling to breathe creates a suction effect in the back of the throat at the opening to the windpipe. This opening into the windpipe is called the larynx (or voice box in humans) and it has a tough cartilage frame that keeps it open wide. However, constant suction in this area over a period of months or years can cause it to fold inwards that narrows the airway even further and really does cause serious breathing difficulty.

This secondary problem is called *laryngeal collapse*. The *laryngeal saccules* are small pouches just inside the larynx. They evert (turn outwards) causing a further obstruction of the airways.

### Symptoms of BAOS

- 🐾 Loud snoring
- 🐾 Noisy breathing – especially during excitement or exercise
- 🐾 Panting
- 🐾 Poor ability to exercise
- 🐾 Intolerance to heat
- 🐾 Choking on food
- 🐾 Regurgitating
- 🐾 Laboured breathing
- 🐾 Blue gums or tongue
- 🐾 Fainting

Affected dogs may also suffer from:

* 🐾 Difficulty swallowing
* 🐾 Strange body posture as he tries to breathe more efficiently
* 🐾 Tooth or gum disease
* 🐾 Increased eye problems
* 🐾 Infections in the facial skin folds

Unfortunately, a high percentage of brachycephalic dogs show a mild form of some of these symptoms in their daily lives. Some vets believe that our tolerance of what is acceptable in Bulldogs has shifted to think that the above signs are normal. They are, however, all signs that the respiratory system is not functioning efficiently.

 *Another problem for the stoic Bulldog is that he has an extremely high tolerance to pain, which may hide the fact that he is in distress.*

These symptoms are not normal and if your Bulldog is displaying some of them then he needs help. If you are thinking of getting a puppy, avoid one exhibiting any of the above symptoms.

## Treatment

There are various forms of surgery that can reduce the breathing problems associated with this syndrome. These procedures improve the flow of air, helping the dog to breathe more easily and improving his quality of life and ability to exercise. Exercise is important to avoid obesity, which can make things much worse.

One of the most important factors in deciding outcomes is how early the problem is diagnosed. Tackling breathing issues early in a Bulldog's life helps to reduce the amount of suction at the back of the throat and to prevent or delay the development of the very serious *laryngeal collapse,* for which there are only limited options.

A small flexible camera called an **endoscope** may be used to examine the throat, larynx and possibly the windpipe. Many vets prefer to perform corrective surgery to remodel the soft tissue at the same time, so that the dog is only knocked out once. He or she may also take a small tissue sample, or biopsy, and blood sample to check carbon dioxide and alkaline levels. Here are some of the options your vet may discuss with you:

*Stenotic nares, pictured before and after surgery,* can be surgically opened by removing a wedge of tissue from the nares allowing better airflow through the nose.

*An elongated soft-palate* can be surgically shortened so it no longer protrudes into the back of the throat.

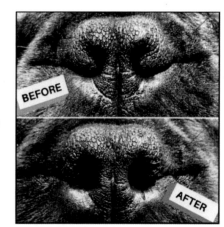

*Everted laryngeal saccules* can be surgically removed to increase the size of the laryngeal airway.

With today's laser technology some of these procedures can be performed with a minimal amount of bleeding and no need for stitches. The level of success depends on the age of the animal and when these procedures are performed. The earlier BAOS is diagnosed and treated, the better, as the condition can worsen with time and cause other abnormalities.

Everted laryngeal saccules and a weakening of the windpipe can result when the Bulldog has to breathe through a restrictive airway for a long time. If the vet can increase the size of the airway and decrease the inspiratory (breathing in) pressure before the airway is damaged, then the dog can breathe much easier.

The key here is to keep a lookout for the tell-tale signs and if you are at all worried that your dog is showing one or several of the symptoms, then consult a vet straight away; the earlier the better.

 *All Bulldogs have narrow airways, which means that anaesthesia can pose a risk to life. Discuss all options thoroughly with your vet before agreeing to surgery.*

..........................................................................................................................................

# Hip Dysplasia

Hip Dysplasia (HD), or Canine Hip Dysplasia (CHD), is the most common inherited orthopaedic problem in dogs of all breeds. The Bulldog ranks No.2 for the disease after the Pug. The latest OFA (Orthopedic Foundation for Animals) statistics show that of more than 1,000 Bulldogs tested, 70% of them had abnormal hips. www.ofa.org/diseases/breed-statistics#detail

The hips are the uppermost joints on the rear legs of a dog, either side of the tail, and *"Dysplasia"* means *"abnormal development."* Dogs with this condition develop painful degenerative arthritis of the hip joints.

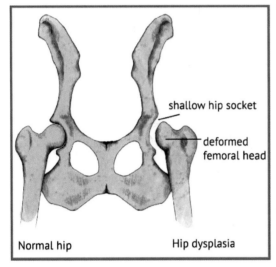

shallow hip socket

deformed femoral head

Normal hip          Hip dysplasia

The hip is a ball and socket joint. Hip dysplasia is caused when the head of the femur, or thigh bone, fits loosely into a shallow and poorly developed socket in the pelvis.

Most dogs with dysplasia are born with normal hips, but due to their genetic make-up, and sometimes worsened by factors such as diet, obesity or over-exercising when young, the soft tissues that surround the joint develop abnormally.

The joint carrying the weight of the dog becomes loose and unstable, muscle growth slows and degenerative joint disease often follows.

Symptoms often start to show at five to 18 months of age. Occasionally, an affected dog will display no symptoms at all, while others may experience anything from mild discomfort to extreme pain. Diagnosis is made by X-ray, and an early diagnosis gives a vet the best chance to tackle HD, minimising the chance of arthritis developing.

**Look Out For:**

- 🐾 Hind leg lameness, particularly after exercise
- 🐾 Difficulty or stiffness when getting up, climbing stairs or walking uphill
- 🐾 A reluctance to jump, exercise or climb stairs
- 🐾 A "bunny hop" gait or waddling gait
- 🐾 A painful reaction to stretching the hind legs, resulting in a short stride
- 🐾 Side-to-side swaying of the croup (area above the tail)
- 🐾 Wastage of the thigh muscles

*While hip dysplasia is usually inherited, other factors can trigger or worsen it, including:*

- 🐾 Too much exercise, especially while the dog is still growing
- 🐾 Extended periods without exercise
- 🐾 Overfeeding, especially on a diet high in protein and calories, or too much calcium
- 🐾 Obesity
- 🐾 Damp or cold weather

 *During their first year or so of life, it is very important that Bulldog puppies are fed a diet containing the right balance of calories, minerals and protein. Too much impact exercise for puppies can also be a trigger. The key is moderate, low impact exercise for young dogs.*

High impact activities that apply a lot of force to the joint - such as jumping and catching Frisbees, are not recommended, however energetic young Bulldogs are. See **Chapter 10. Exercise** and www.bva.co.uk/Canine-Health-Schemes/Hip-Scheme for more information.

## Prevention and Treatment

The most common cause of hip dysplasia is genetic. There is, however, a system called *hip scoring,* which is run by the BVA (British Veterinary Association) and Kennel Club in the UK and PennHIP in the USA. A UK dog's hips are X-rayed at a minimum age of 12 months; in the US, dogs must be 24 months old before they can receive their final hip certification.

In the UK, the X-rays are submitted to a specialist panel at the BVA who assess nine features of each hip, giving each feature a score. **The lower the score, the better the hips,** so the range can be from **0** CLEAR to **106** BADLY DYSPLASTIC. A hip certificate shows the individual score for each hip.

It is far better if the dog has evenly matched hips, rather than a low score for one and a high score for the other. Listed here are the American ratings, with the UK ratings in brackets:

**Excellent** (0-4, with no hip higher than 3)

**Good** (5-10, with no hip higher than 6)

**Fair** (11-18) *This is the breed average*

**Borderline** (19-25)

**Mild** (26-35)

**Moderate** (36-50)

**Severe** (51-106)

*This section of BVA certificate, pictured, shows a hip score of 10*

**Section C** – TO BE COMPLETED BY SCRUTINEERS

**CERTIFICATE OF SCORING**

| HIP JOINT | Score Range | Right | Left |
|---|---|---|---|
| Norberg angle | 0-6 | 0 | 1 |
| Subluxation | 0-6 | 2 | 3 |
| Cranial acetabular edge | 0-6 | 2 | 2 |
| Dorsal acetabular edge | 0-6 | — | — |
| Cranial effective acetabular rim | 0-6 | — | |
| Acetabular fossa | 0-6 | — | |
| Caudal acetabular edge | 0-5 | — | |
| Femoral head/neck exostosis | 0-6 | — | |
| Femoral head recontouring | 0-6 | — | |
| TOTALS (max possible 53 per column) | | 4 | 6 | 10 |

**FACT** ▶ *In the UK, the Breed Median (middle) Score of the Bulldog, is very high at 32, i.e. 50% of dogs have better scores and 50% are worse. The Breed Mean (average) Score is even higher at 43.6. Sadly, the latest statistics show that the condition is getting worse, not better, in Bulldogs.*

This is probably due to increasing numbers of people producing puppies from their Bulldogs without first carrying out hip scoring on their breeding dogs.

The BVA (British Veterinary Association) says: "Ideally, breeders should choose breeding stock with hip scores WELL BELOW the Breed Mean Score (BMS) and ideally below the Median for their breed."

One UK breeder added: "I test for hip scores, but hip scores should not be looked at on their own. They should be looked at with the Kennel Club tool called Estimated Breeding Values, where you can put the name of the dog into the box and the estimated value will be shown. This is a more accurate indicator of the risk of dogs passing on genes for hip and elbow dysplasia."

 *Ask the breeder to show you certificates for both dam and sire. You are ideally looking for parents with below average hip scores; avoid buying a puppy from parents with high combined or individual hip scores.*

There is no 100% guarantee that a puppy from low scoring parents will not develop hip dysplasia, as the condition is caused by a combination of genes, rather than just one. However, the chances are significantly reduced with good hip scores.

Treatment is geared towards preventing the hip joint getting worse. Vets usually recommend restricting exercise, keeping body weight down and managing pain with analgesics and anti-inflammatory drugs.

Various medical and surgical treatments are now available to ease discomfort and restore some mobility. They depend on factors such as age, how bad the problem is and, sadly, sometimes how much money you can afford – another reason for taking out early insurance.

Cortisone can be injected directly into the affected hip to provide almost immediate relief for a tender, swollen joint. In severe cases, surgery may be an option.

## Elbow Dysplasia

The elbow is at the top of a dog's front leg, near the body, and bends backwards. Elbow Dysplasia is a broad term to describe a complex genetic disorder that occurs when cells, tissue or bone don't develop correctly. This causes the joint to form abnormally then to degenerate. All breeding Bulldogs should be screened for Elbow Dysplasia. Results are graded from 0 (best) to 3 (most severe).

**FACT** *Latest figures from the OFA show that the Bulldog is rated 5th worst breed for Elbow Dysplasia, with over one-third of all dogs tested showing signs. Results (graded I, II and III) are very similar in the USA.*

Elbow dysplasia is the most common cause of elbow pain and one of the main reasons for front leg lameness in big or heavy breeds. It affects more males than females, possibly due to their increased size and weight. Symptoms begin typically at four to 10 months of age, although not all affected dogs show signs this early. Look out for:

- Stiffness followed by temporary or permanent lameness aggravated by exercise
- Pain when extending or flexing the elbow
- Holding the affected leg away from the body
- Groaning when getting up
- Swelling around the joint
- In advanced cases, grating of bone and joint when moving

There are several types of Elbow Dysplasia. Diagnosis is made by a veterinary examination and X-rays, requiring the dog to be anaesthetised. Treatment depends on age and severity, and may involve Non-steroidal Anti-inflammatory Drugs (NSAIDs) or injections. An elbow brace) can help to reduce pain in some cases.

Thanks to advances in veterinary medicine, surgery is now an option for many dogs. Depending on the severity, it may cost anything from $1,500-$4,000, and results in partial or full improvement in the vast majority of cases.

As with Hip Dysplasia and other joint diseases, feeding the right diet and keeping your dog's weight in check are important. Supplements such as omega-3-fatty acids, glucosamine and chondroitin sulphate can also help to relieve pain and stiffness.

........................................................................................................................................................

# Eyes

There are several eye disorders that can affect the Bulldog. If you haven't chosen your puppy yet, look for one with bright, clear eyes which fit snugly into the surrounding skin without drooping.

## Cherry Eye

Humans have two eyelids, but dogs have a third eyelid, called a **nictating membrane.** This third eyelid is a thin, opaque tissue with a tear gland which rests in the inner corner of the eye. Its purpose is to provide additional protection for the eye and to spread tears over the eyeball.

Usually it is retracted and therefore you can't see it, although you may notice it when your dog is relaxed and falling asleep. When the third eyelid becomes visible it may be a sign of illness or a painful eye.

Cherry Eye, officially known as **nictitans gland prolapse**, is prolapse of the gland of the third eyelid. The Bulldog is the breed most prone to the condition and it usually develops during puppyhood. If your dog hasn't had it by one year old, there's a good chance he won't get it at all.

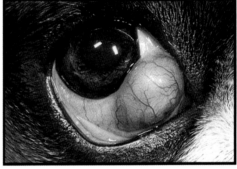

Other susceptible breeds include the Beagle, Bloodhound, Boston Terrier, Bull Terrier, Cocker Spaniel, Lhasa Apso, Saint Bernard and Shar-Pei.

The exact cause of is not known, but it is thought to be due to a weakness of the fibrous tissue which attaches the gland to the surrounding eye. This weakness allows the gland to fall down, or prolapse. It is not known if the condition is inheritable.

Once this has happened and the gland is exposed to the dry air and irritants, it can become infected. There is sometimes a mucous discharge and if the dog rubs or scratches it, he can damage the gland even more and sometimes cause an ulcer on the surface of the eye's surface. The main visible symptom is a red, often swollen, mass in the corner of one or both eyes. It can occur in one or both eyes and although it may look sore, the good news is that it is not it is not usually painful for the dog.

### Treatment

Eye drops may be prescribed to control the condition, and initially you may be able to push the gland back into place yourself, but Cherry Eye is usually eventually dealt with using one of two forms of surgery.

At one time, it was popular to surgically remove the gland to correct this condition. While this was often effective, it could create problems later on. The gland of the third eyelid is important for producing tears, without which dogs can suffer from **dry eye,** also known as **keratoconjunctivitis sicca (KCS).** This can be treated with drops several times a day.

The other option is to surgically reposition the gland by tacking it back into place with a single stitch. There is also another type of operation during which the wedge of tissue is removed from directly over the gland. Tiny dissolving stitches are used to close the gap so that the gland is pushed back into place. After surgery the dog may be placed on antibiotic ointment for a few days.

Mostly, surgery is performed quickly and few dogs experience complications. However, the downside is that the gland often pops back out.

 *It's not unusual for Cherry Eye to develop first in one eye and later in the other. If your young Bully has been diagnosed with the condition, discuss with your vet waiting a few weeks or months before surgery to see if the second eye is affected. This will save the dog being anaesthetised twice - and will save you money.*

........................................................................................................................................

## Eyelid Problems

The Bulldog is susceptible to *Ectropion* and *Entropion.* If you see your dog rubbing his eyes a lot, one of these eyelid disorders could be the cause. Get your dog to the vet quickly so he or she can deal with it successfully before it worsens. Both of these conditions are treatable, but can result in *corneal ulcers* and loss of vision if left untreated and further damage occurs - either naturally or by the dog scratching his eye.

**Entropion** occurs when edge of the lower eyelid rolls inward, causing the dog's fur to rub the surface of the eyeball, or cornea. In rare cases the upper lid can also be affected, and one or both

eyes may be involved. This painful condition is thought to be hereditary and is more commonly found in dog breeds with a wrinkled face, such as the Bulldog, Bloodhound, Pug, Bull Mastiff, Great Dane, Rottweiler and Shar Pei.

The affected dog scratches at his painful eye with his paws and this can lead to further injury. If your Bulldog is to suffer from entropion, he will usually show signs at or before his first birthday. You will notice that his eyes are red and inflamed and they will produce tears. He will probably squint.

The tears typically start off clear and can progress to a thick yellow or green mucus. If left untreated, entropion causes corneal ulcers and you might also notice a milky-white colour develop. This is caused by increased fluid which affects the clarity of the cornea.

For your poor dog, the irritation is constant. Imagine how painful and uncomfortable it would be if you had permanent hairs touching your eyes. It makes my eyes water just thinking about it.

*It's important to get your dog to the vet as soon as you suspect Entropion before your dog scratches his cornea and worsens the problem.*

A vet will make the diagnosis after a painless and relatively simple inspection of your dog's eyes. He or she will first have to rule out other issues that might also be making your Bulldog's eyes red and itchy, such as allergies. That's another reason why it is a good idea to find a vet who is familiar with Bulldogs and their associated health issues.

In mild cases, the vet may successfully prescribe eye drops, ointment or other medication. However, the most common treatment for more severe cases is a fairly straightforward surgical procedure to pin back the lower eyelid, *pictured*. In young Bulldogs, some vets may delay surgery and treat the condition with medication until the dog's face is fully formed to avoid having to repeat the procedure later.

Discuss the severity of the condition and all possible options with your vet before proceeding to surgery; anaesthetic is not without risk for Bulldogs.

**Ectropion** is a condition where the lower lids turn outwards, causing the eyelids to appear droopy and one or both eyes may be involved. It can occur in any breed, but certain breeds, including Bulldogs, Cocker Spaniels, Saint Bernards, Mastiffs, Bassett Hounds, Newfoundlands and Bloodhounds all have a higher incidence of the condition.

The cause is usually genetic. However, *'Acquired ectropion'* can occur in any dog at any age and means that a reason other than genetics has caused the eyelid to sag. These include:

- Facial nerve paralysis
- Hypothyroidism
- Scarring secondary to injury
- Chronic inflammation and infection of the tissues around the eyes
- Surgical overcorrection of ectropion
- Neuromuscular disease

Ectropion causes the lower lid to droop, exposing the conjunctiva and forming a pouch or pocket where pollens, grasses and dust can collect and rub against the sensitive conjunctiva. This is a consistent source of irritation to the dog, and leads to increased redness of the conjunctiva and the production of tears which flow over the lower lid and face, often causing a brownish staining of the fur below the eyes. A thick mucus discharge may appear along the eyelid margin and the dog may rub or scratch his eyes if it becomes uncomfortable.

Diagnosis is usually made with a physical examination. If the dog is older, blood and urine tests may also be done. The vet may also perform corneal staining to see if any ulcers are present.

Many dogs live normal lives with ectropion and some require no treatment at all. However, others develop repeated eye infections due to dirt and dust getting in the eye. It is mostly a minor condition, except when secondary eye infections develop.

If eye irritations do develop, see your vet. Mild cases can be treated with lubricating eye drops and ointments to prevent the cornea and conjunctiva from drying out. Special eye (ophthalmic) antibiotics are used to treat any corneal ulcers.

In severe cases, surgery is undertaken to remove excess tissue to tighten the lids and remove the abnormal pocket which is trapping the dirt, etc. Surgical correction is usually successful. As always, the risks of anaesthesia and surgery for Bulldogs have to be weighed against any potential benefits.

**Distichiasis** is another condition to look out for. It occurs when a few small eyelashes grow on the inner surface or very edge of the eyelids, causing constant irritation. In some cases they are not a problem, but in others they can cause the eye to become red and inflamed and the dog to blink a lot. Symptoms are similar to entropion.

With a placid dog, they can sometimes be removed with tweezers – unless you know what you are doing, we suggest allowing your vet to do this. If that's not possible, the offending lashes can be removed with electrolysis. Some mild cases can be treated with eye drops alone.

**Trichiasis** is when the eyelashes grow inward toward the eyeball. Symptoms are: swollen eyes, excessive tearing, eye twitching and sometimes the iris changes colour. Mild cases are dealt with by trimming the problem eyelashes, while more severe cases require permanent removal by surgery.

......................................................................................................................................

## Dry Eye (Keratoconjunctivitis sicca)

KCS is the technical term for a condition also known as *"dry eye"* when not enough tears are produced, causing a dog's eyes to become irritated and turning the conjunctiva red.

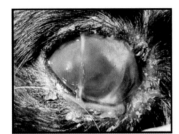

The eyes typically develop a thick, yellowy discharge. Infections are common as tears also have anti-bacterial and cleansing properties, and inadequate lubrication allows dust, pollen and other debris to accumulate. The nerves of these glands may also become damaged. It looks nasty, but is usually relatively easy to control.

In many cases the reason for dry eye is not known, other times it may be caused by injuries to the tear glands, eye infections, reactions to drugs, an immune reaction or even the gland of the third eyelid being surgically removed by mistake. Left untreated, the dog will suffer painful and chronic eye infections.

Treatment usually involves cyclosporine, ophthalmic ointment or drops. In some cases, another eye preparation – Tacrolimus - is also used and may be effective when cyclosporine is not. Sometimes artificial tear solutions are also prescribed. While surgery to re-route the tear gland can be successful in some breeds, it can cause other issues in Bulldogs as the eye produces too many tears which fall in the wrinkles, where bacteria thrive.

You may be able to avoid drugs by bathing your dog's eye every morning and then a further once or twice a day. Use sterilised water and a canine eye cleaner or Optrex, then put artificial tear drops into the eye, or a canine eye gel, to keep the eye lubricated.

......................................................................................................................................

## Eye Care for Bulldogs

Despite the fact that your Bulldog has a strong, beefy head, it needs to be lavished with a great deal of care and attention to remain in tip top condition.

Some eye conditions affecting Bulldogs are inherited, but there are other issues, such as dirt or pollen in the eye, which are environmental. Bulldogs love to root around in all sorts of places and can easily finish up with irritating material in their eyes, causing them to rub or scratch. Other Bullies suffer from allergies which also cause their eyes to become irritated.

The wrinkles attract dirt and are a haven for bacteria and, if your dog is producing too many tears, infections can occur in the folds of the skin.

Whatever the reason, it is a good idea to get into the habit of cleaning your Bulldog's eyes and wrinkles regularly – at least once or twice a week; daily is even better. This also enables you to monitor any changes and, if a problem such as infection, Cherry Eye or an eyelash disorder does occur, to get on top of it right away.

Tear staining is a common problem with Bulldogs, especially with lighter coloured ones. These brownish, wet stains are also a breeding ground for bacteria and yeast.

The most common is Red Yeast, which is usually associated with reddish-brown facial stains, and which may emit an odour.

Tear staining can be related to health and diet as well as genetics. Most vets agree that face staining results from excessive tear production and a damp face.

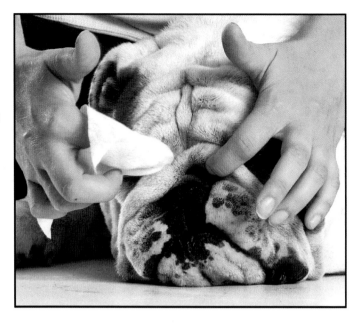

Cleaning your dog's tear stains will also help to avoid infection. To do this, wet a cotton ball with a sterile eye wash, or use eye wipes, to gently rub the folds around your Bulldog's eyes, clearing them of any dried discharge. Repeat the action with clean cotton balls or wipes until the area is clean. There are videos on YouTube which show you how to do this. Remember to dry the wrinkles after cleaning to deter yeast infections.

There are many tear stain removers on the market. Some owners have tried home remedies with some success, but be extremely careful of the substances you put near to your Bulldog's sensitive eyes. If in any doubt at all about a product or remedy, check with your vet.

# Head Tremors

It is well documented that some Bulldogs develop head tremors. They are also referred to as *Idiopathic Head Tremors,* which means that the cause is unknown. Other breeds affected include Pit Bulls, Dachshunds, Boxers, Doberman Pinchers and Chinooks and medical research is continuing into the condition.

It can be distressing for an owner to witness their beloved Bully experiencing head tremors, but vets believe that the dog is not in pain or unduly distressed during the tremors. Typically, an affected Bulldog will bob his head up and down or side to side. To see what this looks like, go to YouTube and type in "Bulldog Head Tremors."

 *Head tremors in Bulldogs are different from seizures, see the section on Epilepsy later in this chapter to read about seizures and their symptoms.*

If your dog has head tremors, the best piece of advice is: REMAIN CALM. Panicking will only make things worse for your dog. If you can, record the episode on your mobile phone to show to your vet later. Notice whether your dog is alert and responsive or in a trance, how long and how often the tremors occur and any other details you think may be relevant.

Many owners say that their Bulldogs are entirely aware during episodes. Their ears stay up as if alert, they respond to calls and commands as usual, and their appetites aren't affected.

*There is anecdotal evidence to suggest that sometimes the head tremors may be triggered either by excitement, stress or pain or by low blood sugars. Sometimes a Bulldog may start to exhibit head tremors some time after surgery, when previously he had none.*

If your dog has a tremor episode, get his attention by calling him over to you and making him sit still so he can focus.

*Some owners give their dogs honey, frozen yoghurts, ice pops or other treats to help release them from the tremors. Vets do not recommend giving seizure medication to treat head tremors.*

The following are extracts from the article *"Head Tremors in the Bulldog - Partial/Focal Seizures, Paroxysmal Dyskinesia"* by Kathy Jacobsen, of Rely-A-Bull Bulldogs, USA:

What qualifies me to discuss such a topic, you might ask? My answer to you would be good old experience. I have been in bulldogs for 25+ years, had seven litters and of those seven litters have had five dogs/bitches who have exhibited one or more of these behaviours.

In my experience, head tremor activity in the Bulldog usually starts around the age of two years old. The motion you will see will almost always be a fast side to side rocking motion (ear to shoulder, ear to shoulder) occurring in rapid succession. Occasionally I have seen an up and down motion (like they are shaking their heads to say yes), but for the most part it is the same fast rocking. The way it was defined to me was that the neuron cluster that controls a certain motor function (in this case head movement) begins to fire continuously. The reason for this rapid fire is truly unknown.

I have not experienced any drooling or other body part involvement. It has always been isolated to the head. When you call the dog's name they can stop the bobbing motion for a few seconds and will look at you, then it will kick in again. They can move their heads and watch you move from place to place, they can even walk around etc.

**Scenario I:** The bully will be sleeping very soundly and all of a sudden the head will start rocking usually from side to side very quickly - occasionally you might experience one bobbing up and down. This sudden head motion will cause the bully to awaken suddenly. An episode will last from 15 to 30 seconds, sometimes longer. It may stop on its own and then as the dog lies down to go back to sleep the head tremor will recur.

**Scenario II:** A bitch will be pre-season or just come into season and can show head tremor activity due to the increase in hormones. In addition, you may witness your males/stud dogs show head bobbing activity. The female hormones can trigger the tremors in the male also due to the excitement from the scent of a girl in season/extra hormonal activity.

**Scenario III:** A bitch is post-whelp, in the milk let-down phase of lactation, and trying to nurse a litter of hungry pups. In this case the bitch has had surgical trauma as the result of a C section, is in pain, is not eating and is trying to make milk. This, in my opinion is different than the head tremors described in Scenario I and II. When you see this what do you do? The first time we experienced this phenomenon was a scenario III post-whelp and I panicked. I grabbed the puppies off the bitch and almost caused one to aspirate.

When I gained a little composure, I called a breeder friend of mine and explained what I was seeing. She told me that it was not uncommon and I should try to get some sugar, honey, Karo corn syrup into her. The thought is that the blood sugar had experienced a sharp drop at that point in time thus stimulating this type of a response. We gave the girl the Karo and lo and behold the tremors stopped within a couple of seconds.

The next time we witnessed this behaviour was a little different. The bitch was not post whelp. However, she was three days prior to coming into season. She had been sleeping on the couch. We gave her honey. It stopped. Started up 15 minutes later we repeated this time with Karo syrup. Same result.

We gave her frozen yogurt, same result. This went on for almost 24 hours with the length of time between episodes varying from 10-15 minutes to as long as a half hour. Needless to say, we packed her up and went off to the vet who said: "This is not unusual in this breed. Normally we don't do anything. Epilepsy meds have proven to be ineffective for the most part; phenobarbital has too many side effects."

The veterinarian stated that they suspect it has something to do with the growth activity at this age or stress, which can cause a sudden drop in glucose levels in the blood. There can be different things or circumstances that can trigger an episode, such as a traumatic experience, an injury, hormones, etc. In this girl's case we have determined that it is a hormone trigger, specifically at the time of a progesterone spike associated with ovulation.

The vet recommended calcium and taurine supplementation twice daily. As you know, calcium is one of the minerals needed for healthy nerve growth and electrical conductivity, Taurine is an amino acid that works with calcium. The vet said she might grow out of it. So, we took that information and we asked for a referral to a neurologist.

The specialist did all of the neurological tests and determined she was fine. She ordered ionized calcium levels along with several other specific blood tests. The results all came back normal. She recommended an MRI to determine if there was an injury or tumor. We declined this step at the time due to finances, but decided if she showed any other neurological symptoms such as falling down or aggression (which could be indicative of an injury or tumor) that we would come back to do the MRI.

Six months went by on the calcium and taurine supplementation to which we added a heaped tablespoon of ricotta cheese every morning, and every couple of days a bowl of frozen vanilla yogurt with honey in the evening. No incidents. The day we bred her (at the time of the progesterone spike indicating ovulation that we were waiting for) she had one mild episode, then nothing for the entire pregnancy.

The episodes started up the second week of lactation when the calcium bolus given at the time of the C-section was gone and six hungry puppies were pulling on her calcium/glucose levels. Five months have since passed and she has been just fine, with no episodes. My recommendations:

1. If your dog exhibits this head bobbing behaviour a. DON'T PANIC!!! This could only worsen the situation by adding additional stress on the dog. Give them a bowl of ice cream or frozen vanilla yogurt with honey to get the situation under control. If you don't have any of those then Ensure, Pediasure, Karo syrup all work because of the sugar and or calcium content. Liquids work quicker because they are absorbed into the mucosa of the mouth.

2. Call your veterinarian and advise of the situation. Schedule an appointment for a visit and have your vet do a health screening with blood work. Odds are the blood work for calcium and sugar will be fine.

3. Keep a record of each episode, every time one occurs describe it in great detail, time it occurred how long, how frequent. Give this info to the vet when you see him.

4. IF they do not get any worse than the head bobs don't do anything else but observe and document. If the behaviour changes in any way, call the vet, you may need additional assistance at this point. Two other behaviours I would like to mention briefly are the fly chasing and the circling behaviours. Fly chasing is just that, the dog seems to be chasing and trying to catch imaginary flies. Again, if you call the dog by name he will stop and look at you then resume the behaviour.

The other is circling. This looks like VERY slow motion tail-chasing, usually in the same direction each time. If you call the dog, they will stop to acknowledge you then start up again. In this case, I go over and give my girl a nudge and she stops and resumes whatever she had started to go outside to do.

5. Distraction helps. Take the dog outside to run around. Throw a ball and play fetch or whatever their favorite game is. The distraction sometimes helps to cut the duration of the tremor down because the dog's focus is elsewhere

6. Lastly, the other thing you can do is nothing. While this is very difficult on the owner, the tremors will stop on their own. They seem to last only as long as the nerve has acetylcholine to cause it to fire. Once it depletes the stores, the tremor or bobbing motion will stop on its own.

There is a study currently in progress on this subject. Hopefully a report with some significant findings will be produced. Up until recently it was not studied as it is not a life-threatening syndrome. Yet it is being seen more and more in the Bulldog as well as other breeds."
**With thanks to Kathy Jacobsen for kind permission to reproduce these extracts.**

......................................................................................................................................................

## Epilepsy

If you have witnessed your dog having a seizure, also called a convulsion or fit, it can be scary. Seizures are not uncommon in dogs, but many dogs have only a single seizure. If your dog has had more than one seizure it may be that he or she is epileptic. Just as with people, there are medications to control seizures, allowing your dog to live a more normal life.

 *Epilepsy means repeated seizures due to abnormal activity in the brain and is caused by an abnormality in the brain itself.*

If seizures happen because of a problem somewhere else in the body, such as heart disease (which stops oxygen reaching the brain), this is not epilepsy. Your vet may do tests to try to find the reason for the epilepsy but in many cases no cause can be identified.

Epilepsy affects around four or five in every 100 dogs and in some breeds it can be hereditary. The Bulldog is not listed as one of the breeds more susceptible to epilepsy, although some do suffer from head tremors, which can be mistaken for epilepsy, but are entirely different.

### Symptoms

Some dogs seem to know when they are about to have a seizure and may behave in a certain way. You will come to recognize these signs as meaning that a seizure is likely. Often dogs just seek out their owner's company and come to sit beside them when a seizure is about to start.

Once the seizure starts, the dog is unconscious – he cannot hear or respond to you (unlike with head tremors). Most dogs become stiff, fall onto their side and make running movements with their legs. Sometimes they will cry out and may lose control of their bowels or bladder.

Most seizures last between one and three minutes - it is worth making a note of the time the seizure starts and ends because it often seems that a seizure goes on for a lot longer than it actually does.

After a seizure, dogs behave in different ways. Some dogs just get up and carry on with what they were doing, while others appear dazed and confused for up to 24 hours afterwards.

Most commonly, dogs will be disoriented for only 10 to 15 minutes before returning to their old self. They often have a set pattern of behaviour that they follow - for example going for a drink of water or asking to go outside to the toilet. If your dog has had more than one seizure, you may well start to notice a pattern of behaviour which is typically repeated.

Most seizures occur while the dog is relaxed and resting quietly. It is very rare for a seizure to occur while exercising. Often seizures occur in the evening or at night. In a few dogs, seizures seem to be triggered by particular events or stress.

It is common for a pattern to develop and, if your dog suffers from epilepsy, you will gradually recognise this as specific to your dog.

## What Should I Do?

The most important thing is to **STAY CALM**. Remember that your dog is unconscious during the seizure and is not in pain or distressed. It is likely to be more distressing for you than for him. Make sure that he is not in a position to injure himself, for example by falling down the stairs, but otherwise do not try to interfere with him.

**Never try to put your hand inside his mouth during a seizure or you are very likely to get bitten.**

The damage caused is cumulative and after a lot of seizures, there may be enough brain damage to cause early senility - with loss of learned behaviour and housetraining or behavioural changes. It is very rare for dogs to injure themselves during a seizure. Occasionally they may bite their tongue and there may appear to be a lot of blood, but is unlikely to be serious; your dog will not swallow his tongue.

If a seizure goes on for a very long time (more than 10 minutes), his body temperature will rise and this can cause damage to other organs such as the liver and kidneys as well as the brain. In very extreme cases, some dogs may be left in a coma after severe seizures.

Generally, if your dog has a seizure lasting more than five minutes, or is having more than two or three a day, you should contact your vet.

 *If you can, record your dog's seizure on your mobile phone. Then take notes afterwards describing how long the fit lasted and your dog's actions during and afterwards. This will be extremely useful for the vet.*

When your dog starts a seizure, make a note of the time. If he comes out of it within five minutes, allow him time to recover quietly before contacting your vet. It is far better for him to recover quietly at home rather than be bundled into the car and carted off to the vet right away.

However, if your dog does not come out of the seizure within five minutes, or has repeated seizures close together, contact your vet immediately, as he or she will want to see your dog as soon as possible. If this is his first seizure, your vet may ask you to bring him in for a check and some routine blood tests. Always call your vet before setting off to be sure that there is someone there who can help your dog.

**FACT** ❯ *There are many things other than epilepsy which cause seizures in dogs. When your vet first examines your dog, he or she will not know whether your dog has epilepsy or another illness.*

It's unlikely that the vet will see your dog during a seizure, so it is **vital** that you're able to describe in some detail just what happens. Epilepsy usually starts when the dog is aged between one and five. So, if your dog is older or younger, it's more likely he has a different problem.

The vet may need to run a range of tests to ensure that there is no other cause of the seizures. These may include blood tests, possibly X-rays, and maybe even a scan (MRI) of your dog's brain. If no other cause can be found, then a diagnosis of epilepsy may be made. If your Bulldog already has epilepsy, remember these key points:

- 🐾 **Don't change or stop any medication without consulting your vet**
- 🐾 **See your vet at least once a year for follow-up visits**
- 🐾 **Be sceptical of "magic cure" treatments**

Remember, live **with** epilepsy not **for** epilepsy. With the proper medical treatment, most epileptic dogs have far more good days than bad ones. Enjoy all those good days.

### Treatment

Treatment will not cure the disease, but it will manage the signs – even a well-controlled epileptic may have occasional seizures. Sadly, as yet there is no miracle cure for epilepsy, so don't be tempted with *"instant cures"* from the internet.

Two of the most common drugs used to treat epilepsy are Phenobarbital and Potassium Bromide. Many epileptic dogs require a combination of one or more drugs to achieve the best results. Treatment is decided on an individual basis and it may take some time to find the best combination and dose of drugs for your pet. It will be based on the severity and frequency of the seizures and how they respond to different medications.

*You need patience when managing an epileptic dog.*

It is important that medication is given at the same time each day. Once your dog has been on treatment for a while, he will become dependent on the levels of drug in his blood at all times to control seizures. If you miss a dose, blood levels can drop and this can trigger a seizure.

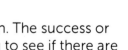

Keep a record of events in your dog's life, note down dates and times of seizures and record when you have given medication. Each time you visit your vet, take this diary along with you so he or she can see how your dog has been since his last check-up.

If seizures become more frequent, it may be necessary to change the medication. The success or otherwise of treatment may depend on you keeping a close eye on your Bulldog to see if there are any physical or behavioural changes.

It is rare for epileptic dogs to stop having seizures altogether. However, provided your dog is checked regularly by your vet to make sure that the drugs are not causing any side-effects, there is a good chance that he will live a full and happy life. Visit www.canineepilepsy.co.uk for more information.

### The Urinary Tract

Urinary Tract Infections (UTIs) are very common in Bulldogs. They are often caused by bacteria, especially in females - but there are also two hereditary diseases that affect Bulldogs.

**Cystinuria** is an inherited disorder that prevents a dog from effectively filtering cystine out of urine, causing stones to form. These tiny objects can get stuck anywhere in the urinary tract, including the kidneys, bladder and ureter, which carries urine from the kidneys to the bladder.

**Hyperuricosuria (HUU)** is also genetic and means elevated levels of uric acid in the urine. This trait predisposes dogs of certain breeds, including Bulldogs, to form stones in their bladders or sometimes kidneys. They can be difficult to treat and often have to be surgically removed.

The Bulldog Canine Health Information Center (CHIC) and Ambassador For Health Programs recommend that breeders carry out the available DNA tests on their breeding stock for both of these diseases.

In terms of infections, it has been estimated that 14% of dogs of all breeds will have a UTI at some time in their lives. The infection may be picked up from the environment or from the dog's own poop. It usually enters through the urethra and works its way up into the bladder. Sometimes the bacteria pass from the bladder through the ureters to the kidneys.

There are a few other causes of urinary tract infections in dogs, but they are much less common than bacterial infection, which is also referred to as "bacterial cystitis."

**FACT** ⟩ *The urinary system is responsible for filtering wastes from the blood and for forming and getting rid of urine. These functions help the body to maintain the right balance and volume of fluids.*

Although it has far-reaching effects, the urinary tract is relatively simple and consists of the kidneys, ureter, bladder and urethra (the tube carrying urine from the bladder to the outside).

### Symptoms and Treatment

Some dogs with a UTI may not show any signs of disease, while others may show one or more of the following:

- Frequently urinating small amounts (pollakiuria)
- Painful urination (dysuria)
- Blood in the urine (haematuria)
- "Accidents"

A vet will carry out a urine analysis to confirm the diagnosis of UTI. Treatment is usually a course of antibiotics. If the infection does not respond, it may be that the bacterial strain is resistant to a particular antibiotic, or there may be another underlying cause, such as bladder stones, diabetes mellitus or a suppressed immune system.

It is important that owners ensure that their Bulldog completes the full course of antibiotics to get rid of the infection. Stopping part way through because your dog seems OK may cause the infection to return.

 *Owners should make sure their dog drinks plenty of water to help flush out the bacteria, as with any infection. Consider adding a spoonful of live yoghurt to one or both meals to boost the good bacteria in your dog's system or add a daily urinary tract supplement.*

It's a good idea to have your dog retested as soon as the antibiotics have finished, as UTIs are notoriously stubborn - and expensive - to shift. Better to ensure you get rid of it properly the first time it occurs.

# The Heart

Heart problems are one of the main issues that can shorten the life of a Bulldog.

Heart failure, or congestive heart failure (CHF), occurs when the heart is not able to pump enough blood around the dog's body. The heart is a mechanical pump. It receives blood in one half and forces it through the lungs, then the other half pumps the blood through the entire body.

*Pulmonic Stenosis* is a hereditary disorder issue that affects Bulldogs 19 times more than any other breed (Universities Federation for Animal Welfare).

**Normal**   **Pulmonary stenosis**

Pulmonary valve

Bulldog organisations in North America and the UK recommend that all breeding dogs undergo a heart examination by a vet. If you haven't got your puppy yet, check if the parents were screened and tested Clear.

Pulmonic Stenosis usually occurs when the pulmonic valve is poorly formed, which restricts the blood supply from the right ventricle of the heart to the lungs. In most cases, the fault is in the three-leafed pulmonic valve itself; this is called "Valve Dysplasia." The leaves are too thick or too fused together to allow blood to flow properly through the valve. A less common form is *"annular hypoplasia"* when a ring of tissue around the valve is too narrow.

The right side of the heart - the one that receives blood from the body and pumps it into the lungs - becomes enlarged, as the heart (which is a muscle) has to pump harder to move the blood through this narrowed area.

This disease can be inherited with varying degrees of severity. Some dogs remain symptom-free their whole lives, while others sadly die young when the heart can't move enough blood through the lungs for oxygenation.

A vet will usually make the diagnosis when he or she notices a significant heart murmur during a puppy's first visit. Further tests include a Doppler ultrasound *(pictured)* to show the blood flow. For some dogs, an innocent heart murmur may be the only symptom. In more severe cases, symptoms include:

- ❖ Exercise intolerance, general sluggishness
- ❖ Breathlessness
- ❖ Fainting, especially during excitement, exercise or stress
- ❖ Fluid-build-up in the abdomen (ascites)
- ❖ Sudden death

As long as no other heart problems are present, some severe cases can now be treated with a surgical procedure called "Balloon Valvuloplasty." The good news is that it is minimally invasive - although the dog still has to be anaesthetised.

A catheter or tube with a balloon on the end is placed through the jugular vein in the neck, or a vein in the leg, and the balloon is inflated at the valve to widen the area. Vets claim that 80%-85% of dogs that have this procedure go on to live normal lives.

The bad news is that it is expensive, costing $5,000-$10,000 (£4,000-£8,000). For owners who cannot afford surgery, beta blockers and other cardiac drugs may decrease the symptoms, alongside managing exercise.

# Heart Murmurs

Heart murmurs are not uncommon in dogs. One of our dogs was diagnosed with one many years ago and, of course, your heart sinks when you get that terrible news from the vet.

But once the shock is over, it's important to realise that there are several different severities of the condition and, at its mildest, it is no great cause for concern. (Our dog lived to 13).

Literally, a heart murmur is a specific sound heard through a stethoscope, it results from the blood flowing faster than normal within the heart itself or in one of the two major arteries. Instead of the normal "lubb dupp" noise, an additional sound can be heard that can vary from a mild "pshhh" to a loud "whoosh." The different grades of heart murmurs are:

Grade 1—barely audible

Grade 2—soft, but easily heard with a stethoscope

Grade 3—intermediate loudness; most murmurs which are related to the mechanics of blood circulation are at least Grade 3

Grade 4—loud murmur that radiates widely, often including opposite side of chest

Grade 5 and Grade 6—very loud, audible with stethoscope barely touching the chest; the vibration is also strong enough to be felt through the animal's chest wall

Murmurs are caused by a number of factors; it may be a problem with the heart valves or could be due to some other condition, such as hypothyroidism, anaemia, or heartworm.

In puppies, there are two major types of heart murmurs, and they will probably be detected by your vet at the first or second vaccinations. The most common type is called an innocent "flow murmur." This type of murmur is soft (typically Grade 2 or less) and is not caused by underlying heart disease. An innocent flow murmur typically disappears by four to five months of age.

However, if a puppy has a loud murmur (Grade 3 or louder), or if the heart murmur is still easily heard with a stethoscope after four or five months of age, the likelihood of the puppy having an underlying congenital (from birth) heart problem becomes much higher.

The thought of a puppy having heart disease is extremely worrying, but it is important to remember that the disease will not affect all puppies' life expectancy or quality of life.

A heart murmur can also develop suddenly in an adult dog with no prior history of the problem. This is typically due to heart disease that develops with age. In Toy and small breeds, a heart murmur may develop in middle-aged to older dogs due to an age-related thickening and degeneration of one of the valves in the heart, the mitral valve.

This thickening of the valve prevents it from closing properly and as a result it starts to leak, this is known as mitral valve disease. The more common type of heart disease affecting larger dog breeds in middle age is Dilated Cardiomyopathy (DCM), also called *enlarged heart.*

This occurs when the ventricles, or heart chambers, become larger and the cardiac muscle surrounding them becomes thinner, causing the heart to change shape. This then restricts muscle contractions and the effectiveness of the valves, which can lead to irregular heartbeats and the backflow or leakage of blood through the valves.

In people, heart disease usually involves the arteries that supply blood to the heart muscle becoming hardened over time, causing the heart muscles to receive less blood than they need. Starved of oxygen, the result is often a heart attack.

**FACT** ❯ *In dogs, hardening of the arteries (arteriosclerosis) and heart attacks are very rare. However, heart disease is common. In dogs, heart disease is often seen as heart failure, which means that the muscles "give out."*

This is usually caused by one chamber or side of the heart being required to do more than it is physically able to do. It may be that excessive force is required to pump the blood through an area and over time the muscles fail. Unlike a heart attack in humans, heart failure in a dog is often a slow process that occurs over months or even years.

## Hypothyroidism

Hypothyroidism is a common hormonal disorder in dogs and is due to the thyroid gland (located on either side of the windpipe in the dog's throat) not producing enough of the hormone *thyroid,* which controls the speed of the metabolism, or the process of turning food into fuel. Dogs with very low thyroid levels have a slow metabolic rate.

*Autoimmune thyroiditis* is the most common cause of primary hypothyroidism in Bulldogs. Symptoms often appear at two to five years of age. It occurs when the autoimmune system attacks the thyroid gland, impairing its function. According to OFA, out of 729 Bulldogs tested, one in 16 had a thyroid problem.

Most forms of hypothyroidism are diagnosed with a simple blood test. US dogs have to pass the thyroid test to qualify for the BCA Ambassador for Health certificate.

Symptoms vary greatly from one dog to the next - and are often similar to other diseases, but these are the usual ones, with the most common being at the top of the list:

- ❧ High blood cholesterol
- ❧ Lethargy and exercise intolerance
- ❧ Hair Loss
- ❧ Weight gain or obesity
- ❧ Dry coat or excessive shedding
- ❧ Hyper pigmentation or darkening of the skin, seen in 25% of cases
- ❧ Intolerance to cold, seen in 15% of dogs with the condition

### Treatment

Although hypothyroidism is a type of auto-immune disease and cannot be prevented, the symptoms can usually be easily diagnosed and treated. Most dogs suffering from hypothyroidism can be well-managed on thyroid hormone replacement tablets.

The dog is normally placed on a daily dose of a synthetic thyroid hormone called thyroxine (levothyroxine). The dose and frequency of administration of the drug varies depending on the severity of the disease and the response of the individual dog to the drug.

A dog is usually given a standard dose for his weight and then blood samples are taken once or twice a year to check his response and the dose is adjusted accordingly. Depending upon your dog's preferences and needs, the medication can be given in different forms, such as a solid tablet, in liquid form, or a gel that can be rubbed into your Bulldog's ears. Once treatment has started, he will have to be on it for the rest of his life.

NOTE: HYPERthyroidism (as opposed to HYPOthyroidism) is caused by the thyroid gland producing too much thyroid hormone. It is quite rare in dogs, being more commonly seen in cats. A common symptom is the dog being ravenously hungry all the time, but actually losing weight.

........................................................................................................................................

## Tails and Spines

There is a difference in the Breed Standards for the Bulldog tail between the UK Kennel Club and the American Kennel Club (AKC)

In the UK, The Kennel Club says that the tail must be straight and stick out, like this little pup in the photo: *"Tail - Set on low, jutting out rather straight and then turning downwards...Lack of tail, inverted or extremely tight tails are undesirable."*

However, the American Kennel Club has a definition which allows the tail to be *"screwed,"* i.e. twisted like a corkscrew. (I'm not sure how a tail can be screwed without being curly or curved), but here is the AKC Breed Standard for tails:

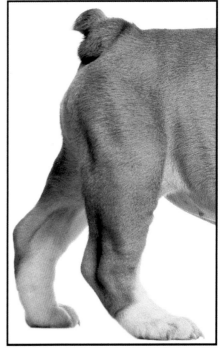

*"The tail may be either straight or "screwed" (but never curved or curly), and in any case must be short, hung low, with decided downward carriage, thick root and fine tip. If straight, the tail should be cylindrical and of uniform taper.*

*"If "screwed," the bends or kinks should be well defined, and they may be abrupt and even knotty, but no portion of the member should be elevated above the base or root."*

If a Bulldog's tail is screwed too tight, or even inverted, less air can circulate and this causes infections. A *"tail pocket"* is a tiny hidden chamber under a Bulldog's tail. Due to the lack of air circulation, these pockets are ideal breeding grounds for bacteria and yeast.

Feel at the base of the tail and see if there is any hidden dark space there. If there is, lift the tail, clean, rinse it and dry it well regularly – no matter how unpleasant you find the task. When you decide to become a Bulldogger, you have to take on all that goes with it! Do not leave the tail pocket moist as this will encourage infection.

In extreme cases of repeated infection, when it is impossible for the owner to keep the area clean without causing distress to the Bulldog, the tail has to be amputated.

*Hemivertebrae* is the name given to a genetic abnormality of the spine which occurs when the puppy is still a foetus in the mother's womb. *"Hemi"* means half and *"vertebrae"* are the series of small bones which link to make up the backbone or spine.

Hemivertebrae occurs when the right and the left halves of the developing spine fail to fuse. The two halves often grow unequally, producing a wedge-shaped vertebral body. Depending on which way the broad side of the wedge is directed, this may cause a top curvature (kyphosis) or a side curvature (scoliosis) of the spine.

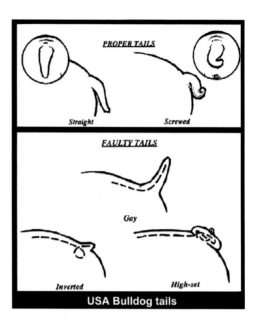

The condition is not uncommon in Bulldogs and other brachycephalic breeds like the French Bulldog that have a screw tail. Most dog breeds have 49 to 53 vertebrae, while a screw-tailed Bulldog may have 10 to 15 fewer, depending on the tail formation. In Bulldogs those tail vertebrae are often deformed.

As the backbone is bent, it can start pressing on the spinal cord, causing
- Pain
- Loss of feeling
- Weakness or paralysis of the hind legs

As this disorder is due to the conformation, or shape, of the Bulldog, problems begin early - as early as three or four months old. You might notice that the puppy has weak back legs or an abnormal gait. It often gets progressively get worse, and loss of bladder and bowel control may follow. Symptoms level off at about nine months when the spine stops growing.

Diagnosis is relatively straightforward. The vet will take X-rays to see if the condition is present in the spine. He or she may then use more advanced technologies like a myelogram, CT scan or MRI to see if there is any compression of the spinal cord.

Because a dog is born with hemivertebrae, it cannot be cured. Mild cases can be managed with supplements, cortisone injections for flare-ups, painkillers and keeping the dog lean, while some more severe cases are suitable for surgery. Hemivertebrae can, however, be a very painful condition for Bulldogs and in extreme cases, it is kinder to have the dog put to sleep.

 *The best way to ensure that your Bulldog does not have hemivertebrae is to get your dog from a responsible breeder who has screened his or her dogs for the problem. And if you are looking at puppies, choose one with a proper tail.*

# Overheating Bulldogs

It's a fact: Bulldogs overheat more easily than any other breed. They certainly do not cope well with warm temperatures and are prone to heatstroke or hyperthermia. They can also suffer from hypothermia if they get too cold.

It's also a fact that dogs can't sweat. Well, only a tiny bit through the pads of their paws. Instead of being able to cool down by sweating all over their body like humans, they have the far less efficient mechanism of panting, which circulates cooling air around their body. Couple this inefficient cooling system with the Bulldog's flat face and you have a recipe for potential disaster. Make no mistake, heat can be a killer

Bulldogs have been bred with shortened facial bone structures to give a pushed-in look. However, the soft tissue inside has stayed the same size, which means that there isn't much room for air to circulate inside the mouth and throat.

Some Bulldogs have elongated palates and extremely narrow nostrils (stenotic nares), which make breathing difficult, and especially so when they are hot and need to pant. When they try to pant quickly, foam can be produced, which in turn blocks the throat and causes laboured breathing.

Eventually, they may begin to roar as they try to breathe through the blockage. A dog's normal body temperature is around 100-102.5ºF, (a puppy's normal rectal temperature is 96-100ºF), if this rises to over 106ºF, the dog is suffering from severe heatstroke and can die.

**Escalating Symptoms**

- Panting rapidly and "heaving"
- This will develop into a roar
- The tongue will be bright red and floppy
- Gums may be discoloured
- He will look tired and distressed, perhaps becoming dizzy
- He will produce a thick, sticky saliva or foam as his airways become blocked
- He may have diarrhoea or begin vomiting - sometimes with blood
- Shock
- Coma

STAY CALM! Your dog will pick up on your fear if you panic, causing him more stress. Remove the dog from the hot area immediately. Lower his temperature by wetting him thoroughly with cool water then increase air movement around him with a fan. Part his fur with your fingers to let the cooling air get to his body.

CAUTION: Using very cold water can actually be counterproductive. Cooling too quickly and especially allowing the dog's body temperature to become too low can cause other life-threatening medical conditions. Similarly, some Bulldog owners recommend using ice on the body to cool the dog, but many vets advise against this, as it closes the skin pores and could potentially make the situation worse.

Other suggestions from owners include getting your Bulldog used to eating ice cubes, ice pops or frozen yoghurts from an early age so that if he does start to overheat, you can feed him these and he will readily take them.

Another suggestion is that if your dog has started foaming, squirt lemon juice from a plastic lemon into the back of his throat – he will hate it, but the lemon juice will help to break down the foam and clear the throat.

 *Many owners have found certain products, such as cooling jackets, pictured, cooling or ice collars and cooling blankets to be helpful.*

The temperature of an overheated dog should be checked every five minutes. If you use a rectal thermometer, do it very carefully, preferably with somebody holding him steady; Bulldogs have been known to "suck in" the thermometer.

Once the body temperature is down to 103ºF, the cooling measures should be stopped and the dog should be dried thoroughly and covered so he does not continue to lose heat. Even if the dog appears to be recovering, take him to your vet as soon as possible. He should still be examined as he may be dehydrated or have other complications. Allow him access to water or an electrolyte rehydrating solution if he can drink on his own. Do not try to force-feed cold water as he may inhale it or choke.

The vet will lower your dog's body temperature to a safe range, if you have not already done so, and continue to monitor it. He or she may administer fluids, and possibly oxygen and may take blood samples to test for clotting. The dog will be monitored for shock, respiratory distress, kidney failure, heart abnormalities and other complications, and treated accordingly.

Dogs with moderate heatstroke often recover without complicated health problems. However, severe heatstroke can cause organ damage that might need ongoing care, such as a special diet prescribed by the vet. Dogs who suffer from heatstroke once have an increased risk of getting it again, so steps must be taken to prevent it.

## 15 Tips to Prevent Overheating

The main factor in determining whether your Bulldog gets heatstroke is YOU. Being aware of your dog's susceptibility to heat is the first step, taking action to prevent it is the second essential step. Bulldogs can overheat alarmingly quickly, here are some preventative measures:

1. Make sure your Bulldog has a cool place indoors and shade outdoors at all times.

2. Reduce exercise in warm weather. Only take your dog outside for short periods – early in the morning and in the evening when temperatures are lower are the best times. For some Bulldogs, anything in the 70s is hot, while others may be fine outdoors for short periods at temperatures up to 80ºF.

3. Make sure your dog has access to water 24/7.

4. If your dog does not want to go outside in hot weather, do not force him.

5. Have a shady toilet area in your yard or garden for your Bulldog.

6. Always take water with you on your walks in warm weather. Watch your dog carefully for indications that he is over-heating, such as heavy panting, loss of energy, and any weakness or stumbling. If he shows signs, stop in a shady spot and give him some water. If symptoms don't subside, take him home and ring the vet.

7. NEVER muzzle your dog.

8. NEVER leave your pet in a parked car, even if you're in the shade or will only be gone a short time. The temperature inside a parked car can quickly reach up to 140ºF. Also, there is a high incidence of Bulldog theft, especially in the USA.

9. Avoid places like the beach in warm weather and concrete or asphalt areas, where heat is reflected and there is no access to shade.

10. Put your dog in a cool area of the house. Air conditioning is one of the best ways to keep a dog cool. You can freeze water in plastic bottles, or place ice and a small amount of water in several resealable food storage bags, wrap them in a towel or tube sock and put them on the floor for your dog to lie on.

11. Don't let your dog become over-excited in warm weather, and avoid strenuous games and exercise.

12. Don't go jogging with a Bulldog. Most dogs will try to keep up with their owners and this can put stress on the heart or cause them to overheat.

13. Dogs are susceptible to sunburn, especially ones with white faces. This can lead to painful blistering and sores, and long-term exposure can even lead to skin cancers. Apply pet sunscreen to the hairless areas on the end of the ears and nose. It's also advisable to keep white-faced dogs indoors during the heat of the afternoon.

14. By the time your Bulldog starts to feel hot, he is probably already overheating. Keep an eye on your dog, especially puppies and young dogs who may want to run and play for hours. Monitor exercise and play time.

15. Keep your Bully at a healthy weight; an obese dog is more likely to suffer from heatstroke.

# Canine Diabetes

This is not an issue which particularly affects Bulldogs any more than any other breed. It does, however, affect overweight dogs more than lean ones and the Bulldog's love of food makes him a candidate for obesity if his diet isn't strictly controlled.

Diabetes can affect dogs of all sizes and both genders. There are two types: *diabetes mellitus* and *diabetes insipidus. Diabetes insipidus* is caused by a lack of vasopressin, a hormone that controls the kidneys' absorption of water. *Diabetes mellitus* occurs when the dog's body does not produce enough insulin and therefore cannot successfully process sugars.

Dogs, like us, get their energy by converting the food they eat into sugars, mainly glucose. This travels in the bloodstream and then, using a protein called *insulin,* cells remove some of the glucose from the blood to use for energy. Almost all diabetic dogs have Type 1 diabetes; their pancreas does not produce any insulin. Without it, the cells can't use the glucose that is in the bloodstream, so they *"starve"* while the glucose level in the blood rises.

*Diabetes mellitus* (sugar diabetes) is the most common form and affects mostly middle-aged and older dogs. Both males and females can develop it, although unspayed females have a slightly higher risk. Vets take blood and urine samples in order to diagnose diabetes. Early treatment helps to prevent further complications developing.

 *The condition is treatable and need not shorten a dog's lifespan or interfere greatly with quality of life. Due to advances in veterinary science, diabetic dogs undergoing treatment now have the same life expectancy as non-diabetic dogs of the same age and gender.*

Symptoms of Diabetes Mellitus:

- Extreme thirst
- Excessive urination
- Weight loss
- Increased appetite
- Coat in poor condition

- 🐾 Lethargy
- 🐾 Vision problems due to cataracts

If left untreated, diabetes can lead to cataracts or other ailments.

## Treatment and Exercise

Many cases of canine diabetes can be successfully treated with a combination of a diet low in fat and sugars, and medication, while more severe cases may require insulin injections. In the newly-diagnosed dog, insulin therapy is done at home after a vet has explained to the owner how to prepare and inject insulin.

Normally, after a week of treatment, you return to the vet for a series of blood sugar tests over a 12 to 14-hour period to see when the blood glucose peaks and troughs. Adjustments are made to the dosage and timing of the injections. You may also be asked to collect urine samples using a test strip of paper that indicates the glucose levels in urine.

 *If your dog is already having insulin injections, beware of a "miracle cure" offered on the internet. It does not exist. There is no diet or vitamin supplement that can reduce a dog's dependence on insulin injections, because vitamins and minerals cannot do what insulin does in the dog's body.*

If you think that your dog needs a supplement, discuss it with your vet first to make sure that it does not interfere with any other medication.

Managing a dog's diabetes also means managing his activity level. Exercise burns up blood glucose the same way that insulin does. If your dog is on insulin, any active exercise on top of the insulin might cause him to have a severe low blood glucose episode, called *"hypoglycaemia."*

Keep your dog on a consistent exercise routine. Your usual insulin dose will take that amount of exercise into account. If you plan to take your dog out for some demanding exercise, such as running around with other dogs, you may need to reduce his usual insulin dose.

## Tips

- 🐾 Specially-formulated diabetes dog food is available from most vets

- 🐾 Feed the same type and amount of food at the same times every day

- 🐾 Most vets recommend twice-a-day feeding for diabetic pets (it's OK if your dog prefers to eat more often)

- 🐾 Help your dog to achieve the best possible blood glucose control by not feeding table scraps or treats between meals

- 🐾 Watch for signs that your dog is starting to drink more water than usual. Call the vet if you see this happening, as it may mean that the insulin dose needs adjusting

*Food raises blood glucose - Insulin and exercise lower blood glucose - Keep them in balance*

For more information visit www.caninediabetes.org

# Canine Cancer

This is the biggest single killer and will claim the lives of one in four dogs, regardless of breed. It is the cause of nearly half the deaths of all dogs aged 10 years and older, according to the American Veterinary Medical Association.

While the Bulldog can suffer from a range of illnesses, he is no more prone to cancer than many other breeds. The common types of cancer that might affect a Bulldog include mast cell tumours, which present as skin cancer (especially in white or light-coloured dogs), mammary gland tumours (the equivalent of breast cancer), and lymphoma, a type of blood cancer that develops when white blood cells called lymphocytes grow out of control.

Symptoms of different types of cancer include:

- Swellings anywhere on the body or around the anus
- Sores that don't heal
- Weight loss
- Lameness, which may be a sign of bone cancer, with or without a visible lump
- Laboured breathing
- Changes in exercise or stamina level
- Change in bowel or bladder habits
- Increased drinking or urination
- Bad breath, which can be a sign of oral cancer
- Poor appetite, difficulty swallowing or excessive drooling
- Vomiting

If your dog has been spayed or neutered, there is evidence that the risk of certain cancers decreases. These cancers include uterine and breast/mammary cancer in females, and testicular cancer in males, if the dog was neutered before he was six months old. However, recent studies also show that some dogs may have a higher risk of certain cancers after early neutering. Spaying prevents mammary cancer in female dogs, which is fatal in about 50% of all cases.

## Treatment and Reducing the Risk

Just because your dog has a skin growth doesn't mean that it's cancerous. Your vet will probably confirm the tumour using X-rays, blood tests or a biopsy. Often these are benign (harmless), but if you discover one you should get it checked out by a vet, as they can sometimes be malignant (cancerous).

If your dog is diagnosed with cancer, there is hope. Advances in veterinary medicine and technology offer various treatment options, including chemotherapy, radiation and surgery. Unlike with humans, a dog's hair does not fall out with chemotherapy.

We have all become aware of the risk factors for human cancer - stopping smoking, protecting ourselves from over-exposure to strong sunlight and eating a healthy, balanced diet all help to reduce cancer rates. We know to keep a close eye on ourselves, go for regular health checks and report any lumps to our doctors as soon as they appear. *The same is true with your dog.*

 *Every time you groom your dog, check him over for lumps of anything out of the ordinary. As with any illness, early detection often leads to a better outcome.*

If you notice any new lumps, for example, monitor them for the next few days to see if there is any change in their appearance or size. If there is, then make an appointment to see your vet as soon as possible. It might only be a cyst, but better to be safe than sorry.

Many older dogs develop fatty lumps, or *lipomas,* which are often harmless, but it's still advisable to have the first one checked.

The outcome depends on the type of cancer, treatment used and, importantly, how early the tumour is found. The sooner treatment begins, the greater the chances of success. While it is impossible to completely prevent cancer, the following points may help to reduce the risk:

- Feed a healthy diet with few or no preservatives
- Consider dietary supplements, such as antioxidants, Vitamins, A, C, E, beta carotene, lycopene or selenium, or coconut oil – check compatibility with any other treatments
- Don't let your Bulldog get overweight
- Give your Bully daily exercise (within his limits)
- Keep your dog away from chemicals, pesticides, cleaning products, etc. around the garden and home
- Don't let you dog spend too much time in bright sunshine
- Avoid passive smoking
- Give pure, filtered or bottled water (fluoride-free) for drinking
- Consider natural flea remedies (check they are working) and avoid unnecessary vaccinations
- Check your dog regularly for lumps and any other physical or behavioural changes

One of our dogs was diagnosed with T-cell lymphoma - a particularly aggressive form of cancer - when he was four years old. We had noticed a small lump on his anus, which grew to the size of a small grape within a couple of days. We rushed him down to the vet and he had surgery the following day. He died, aged 13, having lived a further nine very happy years.

If your dog is diagnosed with cancer, do not despair, there are many options and new, improved treatments are constantly being introduced. Research is being conducted all over the world, and medical advances are producing a steady flow of new tests and treatments, and survival rates are improving all the time.

Disclaimer: The author is not a vet. This chapter is intended to give owners an outline of some of the health issues and symptoms that may affect their dog(s). If you have any concerns regarding your dog's health, our advice is always the same: consult a veterinarian.

# 12. Skin and Allergies

Allergies are a growing concern for owners of many dogs. Visit any busy veterinary clinic these days – especially in spring and summer – and it's likely that one or more of the dogs is there because of some type of sensitivity. Bulldogs can develop skin issues and food intolerances as well as seasonal or other allergies.

......................................................................................................................................................

Any individual dog can have issues. Skin conditions, allergies and intolerances are on the increase in the canine world as well as the human world.

How many children did you hear of having asthma or a peanut allergy when you were at school? Not too many, I'll bet. Yet allergies and adverse reactions are now relatively common – and it's the same with dogs. The reasons are not clear; it could be connected to breeding, feeding, over-vaccination – or a combination, but as yet, there is no clear scientific evidence to back this up.

**FACT** ❯ *White or light-coloured dogs of all breeds may have a statistically higher chance of allergies, which may be related to them having less pigment in their skin.*

The skin is a complicated topic and a whole book could be written on this subject alone. While many dogs have no problems at all, some suffer from sensitive, itchy, dry or oily skin, hot spots, yeast infections or other skin disorders, causing them to scratch, bite or lick themselves excessively. Symptoms may vary from mild itchiness to a chronic reaction.

## Canine Skin

The skin is the dog's largest organ. It acts as the protective barrier between your dog's internal organs and the outside world; it also regulates temperature and provides the sense of touch. Surprisingly, a dog's skin is actually thinner than ours, and it is made up of three layers:

1. **Epidermis** or outer layer, the one that bears the brunt of your dog's contact with the outside world.

2. **Dermis** is the extremely tough layer mostly made up of collagen, a strong and fibrous protein. This is where blood vessels deliver nutrients and oxygen to the skin, and it also acts as your dog's thermostat by allowing her body to release or keep in heat, depending on the outside temperature and your dog's activity level.

3. **Subcutis** is a dense layer of fatty tissue that allows your dog's skin to move independently from the muscle layers below it, as well as providing insulation and support for the skin.

**FACT** ❯ *Human allergies often trigger a reaction within the respiratory system, causing us to wheeze or sneeze, whereas allergies or hypersensitivities in a dog often cause a reaction in her SKIN.*

- Skin can be affected from the INSIDE by things that your dog eats or drinks

- Skin can be affected from the OUTSIDE by fleas, parasites, or inhaled and contact allergies triggered by grass, pollen, man-made chemicals, dust, mould, etc.

Like all dogs, Bulldogs can suffer from food intolerances as well as environmental allergies. Canine skin disorders are complicated. Some dogs can wander through fields, dig holes and roll around in long grass with no after-effects at all. Others may spend more time indoors and have an excellent diet, but still experience severe itching and/or bald spots. Some dogs can eat almost anything and everything with no issues at all, while owners of others spend much of their time trying to find the magic bullet – the ideal food for their dog's sensitive stomach.

 *Because of the Bulldog's skin folds, or wrinkles, the breed is more prone to skin issues than many others.*

It's by no means possible to cover all of the issues and causes in this chapter. The aim here is to give a broad outline of some of the ailments most likely to affect your Bulldog and how to deal with them. We have also included remedies tried with some success by ourselves (we had a dog with skin issues) and other owners of affected dogs, as well as advice from a holistic specialist.

This information is not intended to take the place of professional help; always contact your vet if your dog appears physically unwell or uncomfortable. This is particularly true with skin conditions:

 *SEEK TREATMENT AS SOON AS POSSIBLE. If you can find the source(s) of the problem early, you reduce the chances of it taking hold and causing secondary issues and infections.*

Whatever the cause, before a vet can make a diagnosis, you'll have to give details of your dog's diet, exercise regime, habits, medical history and local environment. The vet will then carry out a physical examination, possibly followed by further (expensive) tests, before a course of treatment can be prescribed. You'll have to decide whether these tests are worth it and whether they are likely to discover the exact root of the problem.

One of the difficulties with skin ailments is that the exact cause is often difficult to diagnose, as the symptoms are similar to other issues.

If environmental allergies are involved, specific and expensive tests are available. You'll have to take your vet's advice on this, as the tests are not always conclusive. And if the answer is dust or pollen, it can be difficult – if not downright impossible - to keep your dog away from the triggers while still having a normal life.

If the cause IS related to the outdoor environment, it is often a question of managing - rather than curing - the condition.

There are many things you as an owner can do to reduce the allergen load – and many natural remedies and supplements that can help as well as veterinary medications.

Another issue reported by some Bulldog owners is food allergy or intolerance (there is a difference), which often results in a skin condition. See **Chapter 6. Feeding a Bulldog** for more information.

# Types of Allergies

*"Canine dermatitis"* means inflammation of a dog's skin and it can be triggered by numerous things, but the most common by far is allergies. Vets estimate that as many as one in four dogs they see has some kind of allergy. Symptoms are:

- Chewing her feet

- Rubbing her face on the floor

- Scratching

- Trying to scratch or bite the anus (Bulldogs can't reach that far round so may scoot across the floor)

- Itchy ears, head shaking

- Hair loss

- Mutilated skin with sore or discoloured patches or hot spots

A Bulldog who is allergic to something will show it through skin problems and itching; your vet may call this *"pruritus."* It may seem logical that if a dog is allergic to something inhaled, like certain pollen grains, her nose will run; if she's allergic to something she eats, she may vomit, or if allergic to an insect bite, she may develop a swelling. But in practice this is seldom the case.

**FACT** ❯ *In dogs, the skin is the organ most affected by allergies, often resulting in a mild to severe itching sensation over the body and possibly a recurring ear infection. Reddish coloured tear stains can also be a sign of a yeast infection.*

Dogs with allergies often chew their feet until they are sore and red. You may see yours rubbing her face on the carpet or couch, or scratching her belly and flanks. Because the ear glands produce too much wax in response to the allergy, ear infections can occur - with bacteria and yeast (which is a fungus) often thriving in the excessive wax and debris.

Digestive health can play an important role. Holistic vet Dr Jodie Gruenstern says: "It's estimated that up to 80% of the immune system resides within the gastrointestinal system; building a healthy gut supports a more appropriate immune response. The importance of choosing fresh proteins and healthy fats over processed, starchy diets (such as kibble) can't be overemphasized. Grains and other starches have a negative impact on gut health, creating insulin resistance and inflammation."

An allergic dog may cause skin lesions or *hot spots* by constant chewing and scratching. Sometimes she will lose hair, which can be patchy, leaving a mottled appearance. The skin itself may be dry and crusty, reddened, swollen or oily, depending on the dog. It is very common to get secondary bacterial skin infections due to these self-inflicted wounds.

An allergic dog's body is reacting to certain molecules called *allergens.* These may come from:

- Chemical products used around the home or garden

- House dust and dust mites

- Mould

- Fabrics, such as wool or nylon

- 🐾 Rubber and plastics
- 🐾 Trees or grass
- 🐾 Other pollens
- 🐾 Flea bites
- 🐾 A specific food or additive, such as a grain, type of meat, colouring or preservative
- 🐾 Milk products

 *These allergens may be INHALED as the dog breathes, INGESTED as the dog eats, or caused by CONTACT with the dog's body when she walks or rolls.*

Regardless of how they arrive, they all cause the immune system to produce a protein called IgE, which releases irritating chemicals like histamine inside the skin, hence the scratching.

Managing allergies is all about **REDUCING THE ALLERGEN LOAD.**

## Inhalant Allergies

When a dog is allergic to something breathed in from the environment, this is called *Atopy* or *Atopic Dermatitis.*

In fact, the most common allergies affecting many dogs are inhalant - and often seasonal, at least at first; some allergies may develop and worsen. Substances that can cause an allergic reaction in dogs are similar to those causing problems for humans. All breeds can suffer from them, although Bulldogs are particularly susceptible.

A clue to diagnosing these allergies is to look at the timing of the reaction. Does it happen all year round? If so, this may be mould, dust or some other trigger that is permanently in the environment. If the reaction is seasonal, then pollens may well be the culprit. A diagnosis can be made by one of three methods of *allergy testing.*

The most common is a blood test for antibodies caused by antigens in the dog's blood, and there are two standard tests: a *RAST* test and an *ELISA* test. Many vets feel that the ELISA test gives more accurate results.

The other type of testing is intradermal skin testing where a small amount of antigen is injected into the skin of the animal and after a short period of time, the area around the injection site is inspected to see if the dog has had an allergic reaction in the form of a bump. This method has been more widely used in the USA than the UK to date. Intradermal skin testing is regarded as *"the gold standard"* of allergy testing for atopy. However, the dog has to be anaesthetised and this is always a risk with Bulldogs and other flat-faced breeds

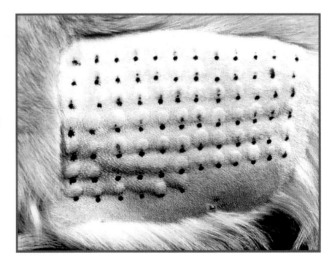

*Our photo shows a Golden Retriever that has undergone intradermal skin testing.* In this particular case, the dog has been tested for more than 70 different allergens, which is a lot; 40 to 60 is more usual.

The resulting immunotherapy treatment, or *"hyposensitisation,"* is expensive. It is a series of injections made specifically for your dog and administered over months (or even longer) to make her more tolerant of specific allergens. Vets in the US claim that success rates can be as high as 75%. Before you get to the stage of considering allergy testing, a vet has to rule out other potential causes, such as fleas or mites, fungal, yeast or bacterial infections and hypothyroidism.

 **FACT** ❯ *As skin testing is expensive and time-consuming, in practice, vets often treat mild cases of allergies with a combination of avoidance, fatty acids, tablets, and steroid injections for flare-ups.*

A less invasive option, although not as reliable, is a single blood test, which can be done during a routine visit to the vet. The dog does not have to be shaved or sedated. Many owners of dogs with allergies also consider changing to an unprocessed diet (raw or cooked) and use natural alternatives to the long-term use of steroids, which can cause other health issues.

## Environmental or Contact Irritations

These are a direct reaction to something the dog physically comes into contact with, and the triggers are similar to inhalant allergies. If grass or pollen is the issue, the allergies are often seasonal. An affected dog may be given treatments such as tablets, shampoo or localised cortisone spray for spring and summer – with a steroid injection to control a flare-up - but be perfectly fine the rest of the year. This was the case with our dog with allergies.

**Tip** *If you suspect your Bulldog has outdoor contact allergies, hosing or rinsing her feet and belly after a walk will definitely get rid of some of the pollen and other allergens, which in turn reduces scratching and biting.*

The problem may be localised - such as the paws or belly. Symptoms are a general skin irritation or specific hotspots - itching (pruritus) and sometimes hair loss. A Bulldog might incessantly lick one part of the body, often the paws, legs or belly. She might also have itchy ears or face.

## Flea Bite Allergies

These are a common canine allergy affecting lots of Bulldogs. Flea bite allergy is typically seasonal, worse during summer and autumn - peak time for fleas - and in warmer climates where fleas are prevalent. Unfortunately, some dogs with flea allergies also have inhalant allergies.

This allergy is not to the flea itself, but to proteins in flea saliva left under the dog's skin when the insect feeds. Just one bite to an allergic dog will cause red, crusty bumps *(pictured)* and intense itching.

If affected, the dog will itch at the base of her tail and other parts of the body. Much of the skin damage is done by the dog's scratching, rather than the flea bite, and can result in hair falling out or

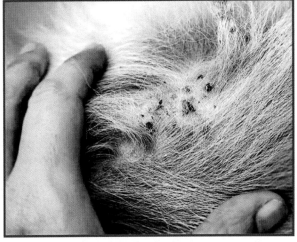

skin abrasions. Some dogs also develop hot spots, often along the base of the tail and back.

Flea bite allergies can only be totally prevented by keeping all fleas away from the dog. Various flea prevention treatments are available – see the section on **Parasites**. A vet can make a diagnosis with a simple blood test. If fleas are the cause, you'll also have to make sure her bedding and your home are flea-free zones.

## Acute Moist Dermatitis (Hot Spots)

*Acute moist dermatitis* or *hot spots* are not uncommon in Bulldogs and other wrinkly dogs, often cropping up in warm, moist areas, such as skin folds. They are inflamed or infected lesions on the skin and if a dog continually licks or chews them, they become like a wet scab and ooze pus.

Hot spots are painful and bacterial infection can spread easily. Because dogs often lick, scratch or bite them, it can be hard for them to heal on their own and they can become large, red, irritated lesions in a short pace of time.

The cause is often a local reaction to an insect bite - fleas, ticks, biting flies or mosquitoes. Other causes of hot spots include:

- Allergies – inhalant, contact and food allergies
- Mites
- Ear infections
- Poor grooming
- Burs or plant awns
- Anal gland disease

If you can't get to the vet right away, clean the area with warm water, pat gently dry with a towel and apply over-the-counter hydrocortisone cream. Don't cover the sore, it needs air, but your dog will need an E-collar (cone of shame) to stop her licking it.

Once diagnosed by a vet and with the right treatment for the underlying cause, hot spots can soon disappear. Treatments may come in the form of injections, tablets or creams – or a combination of all three. The affected area is clipped and cleaned by the vet to help the effectiveness of any spray or ointment. The dog might also have to wear an E-collar until the condition subsides, but usually not for long.

 *Some owners have reported good results after dabbing hot spots, interdigital cysts and other skin irritations with an equal mixture of Listerine (the amber-coloured Original, pictured, above), baby oil and water. US owners have also reported success with Gold Bond Powder.*

## Interdigital Cysts

Unfortunately, these are all too common in Bulldogs. If your dog gets a fleshy red lump between the toes that looks like an ulcerated sore or a hairless bump, then it's probably an interdigital cyst - or *interdigital furuncle* to give the condition its correct medical term.

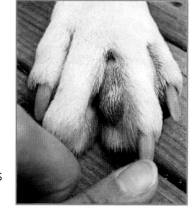

**FACT** ❯ *They can be very difficult to get rid of, since they are often not the main problem, but a symptom of some other ailment. They are not cysts, but the result of furunculosis, a skin condition that clogs hair follicles and creates chronic infection.*

Interdigital cysts can be caused by a number of factors, including allergies, poor foot conformation, mites, yeast infections, ingrown hairs or other foreign bodies, and obesity. Any dog can suffer from them - and often it's dogs that suffer from other allergies as well.

These nasty-looking bumps are painful for your dog and will probably cause a limp. Vets might recommend a whole range of treatments to get to the root cause of the problem. It can be extremely expensive if your dog is having a barrage of tests or biopsies, and even then you are not guaranteed to find the underlying cause. If your Bully has to wear an E-collar, it's stressful for her and you, as you watch her bumping into door frames and furniture. Some dogs can be resistant to the *"Cone of Shame"* - they may slump down like you've hung a 10-ton weight on their neck or sink into a depression. Fortunately, they don't usually have to wear them for more than a few days.

Consider putting socks on the affected foot or feet instead. This works well while your dog sleeps, but you have to watch her like a hawk when she's awake to stop her licking the affected areas. Here are some remedies your vet may suggest:

- ❧ Antibiotics and/or steroids and/or mite killers

- ❧ Soaking the feet in Epsom salts twice daily to unclog the hair follicles

- ❧ Testing for allergies or thyroid problems

- ❧ Starting a food trial if food allergies are suspected

- ❧ Shampooing the feet

- ❧ Cleaning between the toes with medicated (benzoyl peroxide) wipes

- ❧ A referral to a veterinary dermatologist

- ❧ Surgery (this is an absolute last-resort option)

If you suspect your Bulldog has an interdigital cyst, get to the vet for a correct diagnosis and then discuss the various options. A course of antibiotics may be suggested initially, along with switching to a hypoallergenic diet if a food allergy is suspected. If the condition persists, many owners get discouraged, especially when treatment may go on for many weeks.

 *Be wary of agreeing to a series of steroid injections or repeated courses of antibiotics, as this means that the underlying cause has not been diagnosed. In such cases, it is worth exploring natural diets and remedies – and trying to lower the overall allergen load on your dog.*

Before you resort to any drastic action, first try soaking your Bulldog's affected paw in Epsom salts for five or 10 minutes twice a day. After the soaking, clean the area with medicated wipes, which are antiseptic and control inflammation. In the US these are sold under the brand name Stridex pads.

Surgery is a drastic option. Although it can be effective in solving the immediate problem, it doesn't deal with the underlying ailment. Post-surgery healing is a slow and difficult process, and the dog does not have the same foot as before. Future orthopaedic issues and more interdigital cysts are a couple of problems that can occur afterwards.

*Get the right diagnosis as soon as possible.*

## Bacterial infection (Pyoderma)

Pyoderma literally means **pus in the skin** (yuk)! Early signs of this bacterial infection are itchy red spots filled with yellow pus, similar to pimples or spots in humans. They can sometimes develop into red, ulcerated skin with dry and crusty patches. Fortunately, the condition is not contagious.

Pyoderma is caused by several things: a broken skin surface, a skin wound due to chronic exposure to moisture, altered skin bacteria, or poor blood flow to the skin. Allergies to fleas, food or parasites, yeast or fungal skin infections, thyroid disease, hormonal imbalances, hypothyroidism, heredity and some medications can all increase the risk.

Skin fold pyoderma, **pictured,** is not uncommon, which is why it is so important to clean and dry your Bulldog's wrinkles regularly. Puppies can develop **puppy pyoderma** in thinly-haired areas, such as the groin and underarms.

If you notice symptoms, get to the vet quickly before the condition develops from **superficial pyoderma** into **severe pyoderma**, which is very unpleasant and takes a lot longer to treat.

Superficial and puppy pyoderma is usually treated with a two to six-week course of antibiotic tablets or ointment. Severe or recurring pyoderma looks awful, causes your dog some distress and can take months to completely cure. Medicated shampoos and regular bathing, as instructed by your vet, are also part of the treatment. It's also important to ensure your dog has clean, dry, padded bedding.

Bacterial infection, no matter how bad it may look, usually responds well to medical treatment, which is generally done on an outpatient basis.

## Canine Acne

Acne occurs when oil glands become blocked causing bacterial infection, and these glands are most active in teenagers. Acne is not a major health problem as most of it will clear up once the dog becomes an adult, but it can recur. Typical signs are pimples, blackheads or whiteheads around the muzzle, chest or groin. If the area is irritated, then there may be some bleeding or pus.

## Hormonal Imbalances

These occur in dogs of all breeds, including Bulldogs. They are often difficult to diagnose and occur when a dog is producing either too much (hyper) or too little (hypo) of a particular hormone. One visual sign is often hair loss on both sides of the dog's body, which is not usually itchy. Hormone imbalances can be serious as they are often indicators that glands that affect the dog internally are not working properly. However, some types can be diagnosed by special blood tests and treated effectively.

# Parasites

## Demodex

Demodectic Mange is also known as **Demodex, demodectic mange, red mange, follicular mange** or **puppy mange.** It is caused by the tiny mite Demodex canis, **pictured,** which can only be seen through a microscope.

The mite actually lives inside the hair follicles on the bodies of virtually every adult dog, and most humans, without causing any harm or irritation. In humans, the mites are found in the skin, eyelids and the creases of the nose...try not to think about that!

The Demodex mite spends its entire life on the host dog. Eggs hatch and mature from larvae to nymphs to adults in 20 to 35 days and the mites are transferred directly from the mother to the puppies within the first week of life by direct physical contact.

**FACT** ▶ *Dogs with healthy immune systems rarely get full-blown Demodex. However, a small number with weak immune systems can't combat the mites, and the disease spreads to the face and forelimbs or across the dog's whole body. Affected skin turns blue-grey due to the presence of thousands of blackheads or "comedones."*

Vets currently believe that virtually every mother carries and transfers mites to her puppies, but most are immune to its effects. It is most likely to develop in puppies with parents that have mange, and most lesions develop between three and six months of age.

"*Puppy Mange*" is not usually serious and most cases disappear when the pup's immune system kicks in at about 12 months old. *Demodex* can also occur when females have their first season, which may be due to a slight dip in their immune systems.

**Symptoms** – Bald patches, usually accompanied by crusty, red skin that sometimes appears greasy or wet. Hair loss usually begins around the muzzle, eyes and other areas on the head. The lesions may or may not itch.

In *localised mange*, a few circular crusty areas appear, most frequently on the head and front legs of puppies. With *generalised mange, pictured,* there are bald patches over the entire coat. The skin on the head, side and back is crusty, inflamed and oozes a clear fluid. The skin will often be oily to touch and there is usually a secondary bacterial infection.

 *Some puppies can become quite ill and can develop a fever, lose their appetites and become lethargic. If you suspect your puppy has generalised demodectic mange, (as opposed to local, which only affects the face and front legs), get her to a vet ASAP.*

There is also a condition called *pododermatitis,* when the mange affects a puppy's paws. It can cause bacterial infections and be very uncomfortable, even painful. Symptoms include hair loss on the paws, swelling of the paws (especially around the nail beds) and red, hot or inflamed areas that are often infected. Treatment is always recommended, and it can take several rounds to clear it up.

**Diagnosis and Treatment** – The vet will normally diagnose demodex after taking a skin scraping. Treatment usually involves topical (on the skin) medication and sometimes tablets. In 90% of cases localised demodectic mange resolves itself as the puppy grows. If the dog has just one or two

lesions, these can usually be successfully treated using specific creams and spot treatments. There are also non-chemical treatments, *such as the one pictured*, to relieve symptoms.

With the more serious generalised demodex, treatment can be lengthy and expensive. The vet might prescribe an anti-parasitic dip every two weeks. Owners should always wear rubber gloves when treating their dog, and it should be applied in a room with good ventilation.

Most dogs with a severe case need six to 14 dips every two weeks. After the first three or four dips, the vet takes another skin scraping to check the mites have gone. Dips continue for one month after the mites have disappeared, but dogs are not considered cured until a year after their last treatment.

 *Some dogs can have a bad reaction to anti-parasitic dips. Before proceeding, check with your vet as to whether an anti-parasitic dip is suitable for your dog.*

Other options include the heartworm treatment Ivermectin. This isn't approved by the FDA for treating mange, but is often used to do so. It is usually given orally every one to two days, or by injection, and can be very effective. **Again, some dogs react badly to it.** Another drug is Interceptor (Milbemycin oxime), which can be expensive as it has to be given daily. However, it is effective on up to 80% of the dogs who did not respond to dips – but should be given with caution to pups under 21 weeks of age.

Dogs that have the generalised condition may have underlying skin infections, so antibiotics are often given for the first several weeks of treatment. Because the mite flourishes on dogs with suppressed immune systems, you should try to get to the root cause of immune system disease, especially if your Bulldog is an adult when she first develops demodectic mange.

## Sarcoptic Mange (Scabies)

Also known as canine scabies, this is caused by the parasite *Sarcoptes scabiei.* This microscopic mite can cause a range of skin problems, the most common of which is hair loss and severe itching. The mites can infect other animals such as foxes, cats and even humans, but prefer to live their short lives on dogs. Fortunately, there are several good treatments and it can be easily controlled.

In cool, moist environments, the mites live for up to 22 days. At normal room temperature they live from two to six days, preferring to live on parts of the dog with less hair. Diagnosing canine scabies can be somewhat difficult, and it is often mistaken for inhalant allergies.

Once diagnosed, there are a number of effective treatments, including selamectin (Revolution – again, some dogs can have a bad reaction to this), an on-the-skin solution applied once a month that also provides heartworm prevention, flea control and some tick protection. Various Frontline products are also effective – check with your vet for the correct ones.

There is, however, one product recommended by many breeders and gets excellent reviews, both in terms of effectiveness and also the fact that very few dogs have any reaction to it. It is the *Seresto Flea Collar, pictured,* which provides full body protection against all fleas, ticks, sarcoptic mange, lice and other bloodsucking critters!

The Seresto collar lasts up to eight months and is waterproof. Provided your Bulldog will keep the collar on, I'd recommend it - but it's not cheap, at around £33 in the UK and $50 in the US.

There are also holistic remedies for many skin conditions. Because your dog does not have to come into direct contact with an infected dog to catch scabies, it is difficult to completely protect her. Foxes and their environment can also transmit the mite.

## Fleas

When you see your dog scratching and biting, your first thought is probably: *"She's got fleas!"* and you may well be right. Fleas don't fly, but they do have very strong back legs and they will take any

 opportunity to jump from the ground or another animal into your Bulldog's lovely, warm, sleek coat. You can sometimes see the fleas if you part your dog's hair.

And for every flea that you see on your dog, there is the stomach-churning prospect of hundreds of eggs and larvae in your home.... So, if your dog gets fleas, you'll have to treat your environment as well as the dog in order to completely get rid of them.

*The best form of cure is prevention.* Vets recommend giving dogs a preventative flea treatment every four to eight weeks – although the Seresto Flea Collar lasts for eight months. If you do give a regular skin treatment, the frequency depends on your climate, the season - fleas do not breed as quickly in the cold - and how much time your dog spends outdoors.

To apply topical insecticides like Frontline and Advantix, part the skin and apply drops of the liquid on to a small area on your dog's back, usually near the neck. Some kill fleas and ticks, and others just kill fleas - check the details. It is worth spending the money on a quality treatment, as cheaper brands may not rid your Bulldog completely of fleas, ticks and other parasites.

One UK breeder said that many breeders are opposed to chemical flea treatments, such as Spot On or those from the vet, as they cause a reaction in some dogs - in extreme cases some have been known to have seizures. She added that when she found a flea, she simply washed all of her dogs, one after the other, and then washed every last piece of bedding.

There are also holistic and natural remedies to chemical flea treatments, discussed later in this chapter.

NOTE: There is also anecdotal evidence from owners of various breeds that the US flea and worm tablet *Trifexis* may cause severe side effects in some dogs. You can read some owners' comments at: www.max-the-schnauzer.com/trifexis-side-effects-in-schnauzers.html

## Ticks

A tick is not an insect, but a member of the arachnid family, like the spider. There are over 850 types, some have a hard shell and some a soft one. Ticks don't have wings - they can't fly, they crawl.

They have a sensor called Haller's organ that detects smell, heat and humidity to help them locate food, which in some cases is a Bulldog. A tick's diet consists of one thing and one thing only – blood! They climb up onto tall grass and when they sense an animal is close, crawl on.

Ticks can pass on a number of diseases to animals and humans, the most well-known of which is

 *Lyme Disease*, a serious condition that causes lameness and other problems. Bulldogs don't often get ticks, they are more common on dogs that spend a lot of time outdoors, especially in woods.

If you do find a tick on your Bulldog's coat and are not sure how to get it out, have it removed by a vet or other expert. Inexpertly pulling it out yourself and leaving a bit of the tick behind can be detrimental to your dog's health. Tick prevention treatments are similar to those for fleas. If your Bulldog has sensitive skin or allergies, she might do better with a natural flea or tick remedy.

## Heartworm

Heartworm is a serious and potentially fatal disease affecting pets in North America and many other parts of the world, but not the UK. These foot-long worms live in the heart, lungs and associated blood vessels of affected animals, causing severe lung disease, heart failure and damage to organs.

The dog is a natural host for heartworms, enabling the worms living inside a dog to mature into adults, mate and produce offspring. If untreated, their numbers can increase; dogs have been known to harbour several hundred worms in their bodies.

Heartworm disease causes lasting damage to the heart, lungs and arteries, and can affect the dog's health and quality of life long after the parasites are gone. For this reason, **prevention is by far the best option** and treatment - when needed - should be administered as early as possible.

The mosquito **(pictured below)** plays an essential role in the heartworm life cycle. When a mosquito bites and takes a blood meal from an infected animal, it picks up baby worms that develop and mature into **"infective stage"** larvae over a period of 10 to 14 days.

Then, when it bites another dog, the infective larvae are deposited onto the surface of the animal's skin and enter the new host through the mosquito's bite wound. Once inside the dog, it takes approximately six months for the larvae to develop into adult heartworms. Heartworms can live for five to seven years in a dog.

In the early stages of the disease, many dogs show few or no symptoms. The longer the infection persists, the more likely symptoms will develop. These include:

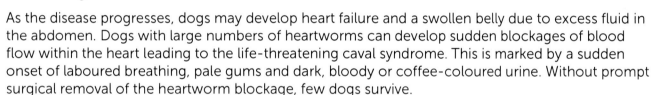

- A mild persistent cough
- Reluctance to exercise
- Tiredness after moderate activity
- Decreased appetite
- Weight loss

As the disease progresses, dogs may develop heart failure and a swollen belly due to excess fluid in the abdomen. Dogs with large numbers of heartworms can develop sudden blockages of blood flow within the heart leading to the life-threatening caval syndrome. This is marked by a sudden onset of laboured breathing, pale gums and dark, bloody or coffee-coloured urine. Without prompt surgical removal of the heartworm blockage, few dogs survive.

Although more common in the south eastern US, heartworm disease has been diagnosed in all 50 states. The American Heartworm Society recommends that you get your dog tested every year and give your dog heartworm preventive treatment for all 12 months of the year. If you live in a risk area, check that your tick and flea medication also prevents heartworm. In the UK, heartworm has only been found in imported dogs.

**Thanks to the American Heartworm Society for assistance with the section.**

..............................................................................................................................................................

## Ringworm

This is not actually a worm, but a fungus and is most commonly seen in puppies and young dogs. It is highly infectious and often found on the face, ears, paws or tail. The ringworm fungus is most prevalent in hot, humid climates but, surprisingly, most cases occur in autumn and winter. But it is not that common; in one study of dogs with active skin problems, less than 3% had ringworm.

Ringworm is transmitted by spores in the soil and by contact with the infected hair of dogs and cats, typically found on carpets, brushes, combs, toys and furniture. Spores from infected animals can be shed into the environment and live for over 18 months, but most healthy adult dogs have some resistance and never develop symptoms.

The fungi live in dead skin, hairs and nails - and the head and legs are the most common areas affected. Tell-tale signs are bald patches with a roughly circular shape *(pictured)*. Ringworm is relatively easy to treat with fungicidal shampoos or antibiotics from a vet.

 *Humans can catch ringworm from pets, and vice versa. Children are especially susceptible, as are adults with suppressed immune systems and those undergoing chemotherapy. Hygiene is extremely important.*

If your Bulldog has ringworm, wear gloves when handling her and wash your hands well afterwards. And if a member of your family catches ringworm, make sure they use separate towels from everyone else or the fungus may spread. As a teenager, I caught ringworm from horses at the local stables where I worked at weekends - much to my mother's horror - and was treated like a leper by the rest of the family until it cleared up!

# Ear Infections

Ear infections are not uncommon in Bulldogs, as the flat head leaves them with a narrowed ear canal. Often an ear infection is a sign of a separate underlying health problem. Or it may be that there's moisture in the dog's ear canal, which has created the warm, damp environment much loved by home-hunting bacteria.

**FACT** *The fact that a Bulldog has recurring ear infections does NOT necessarily mean that the ears are the source of the problem – although they might be. They may also be due to inhalant, contact or food allergies or other health issues such as low thyroid function.*

The underlying problem MUST be treated or the dog will continue to have long-term ear problems. Tell-tale signs include your dog shaking her head, scratching or rubbing her ears a lot, or an unpleasant smell from the ears. If you look inside, you may notice a reddy brown or yellow discharge, it may also be red and inflamed with a lot of wax.

Sometimes a dog may appear depressed or irritable; ear infections are painful. In chronic cases, the inside of her ears may become crusty or thickened. Treatment depends on the cause and what – if any - other conditions your dog may have.

**FACT** *Regular cleaning and drying of your Bulldog's ears, wrinkles and tail pocket - daily if possible - will help to keep skin disorders at bay.*

Vets often treat bacterial infections with antibiotics and yeast infections with antifungals. Glucocorticoids, such as dexamethasone, are often included in these medications to reduce the inflammation in the ear. Your vet may also flush out and clean the ear with special drops, something you may have to do daily at home until the infection clears.

A dog's ear canal is L-shaped, which means it can be difficult to get medication into the lower, or horizontal, part of the ear.

*Hold the dog's ear flap with one hand and put the ointment or drops in with the other, tilting the dog's head away from you so the liquid flows downwards <u>with gravity.</u> Holding the ear flap down, massage the medication into the horizontal canal before letting go of your dog, as the first thing she will do is shake her head – and if the ointment or drops aren't massaged in, they will fly out.*

Use large cotton wool balls or wipes and a veterinary-approved ear cleaning solution. DO NOT use cotton buds inside the ear, they are too small and can cause injury, and be very careful not to put anything too far inside. See **Chapter 13. Grooming** for more information and YouTube for various videos of how to clean Bulldog ears without damaging them. (If your dog has a ruptured or weakened eardrum, ear cleansers and medications could do more harm than good).

Most ear infections can be successfully managed if properly diagnosed and treated. If your dog appears to be in pain, has smelly ears, or if her ear canals look inflamed, get her to the vet straight away before the infection becomes entrenched. If you can successfully treat the first infection, there is a chance it will not return.

In extreme cases of recurring ear infection, a surgical procedure called a *lateral ear resection* may be required. This is EXTREMELY painful for the dog and is only carried out as a last resort if the dog is in danger of going deaf otherwise.

# Some Allergy Treatments

Treatments and success rates vary tremendously from dog to dog and from one allergy to another, which is why it is so important to consult a vet at the outset. Earlier diagnosis is more likely to lead to a successful treatment.

Some owners of dogs with recurring skin issues find that a course of antibiotics or steroids works wonders for their dog's sore skin and itching. However, the scratching starts all over again shortly after the treatment stops.

**FACT** *While a single steroid injection is often highly effective in calming down symptoms almost immediately, frequent or long-term steroid use is not a good option as it can lead to serious side effects.*

Food allergies require patience, a change or several changes of diet and maybe even a food trial, and the specific trigger is notoriously difficult to isolate – unless you are lucky and hit on the culprit straight away.

Blood and skin tests are available for inhalant and contact allergies, followed by hyposensitisation treatment. However, these are expensive and often the specific trigger for many dogs remains unknown. So, the reality for many owners of Bulldogs with allergies is that they manage the condition rather than curing it completely.

## Our Experience

After corresponding with numerous other dog owners and consulting our vet, Graham, it seems our experiences with allergies are common. This is borne out by the dozens of dog owners who have contacted our website about their pet's allergy or sensitivities.

According to Graham, more and more dogs are appearing in his waiting room with various types of allergies. Whether this is connected to how we breed our dogs remains to be seen.

Our dog Max was perfectly fine until he was about two years old, when he began to scratch a lot. He scratched more in spring and summer, which meant that his allergies were almost certainly inhalant or contact-based and related to pollens, grasses or other outdoor triggers. We decided not to have a lot of tests - not because of the cost - but because the vet said it was highly likely that he was allergic to pollens.

Max was an active dog and if we had confirmed pollen allergy confirmed, we were not going to stop taking him out for thrice-daily walks.

As already mentioned, it's definitely beneficial to have a hose or bath outside to rinse the dog's paws and underbelly after a walk. Regarding medications, Max was at first put on to a tiny dose of Piriton *(pictured),* an antihistamine for hay fever sufferers (human and canine) and for the first few springs and summers, this worked well.

Allergies can change and a dog can build up a tolerance to a treatment, which is why they can be so difficult to treat. Max's symptoms changed from season to season, although the main ones were: general scratching, paw biting and ear infections.

One year he bit the skin under his tail a lot– he would jump around like he had been stung by a bee and bite frenetically. This was treated effectively with a single steroid injection, followed by spraying the area with cortisone once a day at home for a period. This type of spray can be very effective if the itchy area is small, but no good for spraying all over a dog's body.

A few years ago, he started nibbling his paws for the first time - a habit he persisted with. Over the years we tried a number of treatments, all of which worked for a while, before he came off the medication in September or October when pollen levels fell. He managed perfectly fine the rest of the year without any treatment at all.

Not every owner wants to treat his or her dog with chemicals, nor feed a diet that includes preservatives, which is why this book includes alternatives. Also, 15 years ago, when we were starting out on the *"Allergy Trail,"* there were far fewer options than there are now.

We fed Max a high quality hypoallergenic dry food. If we were starting again from scratch with an allergic dog, knowing what we know now, I'd look into a raw or home-cooked diet (which is what he was fed towards the end of his life), if necessary in combination with holistic remedies.

One season the vet put him on a short course of steroids. These worked very well for five months, but steroids are not a long-term solution. Another spring, we were prescribed Atopica, a non-steroid daily tablet only sold in the UK through vets. The active ingredient is **cyclosporine**, which suppresses the immune system. Some dogs can get side effects, although ours didn't.

This treatment was expensive, but initially extremely effective – so much so that we thought we had cured the problem completely. However, after a couple of seasons on cyclosporine he developed a tolerance to the drug and started scratching again.

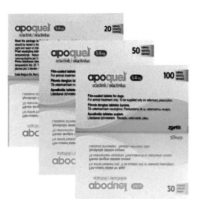

A few years ago, he went back on the antihistamine Piriton, a higher dose than when he was two years old, and this worked very well again. One advantage of this drug is that is it manufactured by the million and is therefore very inexpensive.

## Apoquel

In 2013 the FDA approved **Apoquel** (oclacitinib) *– pictured -* to control itching and inflammation in allergic dogs. Like most allergy drugs, it acts by suppressing the immune system, rather than addressing the root cause. It has, however, proved to be highly effective in treating tens of thousands of dogs with allergies.

It proved so popular in the UK and North America that in the two years after release there was a shortage, as the manufacturers weren't able to produce it fast enough.

We tried Apoquel with excellent results. There was some initial tweaking to get the daily dose right, but it proved highly effective. The tablets are administered according to body weight – half a 19mg daily tablet for a dog weighing 30lb-45lb and two 5.4mg tablets daily for dogs weighting 45lb-60lb. It's not cheap, but can work miracles with some dogs.

 *Side effects have been reported in some dogs, and holistic practitioners and Dogs Naturally magazine believe that it is harmful to the dog.*

Allergies are often complex and difficult to treat; you should weigh up the pros and cons in the best interests of your own dog. Max's allergies were manageable; he loved his food, was full of energy and otherwise healthy, and lived a happy life into his teens.

## Other Options

Vets often recommend adding fish oils, which contain Omega-3 fatty acids, to a daily feed to keep your dog's skin and coat healthy all year round – whether or not she has problems.

We added a liquid supplement called Yumega Plus, which contains Omegas 3 and 6, to one of the two daily feeds all year round. When the scratching got particularly bad, we bathed our dog in an antiseborrheic shampoo called Malaseb, *pictured,* twice a week for a limited time. This also helped, although was not necessary once on Apoquel.

Most allergies are manageable, although they may change throughout the life of the dog and you may have to alter the treatment. Here are some suggestions:

**Bathing** - bathing your dog using shampoos that break down the oils that plug the hair follicles. These shampoos contain antiseborrheic ingredients such as benzoyl peroxide, salicylic acid, sulphur or tar. One example is Sulfoxydex shampoo, which can be followed by a cream rinse such as Episoothe Rinse afterwards to prevent the skin from drying out.

**Dabbing** – Using an astringent such as witch hazel or alcohol on affected areas. We have heard of zinc oxide cream being used to some effect. In the human world, this is rubbed on to mild skin abrasions and acts as a protective coating. It can help the healing of chapped skin and nappy rash in babies. Zinc oxide works as a mild astringent and has some antiseptic properties and is safe to use on dogs, *as long as you do not allow the dog to lick it off*.

**Daily supplements** - Vitamin E, vitamin A, zinc and omega oils all help to make a dog's skin healthy. Feed a daily supplement that contains some of these, such as fish oil, which provides omega.

Many owners have tried coconut oil *(pictured)* with some success. Here is a link to an article on the benefits of coconut oils and fish oils, check with your vet first: www.dogsnaturallymagazine.com/the-health-benefits-of-coconut-oil

 *If you suspect your dog has a skin problem, ear infection or allergy, get her to the vet straight away. You can hopefully nip it in the bud before secondary infections develop – and save a lot of heartache and money in the long run.*

# The Holistic Approach

As canine allergies become increasingly common, more and more owners of dogs with allergies and sensitivities are looking towards natural foods and remedies to help deal with the issues.

Others are finding that their dog does well for a time with injections or medication, but then the symptoms slowly start to reappear. A holistic practitioner looks at finding the root cause of the problem and treating that, rather than just treating the symptoms.

Dr Sara Skiwski is a holistic vet working in California. She writes here about canine environmental allergies: "Here in California, with our mild weather and no hard freeze in Winter, environmental allergens can build up and cause nearly year-round issues for our beloved pets. Also, seasonal allergies, when left unaddressed, can lead to year-round allergies. Unlike humans, whose allergy symptoms seem to affect mostly the respiratory tract, seasonal allergies in dogs often take the form of skin irritation/inflammation.

"Allergic reactions are produced by the immune system. The way the immune system functions is a result of both genetics and the environment: Nature versus Nurture. Let's look at a typical case. A puppy starts showing mild seasonal allergy symptoms, for instance a red tummy and mild itching in Spring. Off to the vet!

"The treatment prescribed is symptomatic to provide relief, such as a topical spray. The next year when the weather warms up, the patient is back again - same symptoms but more severe this time. This time the dog has very itchy skin. Again, the treatment is symptomatic - antibiotics, topical spray (hopefully no steroids), until the symptoms resolve with the season change. Fast forward to another Spring...on the third year, the patient is back again but this time the symptoms last longer, (not just Spring but also through most of Summer and into Fall).

"By Year Five, all the symptoms are significantly worse and are occurring year-round. This is what happens with seasonal environmental allergies. The more your pet is exposed to the allergens they are sensitive to, the more the immune system over-reacts and the more intense and long-lasting the allergic response becomes. What to do?

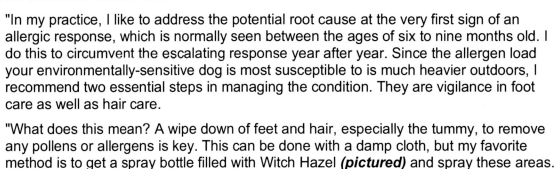

"In my practice, I like to address the potential root cause at the very first sign of an allergic response, which is normally seen between the ages of six to nine months old. I do this to circumvent the escalating response year after year. Since the allergen load your environmentally-sensitive dog is most susceptible to is much heavier outdoors, I recommend two essential steps in managing the condition. They are vigilance in foot care as well as hair care.

"What does this mean? A wipe down of feet and hair, especially the tummy, to remove any pollens or allergens is key. This can be done with a damp cloth, but my favorite method is to get a spray bottle filled with Witch Hazel *(pictured)* and spray these areas.

"First, spray the feet then wipe them off with a cloth, and then spray and wipe down the tummy and sides. This is best done right after the pup has been outside playing or walking. This will help keep your pet from tracking the environmental allergens into the home and into their beds. If the feet end up still being itchy, I suggest adding foot soaks in Epsom salts."

Dr Sara also stresses the importance of keeping the immune system healthy by avoiding unnecessary vaccinations or drugs:

"The vaccine stimulates the immune system, which is the last thing your pet with seasonal environmental allergies needs. I also will move the pet to an anti-inflammatory diet. Foods that create or worsen inflammation are high in carbohydrates. An allergic pet's diet should be very low in carbohydrates, especially grains. Research has shown that 'leaky gut,' or dysbiosis, is a root cause of immune system overreactions in both dog and cats (and some humans).

"Feed a diet that is not processed, or minimally processed; one that doesn't have grain and takes a little longer to get absorbed and assimilated through the gut. Slowing the assimilation assures that there are not large spikes of nutrients and proteins that come into the body all at once and overtax the pancreas and liver, creating inflammation.

"A lot of commercial diets are too high in grains and carbohydrates. These foods create inflammation that overtaxes the body and leads not just to skin inflammation, but also to other inflammatory conditions, such as colitis, pancreatitis, arthritis, inflammatory bowel disease and ear infections. Also, these diets are too low in protein, which is needed to make blood. This causes a decreased blood reserve in the body and in some of these animals this can lead to the skin not being properly nourished, starting a cycle of chronic skin infections which produce more itching."

After looking at diet, check that your dog is free from fleas and then these are some of Dr Sara's suggested supplements:

✓ **Raw (Unpasteurised) Local Honey** - an alkaline-forming food containing natural vitamins, enzymes, powerful antioxidants and other important natural nutrients, which are destroyed during the heating and pasteurisation processes. Raw honey has anti-viral, anti-bacterial and anti-fungal properties. It promotes body and digestive health, is a powerful antioxidant, strengthens the immune system, eliminates allergies, and is an excellent remedy for skin wounds and all types of infections. Bees collect pollen from local plants and their honey often acts as an immune booster for dogs living in the locality.

Dr Sara says: "It may seem odd that straight exposure to pollen often triggers allergies, but that exposure to pollen in the honey usually has the opposite effect. But this is typically what we see. In honey, the allergens are delivered in small, manageable doses and the effect over time is very much like that from undergoing a whole series of allergy immunology injections."

✓ **Mushrooms -** make sure you choose the non-poisonous ones! Dogs don't like the taste, so may have to mask it with another food. Medicinal mushrooms are used to treat and prevent a wide array of illnesses through their use as immune stimulants and modulators, and antioxidants. The most well-known and researched are reishi, maitake, cordyceps, blazei, split-gill, turkey tail and shiitake. Histamine is what causes much of the inflammation, redness and irritation in allergies. By helping to control histamine production, the mushrooms can moderate the effects of inflammation and even help prevent allergies in the first place.

*WARNING! Mushrooms can interact with some over-the-counter and prescription drugs, so do your research as well as checking with your vet first.*

✓ **Stinging Nettles -** contain biologically active compounds that reduce inflammation. Nettles can reduce the amount of histamine the body produces in response to an allergen. Nettle tea or extract can help with itching. Nettles not only help directly to decrease the itch, but also work overtime to desensitise the body to allergens.

✓ **Quercetin** – is an over-the-counter supplement with anti-inflammatory properties. It is a strong antioxidant and reduces the body's production of histamines.

✓ **Omega-3 Fatty Acids -** these help decrease inflammation throughout the body. Adding them into the diet of all pets - particularly those struggling with seasonal environmental allergies – is very beneficial. If your dog has more itching along the top of their back and on their sides, add in a fish oil supplement. Fish oil helps to decrease the itch and heal skin lesions. The best sources of Omega 3s are krill oil, salmon oil, tuna oil, anchovy oil and other fish body oils, as well as raw organic egg yolks. If using an oil alone, it is important to give a vitamin B complex supplement.

- ✓ **Coconut Oil -** contains lauric acid, which helps decrease the production of yeast, a common opportunistic infection. Using a fish body oil combined with coconut oil before inflammation flares up can help moderate or even suppress your dog's inflammatory response.

Dr Sara adds: "Above are but a few of the over-the-counter remedies I like. In non-responsive cases, Chinese herbs can be used to work with the body to help to decrease the allergy threshold even more than with diet and supplements alone. Most of the animals I work with are on a program of Chinese herbs, diet change and acupuncture.

"So, the next time Fido is showing symptoms of seasonal allergies, consider rethinking your strategy to treat the root cause instead of the symptom."

With thanks to Dr Sara Skiwski, of the Western Dragon Integrated Veterinary Services, San Jose, California, for her kind permission to use her writings as the basis for *The Holistic Approach.*

..................................................................................................................................

**FACT** 〉 *Massage can stimulate your Bulldog's immune system and help to prevent or reduce allergies. It's also good for improving your dog's circulation and flexibility, reducing muscle and arthritis pain and other age-related problems.*

Anybody can do it – we do – and your Bulldog will absolutely love the attention! Type "*Bulldog Massage Therapy*" into Google to read articles and watch videos on techniques and benefits.

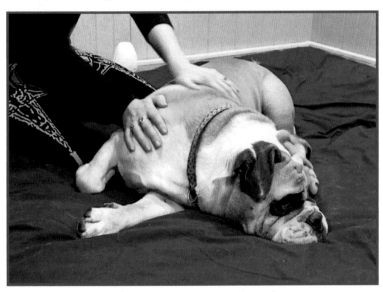

Holistic practitioners also believe that *acupressure* can specifically help dogs with allergies. Google *"Acupressure for Dogs"* to learn the theory behind it and how to apply pressure at specific points on your dog's body. Acupressure can also help nervous and elderly dogs.

If your Bulldog has a skin issue, seek a professional diagnosis as soon as possible before attempting to treat it yourself and it becomes entrenched:

**Early diagnosis and treatment give the best chance of a full recovery.**

Even if a skin condition cannot be completely cured, many can be successfully managed, allowing your dog to live a happy, pain-free life.

 *Remember that a high-quality diet, daily attention to cleanliness, regular grooming and check-overs go a long way in preventing and managing skin problems in Bulldogs.*

..................................................................................................................................

# 13. Grooming

There are so many wonderful aspects to Bulldog ownership. No other breed is quite like the Bully, either in appearance or character. However, they do require a little extra maintenance from their owners to help keep them in tip top condition.

Grooming doesn't just mean giving your Bulldog a quick tickle with a brush a couple of times a month. Regular grooming, cleaning and check-overs are essential to help your Bully look and feel his best.

This all helps to keep his ears, tail and body clean, keep skin-related issues at bay, enable you to spot any potential problems early on, and bond you and your Bully even closer. During routine grooming sessions you can examine his coat, skin, teeth, eyes, ears, paws and nails for signs of problems.

## The Bulldog Coat

A Bulldog has a short, smooth coat with a fine texture and if yours is in good health, it should be sleek and glossy. Heavy shedding can be a sign that something is amiss - such as a skin disorder or intolerance to a certain foodstuff. Even healthy Bulldogs shed a little throughout the year, unlike many breeds which shed seasonally.

There are several different coat colours. The official colours accepted by the Kennel Clubs are listed below in order of popularity. Bulldogs of different colours are not acceptable to the Kennel Clubs and cannot be entered for shows run under Kennel Club or AKC rules, but you can still enter him for other types of show:

- ❧ Red brindle (pictured)
- ❧ All other brindles*
- ❧ Solid white
- ❧ Solid red
- ❧ Fawn or fallow
- ❧ Piebald (irregular patches of two colours, such as brown and white)

**\* Brindle** is a colouring pattern sometimes described as **"tiger striped,"** although the brindle pattern is more subtle than that of a tiger. The colour streaks are irregular and usually darker than the coat's base colour. Very dark markings can still be seen on a coat that is only slightly lighter. Brindles should have a fine and even distribution of colours to be considered perfect.

So-called *"rare colours,"* such as black, blue, lilac, chocolate or merle are not part of the Bulldog DNA, so another breed has been introduced somewhere along the line for the colour. If you don't mind that and want an unusually coloured pup, check that the parents have been health screened – this is far more important than colour. There is some anecdotal evidence from owners that there are more health issues with "rare colour" Bulldogs than those with standard colours. This is probably due to people breeding primarily for colour, rather than health.

If you want a 100% Bully, stick to the Kennel Club and AKC colours. The same goes for markings - there's no such thing as a 100% purebred tri-colour or spotted English Bulldog!

The good news is that Bulldogs require fairly minimal brushing and you don't need a lot of expensive equipment.

Begin at the dog's head and brush backwards towards the tail; brush strokes should always be in the direction that the hair grows, not against the fur. It's easier to do when your Bully is standing. It's OK if he prefers to sit or lie down, just make sure to cover all areas including legs and under the belly. If you gently squirt the coat with a fine spray of water beforehand it prevents the hairs from breaking. Then use a rubber curry comb to remove loose and dead hair, and finally use a bristle brush to remove all the remaining loose hair. Bristle brushes are expensive, but they last forever.

If you do notice an unpleasant smell coming from him (in addition to his normal gassy emissions!) and he hasn't been rolling in animal poop or some other stinky substance, he may have a yeast infection and needs checking out by a vet.

**FACT** ❯ *Other benefits of regular brushing are that it removes dead hair and skin, stimulates blood circulation and spreads natural oils throughout the coat, helping to keep it in good condition. Also, you don't need to bathe your Bulldog very often if you brush him regularly.*

Bulldogs are physically very inflexible due to their short necks and broad bodies, so regular health and hygiene tasks are essential. If you don't think you have time for this extra care several times a week, please don't get a Bulldog.

# Wrinkles, Tails and Nails

Your Bulldog would not be a Bulldog without his distinctive wrinkles. The nose rope, deep facial wrinkles and body skin folds are part of what makes the breed so unique.

However, there are health issues that can arise if the wrinkles are not properly and routinely cleansed. Prevention is better than cure and it's definitely better to keep the skin folds clean than have your Bulldog develop painful problems which later require expensive and time-consuming medical attention.

Some Bulldogs only need their wrinkles cleaning a couple of times a week, while others need a check or a clean every day.

Air cannot circulate in these hidden folds and they can become a breeding ground for yeast or bacteria and the skin in the fold becomes red and infected. Sometimes yellow pus can be seen if the folds are not kept clean and, most important, DRY.

Wipe between the folds of your Bulldog's skin using a medicated pad or baby wipe with lanolin or aloe to keep the crevices free of debris and bacteria – or use a drop of medicated dog shampoo from your vet in a cup of warm water.

Whatever you choose for the task, it is essential that you thoroughly dry the area after cleaning – damp areas are breeding grounds for the aforementioned nasty bugs. Dry with a towel or cloth, don't use talc or corn starch, which can clump.

Overweight dogs are at greater risk of developing a skin infection because the excess fat makes the wrinkles more pronounced.

It's impossible to say exactly how often to clean the wrinkles on any individual Bulldog, but the short answer is: more often than you think. And if a nose-wrinkling smell is coming off your Bully, you're probably not doing it often enough.

Bulldogs cannot clean the area around their own tails – so that job it up to you. It might not be very pleasant, but you owe it to your furry friend to do it for him. Some Bulldog tails, particularly corkscrew ones, actually fold back into the body, leaving a hidden "tail pocket" underneath.

This area is a magnet for bacteria and yeast (which is a fungus) and if your Bulldog has a tail pocket, it needs regular cleaning. It's not always easy to tell whether your dog has a tail pocket. If you're unsure, ask your vet on your next routine visit.

A tail pocket requires regular cleaning and drying in a similar way to the other skin folds. However, the area is extremely sensitive, so proceed gently with caution. Again, use a wet wipe or clean damp cloth to clean the area. Pat the area dry with a towel and then consider applying a protective balm, such as Wrinkle Balm, which has antioxidants as well as anti-inflammatory, antibacterial and anti-fungal properties.

If the tail area becomes red and itchy, your poor dog will not be able to reach it and it will be very uncomfortable for him. If you see him trying to bite it or scoot along the floor, get him to the vet for an anti-fungal treatment ASAP.

If your Bully gets little red pimples on his face and chin, it means he has got acne *(pictured).* He can get acne at any age, not just as a teenager. Plastic bowls can also trigger the condition, which is why stainless steel ones are better.

Often a daily washing followed by an application of an antibiotic cream is enough to get rid of the problem, if it persists it will mean a visit to your vet.

A Bulldog's skin can dry out, especially with artificial heat in the winter months. If you spot any dry patches, for example on the inner thighs, armpits or a cracked nose, massage a little petroleum jelly or baby oil on to the dry patch.

## Nail Trimming

Bulldogs seldom get enough exercise outdoors on hard surfaces to wear their nails down, so they have to be clipped or filed regularly. Nails must be kept short for the paws to remain healthy.

**FACT** *Overly-long nails interfere with a dog's gait, making walking awkward or painful and they can break easily, usually at the base of the nail where blood vessels and nerves are located.*

Get your dog used to having his paws inspected from puppyhood; it's also a good opportunity to check for other problems, such as cracked pads or interdigital cysts. To trim your dog's nails, use a specially designed clipper. Most have safety guards to prevent you cutting the nails too short. Do it before they get too long.

📌 *If you can hear the nails clicking on a hard surface, they're too long.* You want to trim only the ends, before *"the quick,"* which is a blood vessel inside the nail. You can see where the quick ends on a white nail, but not on a dark nail.

Clip only the hook-like part of the nail that turns down. Start trimming gently, a nail or two at a time, and your dog will learn that you're not going to hurt him. If you accidentally cut the quick, stop the bleeding with some styptic powder.

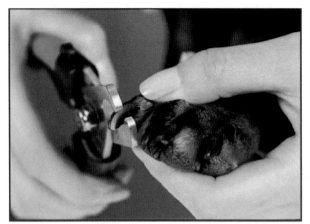

Another option is to file your dog's nails with a nail grinder tool, or Dremel. Some Bulldogs have tough nails that are harder to trim and this may be a less stressful method for your dog, with less chance of pain or bleeding.

The grinder is like an electric nail file and only removes a small amount of nail at a time. Some owners prefer to use one as there is less chance of cutting the quick, and many dogs prefer them to a clipper. Introduce your dog to the grinder gradually - the noise and vibration take some getting used to.

Get your dog used to having his paws inspected from puppyhood. It is also a good opportunity to check for other problems such as cracked pads, thorns and splinters and the Bulldog's nemesis - interdigital cysts. If you find it impossible to clip your dog's nails, or you are at all worried about doing it, take him to a vet or a groomer - and have your Bulldog's anal sacs squeezed, or "expressed," while he's there!

## Anal Glands

While we're discussing the less appealing end of your Bulldog, let's dive straight in and talk about anal sacs. Sometimes called scent glands, these are a pair of glands located inside your dog's anus that give off a scent when he has a bowel movement.

When a dog passes firm stools, the glands normally empty themselves, but soft poop or diarrhoea can mean that not enough pressure is exerted to empty the glands, causing discomfort to the dog. If they get infected, they become swollen and painful. In extreme cases, one or both anal glands can be removed – we had a dog that lived happily for many years with one anal gland.

If your dog drags himself along on his rear end – *"scooting"* - or tries to lick or scratch his anus, he could well have impacted anal glands that need squeezing, either by you if you know how to do it, your vet or a groomer. Scooting can also be a sign of worms or infected tail pocket. Whatever the reason, it pays to keep an eye on both ends of your dog!

## Ear Cleaning

Ear infections affect dogs of all breeds – although dogs with floppy ears tend to be more susceptible to them than dogs with pricked-up ears that allow air to circulate. This is because floppy ears create a warm, moist haven for bacteria and infection. Another reason for Bulldogs getting ear infections is that they are often a sign of allergies.

Ear infections are notorious for recurring once they have taken hold, and can even cause deafness in very severe cases. So, it pays to check your dog's ears regularly while grooming. If yours is one of the few Bulldogs that swims, towel his ears dry inside and out after swimming. Keep an eye out for redness or inflammation at the inner base of the ear, or a build-up of dark wax.

*Never put anything sharp or narrow - like a cotton bud — inside your dog's ears, as you can cause damage.*

Typical signs of an ear infection are the dog:

- Shaking his head a lot
- Scratching his ears
- Rubbing his ears on the floor
- An unpleasant smell coming from the ears, which is a sign of a yeast infection

If your dog exhibits any of these signs, consult your vet ASAP, as simple routine cleaning won't solve the problem, and ear infections are notoriously difficult to get rid of once your dog's had one. Keep your dog's ears clean and dry right from puppyhood and hopefully he will never get one.

## Teeth Cleaning

Veterinary studies show that by the age of three, 80% of dogs show signs of gum or dental disease. Symptoms include yellow and brown build-up of tartar along the gum line, red inflamed gums and persistent bad breath.

Because they have so much packed into their mouths, Bullies are more prone to dental problems than some other breeds. You can keep their dogs' teeth clean by giving him an occasional bone, or regularly feeding bully sticks or other natural treats.

*If your Bulldog has to be anaesthetised for anything, ask your vet to clean the dog's teeth at the same time. Also, avoid cheap foods, which increase plaque and tartar.*

The most effective way of keeping your dog's teeth clean is to brush them regularly. It's not always easy, so take things slowly in the beginning and give lots of praise. Once used to the process, dogs often love the attention - especially if they like the flavour of the toothpaste!

Use a pet toothpaste, as the human variety can upset a canine's stomach. The real benefit comes from the actual action of the brush on the teeth, and various brushes, sponges and pads are available - the choice depends on factors such as the health of your dog's gums, the size of his mouth and how good you are at teeth cleaning.

Get him used to the toothpaste by letting him lick some off your finger when he is young. If he doesn't like the flavour, try a different one. Continue this until he enjoys licking the paste - it might be instant or take days.

Put a small amount on your finger and gently rub it on one of the big canine teeth at the front of his mouth. Then get him used to the toothbrush or dental sponge - praise him when he licks it - for several days. The next step is to actually start brushing.

Lift his upper lip gently and place the brush at a 45° angle to the gum line. Gently move the brush backwards and forwards. Start just with his front teeth and then gradually do a few more. Most Bulldogs have an underbite and protruding lower front teeth, so these are relatively easy to do. You don't need to brush the inside of his teeth as his tongue keeps them relatively free of plaque.

## Eye Care

Like all dogs, a Bulldog's eyes should be clean and clear. Cloudy eyes, particularly in an older dog, could be early signs of cataracts. Red or swollen tissue in the corner of the eye could be a symptom of cherry eye. If your Bully gets dust or dirt in his eyes, gently clean them with warm water and cotton wool — never put anything sharp anywhere near your dog's eyes.

Many Bulldogs suffer from tear staining *(pictured),* often reddish-brown, and most obvious on white or light-coloured dogs and those with more pronounced wrinkles. Causes include:

- A genetic predisposition caused by the physical structure of the eye
- The eyes reacting to an allergen or irritant, such as pollen, dust, chemicals
- An over-active tear duct
- Diet, often involving grain
- An infected tear duct
- A pH imbalance

Excessive tearing results in damp facial hair, which becomes a breeding ground for bacteria and yeast, the most common of which is *"red yeast*." This often makes the tear stains a stronger red-brown colour and may emit a moderate to strong smell. Vets can prescribe medication to treat bacterial and yeast infections. If the tear staining is related to diet, it may take some time to get to the root cause of the problem, see **Chapter 6. Feeding a Bulldog.**

There are various manufactured products available as well as a number of home remedies. Make sure your dog has stainless steel water and food bowls, not plastic. Clean them every couple of days to get rid of the slime and bacteria, and give him distilled or purified water to drink. One option for a pH imbalance is to add a teaspoon of white cider vinegar to the water to alter his internal pH. It may take a bit of getting used to the new flavour, so start with a tiny bit at a time.

One home remedy is to take an equal volume of plain white milk of magnesia and peroxide and mix them into a thick paste with corn starch. Work this into the stained area and let it dry. After three or four hours, wash it off and apply a little Wrinkle Balm or baby rash ointment. Repeat for several days, preferably every other day, until tear staining is gone. Always be extremely careful with peroxide or bleach near your dog's eyes and check with your vet before trying any home remedy.

## Bathing your Bulldog

If you regularly groom your Bulldog and clean his skin folds, you shouldn't need to bath your dog very often – unless he's been rolling is something horrible.

If a Bulldog's coat and skin is allowed to get dirty it can cause irritation, leading to scratching and excessive shedding. It's all a question of getting the balance right, and this will to some extent depend on how much outdoor exercise your Bully gets and what sort of areas he's running in. A Bulldog regularly exercising in dirt or mud will need more bathing than one living in an apartment and getting little outdoor exercise.

Bathing your dog too often may wash off the coat's natural protective oils, leading to the skin drying out. Frequency depends very much on the individual Bulldog, his exercise routine and skin condition, but a bath every few weeks should be enough for most. Never use human shampoos on your Bulldog as you will irritate the skin. Instead use a shampoo specially medicated for dogs, preferably one formulated for sensitive skin or allergies, which will be labelled *hypoallergenic.*

So, Bulldogs need a little extra daily care from their owners. It's all part of the deal when you decide to get one of these absolutely unique dogs. But, let's face it, they're worth it!

# 14. The Birds and the Bees

Judging by the number of questions our website receives from owners, there is a lot of confusion about the canine facts of life. Some ask if, and at what age, they should have their dog spayed or neutered, while others want to know whether they should breed their dog.

Owners of females ask when and how often she will come on heat and how long this will last. Sometimes they want to know how you can tell if a female is pregnant or how long a pregnancy lasts. So here, in a nutshell, is a chapter on The Facts of Life as far as Bulldogs are concerned.

## Females and Heat

Just like all other female mammals, including humans, a female Bulldog has a menstrual cycle - or to be more accurate, an oestrus cycle *(estrus* in the US). This is the period of time when she is ready (and willing!) for mating and is more commonly called **heat**, being **in heat**, **on heat** or **in season**.

Large breeds tend to have their first heat cycle later than small breeds. A Bulldog female usually has her first one at six to 9 months old and then twice a year. Every female is different; a few may not have their first heat until 18 months or later, and then have cycles less frequently than every six months.

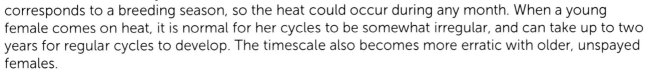

 *Females often follow the pattern of their mother, so if you have a female puppy, ask the breeder at what age the dam had her first heat.*

There is no time of the year that corresponds to a breeding season, so the heat could occur during any month. When a young female comes on heat, it is normal for her cycles to be somewhat irregular, and can take up to two years for regular cycles to develop. The timescale also becomes more erratic with older, unspayed females.

 *Unlike women, female dogs do not stop menstruating when they reach middle age, although the heat becomes shorter and lighter. However, a litter takes a heavy toll on older females.*

### Stages and Signs of Heat

The difference between humans and dogs is that women cannot get pregnant during their period, while female dogs can ONLY get pregnant during their heat. The stages of a heat cycle are:

**Proestrus** – this is the first stage and lasts around nine days. Male dogs are attracted to her, but she is not yet interested, so she may hold her tail close to her body. You will notice that her vulva (external sex organ, or pink bit under her tail) becomes swollen. If you're not sure if she's in heat, hold a tissue against her vulva – does it turn pink or red? The blood is usually light red or brown, turning more watery after a week or so. She may also urinate more frequently.

**Oestrus** - this is when eggs are released from ovaries and the optimum time for breeding. Males are interested in her - and the feelings are very much reciprocated! Oestrus also lasts around nine days.

**Dioestrus -** her body produces hormones whether or not she is pregnant. All the hormones are present; only the puppies are missing, if she hasn't been mated. This can sometimes lead to what is known as a *"false pregnancy."* During this stage she is no longer interested in males.

The canine heat cycle is a complex mix of hormonal, behavioural, and physical changes. Each dog is different. Some show behavioural changes, such as becoming more clingy or irritable, going off their food, shedding hair, mounting other dogs or your leg, or sulking in their beds.

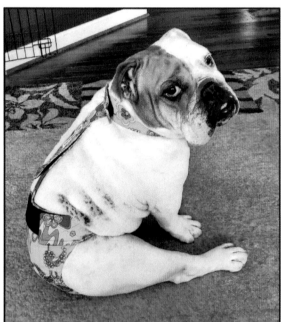

Most dogs lick themselves to keep clean, but many Bulldogs can't reach. They tend to be messier than some other breeds and may leave blood trails around the house. One option is to buy doggie diapers, or nappies *(pictured).* Keep an eye on her until she gets used to one to make sure she doesn't chew it.

Even with a diaper on, leakages occasionally occur and a few female Bulldogs will take advantage and eliminate in them.

**FACT** *When a female is on heat, she produces pheromones that attract male dogs. Because dogs have a sense of smell several hundred times stronger than ours, your girl on heat is a magnet for all the neighbourhood males. It is believed that they can detect the scent of a female on heat up to two miles away!*

They may congregate around your house or follow you around the park - if you are brave or foolish enough to venture out there while she is in season - waiting for their chance to prove their manhood (or mutthood in their case).

It is amazing the lengths some intact males will go to impregnate a female on heat. Travelling great distances to follow her scent, jumping over barriers, digging under fences, chewing through doors or walls and sneaking through hedges are just some of the tactics employed by canine Casanovas on the loose. Love is a powerful thing - and canine lust even more so. A dog living in the same house as a female in heat has even been known to mate with her through the bars of a crate!

To avoid an unwanted pregnancy, you must keep a close eye on her throughout her heat and not allow her to wander unsupervised - and that includes the garden or yard unless you 100% know it is safe. Determined male dogs can jump and scramble over high fences. Keep her on a leash if you go out on walks and definitely don't let her run free anywhere that you might come across other dogs. You can compensate for the restrictions by playing more games at home to keep her mentally and physically active.

The instinct to mate will trump all of her training. Her hormones are raging and, during **her most fertile days, which are Day 9 to 10 of heat for five or more days,** she is ready, able and ... VERY willing! If you do have an intact male, you need to physically keep him in a separate place or kennel.

The desire to mate is all-consuming and can be accompanied by howling or "marking" (urinating) indoors from a frustrated Romeo.

You can also buy a spray that masks the natural oestrus scent. Marketed under such attractive names as "*Bitch Spray,*" these lessen, but don't eliminate, the scent. They may reduce the amount of unwanted attention, but are not a complete deterrent.

There is no canine contraceptive, so if your female is unspayed, you need to keep her under supervision during her heat cycle - which may be as long as three or four weeks.

There is a *"morning after pill"* – actually a series of oestrogen tablets or an injection - which some vets may administer after an unwanted coupling, but side effects can be severe, including Pyometra (a potentially life-threatening infection of the womb), bone marrow suppression and infertility.

# Neutering - Pros and Cons

Once a straightforward subject, this is currently a hot potato in the dog world. Dogs that are kept purely as pets – i.e. not for showing, breeding or working – are often spayed or neutered. There is also the life-threatening risk of *Pyometra* in unspayed middle-aged females. A major argument for neutering of both sexes is that there is already too much indiscriminate breeding of dogs in the world.

One issue all owners have to consider is that both spaying and neutering require the dog to be anaesthetised and this is not without risk for Bulldogs.

As you will read in **Chapter 15. Bulldog Rescue**, it is estimated that 1,000 dogs are put to sleep every hour in the USA alone. It is for this reason that rescue organisations in North America, the UK and Australia neuter all dogs that they rehome.

Some areas in the United States, e.g. LA, have even adopted a compulsory sterilisation policy, aimed at: *"reducing and eventually eliminating the thousands of euthanizations conducted in Los Angeles' animal shelters every year."*

The RSPCA, along with most UK vets, also promotes the benefits of neutering. It is estimated that more than half of all dogs in the UK are spayed or castrated.

Another point is that you may not have a choice. Some breeders' Puppy Contracts may stipulate that, except in special circumstances, you agree to neuter your Bulldog as a Condition of Sale. Others may state that you need the breeder's permission to breed your dog.

**The Science**

While early spay/neuter has been traditionally recommended, there is scientific evidence that for some breeds it may be better to wait until the dog is through puberty. Armed with the facts, it is for each individual owner to decide what is best for their dog – unless there was a Spay/Neuter clause in your Puppy Contract.

Four UC Davis School of Veterinary Medicine studies involving veterinary records for thousands of Golden Retrievers, Labradors and German Shepherds found that spaying or neutering before the age of one increased the risk of one or more of the following: certain cancers, joint disorders and urinary incontinence. The one area where early neutering was beneficial was mammary cancer, the equivalent of breast cancer in women.

A 2018 article, published in The IAABC Journal (International Association of Animal Behavior Consultants), highlights the pros and cons of neutering. It's a bit technical, but worth a read: https://fall2018.iaabcjournal.org/2018/10/31/spay-and-neuter-surgery-effects-on-dogs or Google **"IAABC early neuter in dogs."** Skip to the table at the end to read the major pros and cons. As yet there have been no specific studies involving Bulldogs and neutering.

.....................................................................................................................................................

## Spaying

Spaying is the term traditionally used to describe the sterilisation of a female dog so that she cannot become pregnant. This is normally done by a procedure called an **"ovariohysterectomy"** and

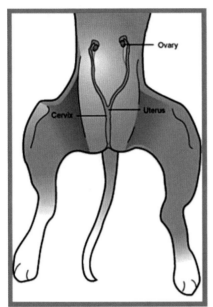

involves the removal of the ovaries and uterus, or womb. Although this is a routine operation, it is major abdominal surgery and she has to be anaesthetised.

One less invasive option offered by some vets is an **"ovariectomy,"** which removes the ovaries, but leaves the womb intact. It requires only a small incision and can even be carried out by laparoscopy, or keyhole surgery.

The dog is anaesthetised for a shorter time and there is less risk of infection or excess bleeding during surgery.

One major reason often given for not opting for an ovariectomy is that the female still runs the risk of Pyometra later in life. However, there is currently little or no scientific evidence of females that have undergone an ovariectomy contracting Pyometra afterwards.

If a female is spayed before her first cycle, she will have an almost zero risk of mammary cancer. Even after the first heat, spaying reduces the risk of this cancer considerably. The risk of mammary cancer in unspayed female dogs can be as high as one in four.

**FACT ❱** *Spaying is a much more serious operation for females than neutering is for males. It involves an internal abdominal operation, whereas the neutering procedure is carried out on the male's testicles, which are outside his abdomen.*

As with any major procedure, there are pros and cons.

**For:**

- 🐾 Spaying prevents infections, cancer and other diseases of the uterus and ovaries. A spayed female will have a greatly reduced risk of mammary cancer

- 🐾 Spaying eliminates the risk of Pyometra, which results from hormonal changes in the female's reproductive tract. It also reduces hormonal changes that can interfere with the treatment of diseases like diabetes or epilepsy

- 🐾 You no longer have to cope with any potential mess caused by bleeding inside the house during heat cycles

- 🐾 You don't have to guard your female against unwanted attention from males

- 🐾 Spaying can reduce behaviour problems, such as roaming, aggression towards other dogs, anxiety or fear (not all canine experts agree)

- 🐾 A spayed dog does not contribute to the pet overpopulation problem

*These photographs are reproduced courtesy of Guy Bunce and Chloe Spencer, of Dizzywaltz Labrador Retrievers, Berkshire, England. The left image shows four-year-old Disney shortly after a full spay (ovariohysterectomy). The right one shows Disney several weeks later.*

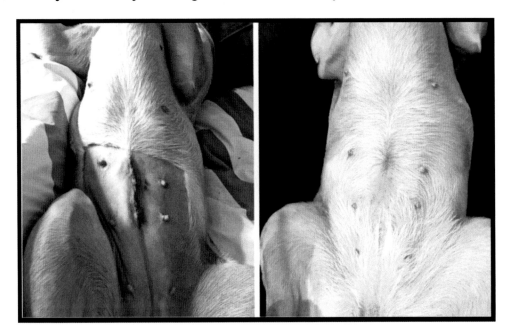

## Against:

❖ Complications can occur, including an abnormal reaction to the anaesthetic, bleeding, stitches breaking and infections; ***these are not common***

❖ Occasionally there can be long-term effects connected to hormonal changes. These include weight gain or less stamina, which can occur years after spaying

❖ Some females may suffer urinary incontinence

❖ Cost. This can range from £100 to £250 in the UK, more for keyhole spaying, and approximately $150-$500 at a vet's clinic in the USA, or from around $50 at a low-cost clinic, for those that qualify

## Neutering

Neutering male dogs involves castration, or the removal of the testicles. This can be a difficult decision for some owners, as it causes a drop in the pet's testosterone levels, which some humans – men in particular! - feel affects the quality of their dog's life. Fortunately, dogs do not think like people, and male dogs do not miss their testicles or the loss of sex.

 *Dogs working in service or for charities are often neutered and this does not impair their ability to perform any of their duties.*

There are countless unwanted puppies, many of which are destroyed. There is also the huge problem of a lack of knowledge from the owners of some dogs, resulting in the production of poor puppies with congenital health or temperament problems.

Technically, neutering can be carried out at any age over eight weeks, provided both testicles have descended. However, recent scientific studies, such as the ones already outlined, are coming down on the side of waiting until the dog is one year or older.

Dogs neutered before puberty tend to grow a little larger than dogs done later. This is because testosterone is involved in the process that stops growth, so the bones grow for longer without testosterone.

Surgery is relatively straightforward, and complications are less common and less severe than with spaying. Although he will feel tender afterwards, your dog should return to his normal self within a couple of days.

When a dog comes out of surgery, his scrotum, or sacs that held the testicles, will be swollen and it may look like nothing has been done. It is normal for these to shrink slowly in the days following surgery. Here are the main pros and cons:

**For:**

- Castration is a simple procedure, and dogs usually make a swift recovery afterwards

- Behaviour problems such as aggression and roaming can be reduced

- Unwanted sexual behaviour, such as mounting people or objects, is usually reduced or eliminated

- Testicular problems such as infections, cancer and torsion (painful rotation of the testicle) are eradicated

- Prostate disease, common in older male dogs, is less likely to occur

- A submissive intact male dog may be targeted by other dogs. After he has been neutered, he will no longer produce testosterone and so will not be regarded as much of a threat by the other males, so he is less likely to be bullied

- A neutered dog is not fathering unwanted puppies

**Against:**

- UCI Davis studies seem to indicate that some dogs neutered before one year old are slightly more likely to have certain health issues

- As with any surgery, there can be bleeding afterwards; you should keep an eye on your dog after the procedure. Infections can also occur, generally caused by the dog licking the wound, so try and prevent him doing this. If he persists, use an E-collar. In the **vast majority** of cases, these problems do not occur

- Some dogs' coats may be affected; this also applies to spaying. Supplementing the diet with fish oil can compensate for this

- Cost - this starts at around £80 in the UK. In the USA this might cost upwards from $100 at a private veterinary clinic, or from $50 at a low cost or Humane Society clinic

**New Techniques**

Two other phrases you may hear are *"tubal ligation"* or *"vasectomy."* *Tubal ligation* is the tying of a female's Fallopian tubes and a *vasectomy* is the clamping shut of the sperm ducts from the male's testicles. Many veterinary papers have been written on these topics, but as yet, not many vets offer them as options, possibly because they have not been trained to carry out these procedures.

In both cases, unlike with spaying and neutering, the dog continues to produce hormones, but is unable to get pregnant or father puppies. With further evidence of the positive effects of hormones, these operations could become more common in the future – although more vets will first have to be trained.

There's a new non-surgical procedure to sterilise male dogs called *"Zeutering."* It involves injecting zinc gluconate into the dog's testicles. Dogs are lightly sedated, but not anaesthetised. It's inexpensive, there's little recovery time and no stitches.

However, studies show that Zeutering is only 99% effective, and its long-term effects are still being researched. And while it makes dogs sterile, they still retain some of their testosterone.

Therefore, habits that usually disappear with traditional castration, such as marking, roaming, following females on heat and aggression towards other males, remain. Zeutering isn't for every dog, but worth discussing with your vet.

**Urban Myths**

**Neutering or spaying will spoil the dog's character -** There is no evidence that any of the positive characteristics of your dog will be altered. He or she will be just as obedient, playful and loyal as before. Neutering may reduce aggression or roaming in male dogs, because they are no longer competing to mate with a female.

**A female needs to have at least one litter -** There is no proven physical or mental benefit to a female having a litter.

**Mating is natural and necessary -** We tend to ascribe human emotions to our dogs, but they do not think emotionally about sex or having and raising a family. Unlike humans, their desire to mate or breed is entirely physical, triggered by the chemicals called hormones within their body. Without these hormones – i.e. after neutering or spaying – the desire disappears or is greatly reduced.

**Male dogs will behave better if they can mate -** This is simply not true; sex does not make a dog behave better. In fact, it can have the opposite effect. Having mated once, a male may show an increased interest in females. He may also consider his status elevated, which may make him harder to control or call back.

 *If you are considering having your dog spayed or neutered, discuss the optimum age for the procedure with your breeder and vet – and do your research. Many vets still promote early spay and neuter.*

## Pregnancy

Regardless of how big or small the dog is, a canine pregnancy lasts for 58 to 65 days; 63 days is average. This is true of all breeds of dog from the Chihuahua to the Great Dane. Sometimes pregnancy is referred to as *"the gestation period."*

A female should have a pre-natal check-up after mating. The vet should answer any questions about type of food, supplements and extra care needed, as well as informing the owner about any physical changes likely to occur in your female.

There is a blood test available that measures levels of **relaxin**. This is a hormone produced by the ovary and the developing placenta, and pregnancy can be detected by monitoring relaxin levels as early as 22 to 27 days after mating. The levels are high throughout pregnancy and then decline rapidly after the female has given birth.

A vet can usually see the puppies (but not how many) using Ultrasound from around the same time. X-rays carried out 45 days into the pregnancy show the puppies' skeletons and give the breeder a good idea of the number of puppies. They can also help to give the vet more information, which is particularly useful if the female has had previous whelping problems.

**Signs of Pregnancy**

- After mating, many females become more affectionate. However, a few may become uncharacteristically irritable and maybe even a little aggressive!

- She may produce a slight clear discharge from her vagina one month after mating

- Three or four weeks after mating, some females experience morning sickness – if this is the case, feed little and often. She may seem more tired than usual

- She may seem slightly depressed or show a drop in appetite. These signs can also mean there are other problems, so you should consult your vet

- Her teats will become more prominent, pink and erect 25 to 30 days into the pregnancy. Later on, you may notice a fluid coming from them

- Her body weight will noticeably increase about 35 days after mating

- Her abdomen will become noticeably larger from around Day 40, although first-time mums and females carrying few puppies may not show as much

- Many pregnant females' appetite will increase in the second half of pregnancy

- Her nesting instincts will kick in as the delivery date approaches. She may seem restless or scratch her bed or the floor - she may even rip and shred items like your comforter, curtains or carpeting!

- During the last week of pregnancy, females often start to look for a safe place for whelping. Some seem to become confused, wanting to be with their owners and at the same time wanting to prepare their nest. If the female is having a C-section, she should still be allowed to nest in a whelping box with layers of newspaper, which she will scratch and dig as the time approaches

 *If your female Bulldog becomes pregnant – either by design or accident - your first step should be to consult a vet.*

Bulldogs often have small litters. Three or four puppies is typical, but it could be more or less. The number depends on factors such as bloodlines, the age of the dam and sire (young and older dogs have smaller litters), health and diet of the dam, and the size of the gene pool; the higher the COI (Coefficient of Inbreeding), the smaller the litter.

## False Pregnancies

Occasionally, unspayed females may display signs of a false pregnancy. Before dogs were domesticated, it was common for female dogs to have false pregnancies and to lactate (produce milk). This female would then nourish puppies if their own mother died.

False pregnancies occur 60 to 80 days after the female was in heat - about the time she would have given birth – and are generally nothing to worry about for an owner. The exact cause is unknown; however, hormonal imbalances are thought to play an important role. Some dogs have shown symptoms within three to four days of spaying; these include:

- ❧ Making a nest
- ❧ Mothering or adopting toys and other objects
- ❧ Producing milk (lactating)
- ❧ Appetite fluctuations
- ❧ Barking or whining a lot
- ❧ Restlessness, depression or anxiety
- ❧ Swollen abdomen
- ❧ She might even appear to go into labour

Under no circumstances should you restrict your Bulldog's water supply to try and prevent her from producing milk. This is dangerous as she can become dehydrated.

Some unspayed females may have a false pregnancy with each heat cycle. Spaying during a false pregnancy may actually prolong the condition, so better to wait until it is over to have her spayed.

 *False pregnancy is not a disease, but an exaggerated response to normal hormonal changes. Even if left untreated, it almost always resolves itself.*

However, if your dog appears physically ill or the behavioural changes are severe enough to worry about, visit your vet. He or she may prescribe *Galastop*, which stops milk production and quickly returns the hormones to normal. In rare cases, hormone treatment may be necessary.

Generally, dogs experiencing false pregnancies do not have serious long-term problems, as the behaviour disappears when the hormones return to their normal levels in two to three weeks.

## Pyometra

One exception is *Pyometra,* a serious and potentially deadly infection of the womb, caused by a hormonal abnormality. It normally follows a heat cycle in which fertilisation did not occur and the dog typically starts showing symptoms within two to four months.

Commonly referred to as *"pyo,"* there are *open* and *closed* forms of the disease. Open pyo is usually easy to identify with a smelly discharge, so prompt treatment is easy. Closed pyo is often harder to identify and you may not even notice anything until your girl becomes feverish and lethargic. When this happens, it is very serious and time is of the essence. Typically, vets will recommend immediate spaying in an effort to save her life.

Signs of Pyometra are excessive drinking and urination, with the female trying to lick a white discharge from her vagina. She may also have a slight temperature. If the condition becomes severe, her back legs will become weak, possibly to the point where she can no longer get up without help.

Pyometra can be fatal. It needs to be dealt with promptly by a vet, who will give the dog intravenous fluids and antibiotics for several days. In most cases this is followed by spaying.

......................................................................................................................................................

## Should I Breed From My Bulldog?

The short and very simple answer is: **NO!** Not unless you do a lot of research, then find a mentor, get expert advice and find a vet experienced with Bulldogs.

More than with any other type of dog, the Bulldog is a breed where specialised knowledge is an absolute must. The pitfalls and risk to life with Bulldog breeding are enormous if you don't really know what you are doing.

 *Breeding is a very expensive, time-consuming and complicated procedure with the Bulldog, which is perhaps the most difficult breed of all to birth.*

Bulldogs are on a "watch list" in the UK of dogs which have had traits bred into them which have inadvertently led to health problems. Today's responsible breeders are continually looking at ways of improving the health of the Bulldog through selective breeding.

When it comes to reproduction, the Bulldog has very specific requirements. You can't just put a male and a female together, let them get on with it and then sit back and wait for a litter of gorgeous wrinkly pups to arrive two months later. It won't.

For a start, most Bulldogs do not mate naturally; instead many females are artificially inseminated with specially stored semen from a syringe. With their deep, heavy chests, short legs and tendency to overheat quickly, most male Bulldogs cannot successfully mate without human assistance.

This may also lead to frustration which can in turn lead to aggression, overheating or even injury. And when the patience of a Bulldog female runs out, she may attack her stud.

In Britain, some breeders use a breeding board or table which keeps the female in place and takes some of the male's weight off her body. Stud dogs are trained in the art of mounting and mating – with human assistance where necessary! Another option is for a third person to hold the female while the stud mates with her - similar to what goes on in the horse world.

A further reason for artificial insemination is that VD and herpes in dogs is as real as it is in humans. Herpes can kill a litter and render the mother unable to breed in future, and artificial insemination removes this risk as all the semen is screened.

**FACT** *According to an in-depth UK study involving 36,000 dogs from 170 breeds published in the Journal of Small Animal Practice, only one in seven Bulldogs give birth naturally, the other 86% have Caesarean or C-Sections – the figure is even higher in the US.*

*Typical veterinary fees for a Bulldog C-section are in four figures - and this is NOT covered by normal pet insurance.*

Physically, Bulldogs are front-loaded with narrow hips, while puppies have relatively massive heads and very wide shoulders, which make passing through the pelvis and birth canal extremely painful – if not downright impossible in most cases.

Well-bred Bulldog puppies cost thousands of dollars or pounds. But despite this, many dedicated Bulldog breeders make little or no money from the practice, due to the high costs of veterinary fees, health screening, stud fees and expensive special nutrition and care for the female and her pups.

Responsible breeding is backed up by genetic information and screening as well as a thorough knowledge of the desired traits of the Bulldog. It is definitely not an occupation for the amateur hobbyist.

 *Breeding is not just about the look or colour of the puppies; health and temperament are very important factors too.*

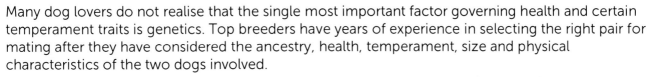

Many dog lovers do not realise that the single most important factor governing health and certain temperament traits is genetics. Top breeders have years of experience in selecting the right pair for mating after they have considered the ancestry, health, temperament, size and physical characteristics of the two dogs involved.

They may travel hundreds of miles to find the right mate for their dog. Some of them also show their dogs. Anyone breeding from their Bulldog must first consider these questions:

- ❧ **Did you get your Bulldog from a good, ethical breeder?** Dogs sold in pet stores and on general sales websites are seldom good specimens and can be unhealthy.

- ❧ **Does your dog conform to the Breed Standard?** Do not breed from a Bulldog that is not an excellent specimen in all respects, hoping that somehow the puppies will turn out better. They won't. Talk with experienced breeders and ask them for an honest assessment of your dog

- ❧ **Do you understand COI and its implications?** COI stands for Coefficient of Inbreeding. It measures the common ancestors of a dam and sire and indicates the probability of how genetically similar they are

- ❧ **Do your dog and the mate both breathe easily?**

- ❧ **Have your dog, the mate and their parents been screened for Bulldog health issues which can be inherited by the puppies?** Has your dog got OFA or BVA certificates for genetic diseases such as hip dysplasia and eye disease?

- ❧ **Have you researched his or her lineage to make sure there are no problems lurking in the background?** Puppies inherit traits from their grandparents and great-grandparents as well as from their mother and father

- ❧ **Are you 100% sure that your dog has no temperament issues which could be inherited by the puppies?**

- ❧ **Are you positive that the same can be said for the dog you are planning on breeding yours with?**

- ❧ **Do you have expert knowledge of Bulldog genetics and health, as well as the know-how and finances to successfully deal with keeping the mother healthy through pregnancy, birthing and C-sections, and care of the puppies and mother after birth?**

- ❦ **Is your female two years old or older and at least in her second heat cycle?** Female Bulldogs should not be bred until they are physically mature, have had their joints screened, and are robust enough to whelp and care for a litter. Even then, not all females are suitable

- ❦ **Giving birth takes a lot out of a female Bulldog - are you prepared to put yours through that?**

- ❦ **Some Bulldogs are poor mothers, which means that you have to look after the puppies 24/7.** Even if they are not, they need daily help from the owner to rear their young

- ❦ **Can you offer a health guarantee against genetic defects or other health issues with each puppy?**

- ❦ **Will you be able to find good homes for all the puppies and are you prepared to take one or more back if necessary?** Good breeders do not let their precious puppies go to just any home. They want to be sure that the new owners will take good care of their dogs for their lifetime

Having said that, experts are not born, they learn their trade over many years. Anyone who is seriously considering getting into the specialised art of breeding Bulldogs should first spend time researching the breed and its genetics. Make sure you are going into Bulldog breeding for the right reasons and not primarily to make money - ask yourself how you intend to improve the breed.

Visit dog shows and make contact with established breeders. Find yourself a mentor, somebody who is already very familiar with the breed and make sure you have a vet who is also familiar with Bulldogs and able to perform a C-section at whatever time of day or night it may be required. If you are determined to breed from your Bulldog - and breed properly - do your research. Read as much as you can; one useful resource is *"Book of the Bitch"* by J. M. Evans and Kay White.

To find a good breeder: In the USA, visit the AKC website and ideally look for a *Bred with H.E.A.R.T.* breeder, or one who has attained Platinum, Gold or Silver status as a Breeder of Merit. Visit the Bulldog Club of America website for a list of events involving Bulldogs, and ask for details of members near you.

In the UK, go to the *Find a Dog Club* page for Bulldogs on the Kennel Club website. You can also find KC Approved Breeders on a county by county basis on the website.

You may have the most wonderful Bulldog in the world, but don't enter the world of canine breeding without knowledge and ethics. Don't do it for the money or the cute factor – or to show the kids "The Miracle of Birth!" Breeding poor examples only brings heartache in the long run when health or temperament issues develop. Our strong advice is: When it comes to Bulldogs, leave it to the experts.

With thanks to Kathy Jacobsen, of Rely-a-Bull Bulldogs, for her invaluable assistance with this chapter.

# 15. Bulldog Rescue

Not everyone who wants a Bulldog gets one as a puppy from a breeder. Some people prefer to offer a good life to a rescue Bulldog. What could be kinder and more rewarding than giving a poor, abandoned dog a loving home for the rest of his life?

Not much really; adoption saves lives and gives unfortunate dogs a second chance of happiness. The problem of homeless dogs is truly depressing. It's a big issue in Britain, but even worse in the US, where the sheer numbers in kill shelters are hard to comprehend. In *"Don't Dump The Dog,"* Randy Grim states that 1,000 dogs are being put to sleep every hour in the States.

If you decide to offer a home to one of these poor souls, do it with your eyes wide open. Offering a home to a rescue Bulldog is not recommended if you are a first-time dog owner. The Bulldog – even a healthy, well behaved one - is a breed which requires specialist knowledge and care.

Some of the most common reasons for giving up a Bulldog for rehoming are:

- ❧ Lifestyle changes, such as new partner, new job, or moving home

- ❧ Finances – the owner can no longer afford to keep the dog

- ❧ Bulldog health issues – the owner has not got the money and/or time needed to deal with them

- ❧ Poor behaviour, such as chewing, biting, not being housetrained, being too rough

- ❧ Lack of time. What may have seemed like a great idea slowly becomes too much of a burden when owners realise how much time and care a Bulldog requires

This is what the Bulldog Club of America Rescue Network (BCARN) has to say:

"A Bulldog may not be the right choice for every family. Living with a Bulldog can be very rewarding, but you must be committed to meeting the Bulldog's particular needs.

**"Some Things to Consider** - Bulldogs are perpetual children: they never grow up. A Bulldog does best in a loving environment, free from fear and neglect. They are happiest when with people and require lots of attention from people. When left alone, Bulldogs can be very destructive. They may chew throughout their lifetimes. They may need to be crated when they are not being supervised. A Bulldog should never be left unattended in your backyard. Not only is it dangerous to your Bulldog's wellbeing, but Bulldogs are often targeted for theft.

**"Possible Health Problems** - Bulldogs have numerous known genetic defects and are subject to various illnesses that affect many breeds. Common Bulldog health problems you may encounter include: elongated soft palate, small trachea, allergies, dermatitis, demodectic mange, eye lid anomalies, hip dysplasia and heart problems. Some of them have a tendency toward self-mutilation (especially if they have itchy skin), so owners should watch carefully for signs of skin irritation and scratching. If you are adopting an older dog, many of these conditions will already have been identified.

"Twenty-four hour care by a qualified veterinarian must be available. Since not all veterinarians are knowledgeable about the health problems Bulldogs may have, you should consult experienced Bulldog owners or the rescue center to find a capable veterinarian. Any veterinarian who will be doing surgery on your Bulldog should have previous experience with putting Bulldogs under anesthesia.

**"Danger of Overheating -** Bulldogs are extremely intolerant of heat. They must be kept in an air-conditioned area with limited trips outside when the outside temperature is over 80 degrees or the humidity is high. Close supervision is required during outside activity, especially in spring and summer to prevent over-exertion leading to over-heating. They also are not usually capable of prolonged physical activity whether the temperature is very warm or cold: a Bulldog is not for someone who enjoys taking a dog for long walks through the countryside.

**"After Adoption -** Although all Bulldogs that we place are subjected to a thorough veterinary examination and are evaluated for soundness of temperament, we do not guarantee that they will not have any problems in their new homes. In fact, a period of adjustment is expected during which the Bulldog and the new owner will be getting acquainted with each other, and the Bulldog will be "settling in" to a new routine.

"If we have any doubts about a Bulldog's ability to deal with certain situations, we put restrictions on the type of home in which it will be placed (for example, by requiring no young children and/or no other pets). We also provide guidelines for the new owners to ensure that they are aware of any special treatment the Bulldog may require. With the application of a little common sense in following the guidelines, new owners will find the transition into owning a rescue Bulldog to be relatively simple."

## An Insight into Temperament

BCARN also produced an AKC Gazette article entitled *The Importance of Temperament* which gives a great insight into the Bulldog and the demands on an owner:

"When selecting a pet, the most important breed characteristic to consider by far is its temperament or disposition. Failure to thoroughly investigate temperament is the biggest mistake anyone can make in selecting a pet, especially a Bulldog.

"In my experience, far too many people select a dog based solely on its physical appearance, and those who do so usually live to regret it. People who shop for a pet the same way they shop for a new car, a piece of furniture or designer jeans should never own one.

"If it is a status symbol you want, please do not even consider buying a Bulldog! You and the dog are sure to be disappointed in each other. For one thing, the modern Bulldog cannot tolerate isolation. Some breeds are able to thrive on only occasional human contact, but Bulldogs simply cannot stand to be ignored. They crave attention, and they will do almost anything to get it.

"To the dismay of their owners, many Bulldogs prefer to pursue the role of a lapdog. They fail to comprehend that some humans find their typical weight of 50 to 60 pounds less than comfortable on their laps.

"It is nearly impossible to lavish too much love and attention on a Bulldog - and only he decides when he has had enough of it. When he has had enough loving, he will finally wander off somewhere to find peace and quiet. If you're not a hands-on type of dog lover who enjoys close and frequent contact and a few wet kisses, a less affectionate pet may better satisfy your needs. The Bulldog's constant craving for attention and the need to entertain humans and be entertained by them is not for everyone.

"There is a limit, however, to how much strenuous physical activity a typical Bulldog can safely tolerate. Their short muzzles and narrow windpipes, relative to the size of their bodies, limits their oxygen intake and causes them to become easily winded. This can result in acute respiratory distress and sometimes death. Like it or not, most Bulldogs do not have great physical endurance. They are more like short-distance sprinters than long-distance runners. Bulldogs don't realize this; your own common sense must prevail.

"Neither do Bulldogs respond obediently to heavy-handed physical discipline. Despite 1,000 years of selective breeding, most Bulldogs I am familiar with, both male and female, instinctively detest and resist violence or the threat of it. This is especially evident with regard to children. A screaming child immediately causes grave concern and routinely triggers a decidedly protective response. They seem to sense trouble, and they are likely to intervene in their own special way to end the disturbance.

"Nonetheless, Bulldogs are not easily provoked by other dogs unless they are seriously threatened or attacked. A Bulldog that has been carefully bred for temperament and lovingly cared for and properly socialized from birth likes to meet other dogs and strangers. Visitors to the household are always welcomed, often enthusiastically. It never occurs to a Bulldog that other dogs and other people might be less than friendly. An intruder might even be a welcome guest, but it is difficult to say what might happen when you are away.

"Modern Bulldogs are not by nature good guard dogs or attack dogs. However, they are fairly reliable watchdogs. They will normally alert you to any unusual activity in the home or yard.

"A common misconception is that Bulldogs are "one-man" dogs. It may sometimes seem apparent that one family member is preferred over another, but Bulldogs regard each family member as their own personal property. Bulldogs can be possessive to a fault. You don't own them, they own you, and don't ever forget it! If you can't appreciate their possessive nature, you certainly will not appreciate their inherent stubbornness and determination. Training takes lots of patience, but they can be successfully trained for obedience and agility competition.

"Unless they choose to behave otherwise, I don't believe there is a more obstinate creature alive. And while a Bulldog might appear to be lazy or stupid, that's only a facade."

There is, however, a ray of sunshine for some of these dogs. Every year many thousands of people in the UK, North America and countries all around the world adopt a rescue dog and the story often has a happy ending.

........................................................................................................................................

## The Dog's Point of View...

If you are serious about adopting a Bulldog, do so with the right motives and with your eyes wide open. If you're expecting a perfect dog, you could be in for a shock. Rescue dogs can and do become wonderful companions, but a lot depends on you.

Bulldogs thrive on lots of attention and love from their owners. Those that end up in rescue centres may be traumatised; some have health problems.

They don't understand why they have been abandoned, neglected or badly treated by their beloved owners and may arrive at your home with "baggage" of their own until they adjust to being part of a loving family again. This may take time. Patience is the key to help the dog to adjust to her new surroundings and family and to learn to love and trust again. Ask yourself a few questions before you take the plunge and fill in the adoption forms:

- 🐾 Are you prepared to accept and deal with any problems - such as bad behaviour, aggression, anxiety, chewing, jumping up or eliminating in the house - which a rescue dog may initially display?

- 🐾 Just how much time can you spend with your new dog to help her integrate back into normal family life?

- 🐾 Can you take time off work to be at home and help her settle in at the beginning?

- 🐾 Are you prepared to take on a new addition to your family that may live for several more years?

- 🐾 Will you guarantee that dog a home for life - even if she later develops health issues?

What could be worse for the unlucky dog than to be abandoned again if things don't work out between you?

## Rescue Groups

Adopting a rescue dog is a big commitment for all involved. It is not a cheap way of getting a Bulldog and shouldn't be viewed as such. It could cost you several hundred dollars - or pounds. You'll have adoption fees to pay and often vaccination and veterinary bills as well as worm and flea medication and spaying or neutering. Make sure you're aware of the full cost before committing. You may even have to wait a while until a suitable dog comes up.

### USA

**The Bulldog Club of America Rescue Network (BCARN)** is the largest umbrella Bulldog rescue organisation in North America, with volunteers in the US and Canada. It only rescues purebred Bulldogs, which are also sometimes referred to as "English" or "British" Bulldogs.

Anyone interested in adopting one will require screening and has to complete the detailed online adoption form before contacting a local BCA Rescue Network representative. This contains a number of questions to help decide if you would be a suitable person or family to adopt a Bulldog. The questions include:

- 🐾 Why do you want to adopt a bulldog?

- 🐾 What age bulldog are you willing to accept – puppy/up to age three/up to age six/any age? (BCARN does not often get puppies offered for adoption)

- 🐾 Must the bulldog be good with children?

- 🐾 Must the bulldog get along with other dogs in your household and/or with visiting dogs?

- 🐾 Are you willing to accept a bulldog needing additional care? (If yes, which level of care are you comfortable providing – Accept (Daily medications, special food, etc), Accept (Frequent medications, house training issues, difficulty walking, behaviour issues, etc) Accept (blindness, deafness, incontinence, spina bifida, seizure disorder, etc) Please Note: ALL Bulldogs require some daily care.

- 🐾 Employment information

- 🐾 Details of household members

- 🐾 Who will be responsible for caring for the Bulldog?

- 🐾 Is anyone in the house allergic to dogs?

- 🐾 Are all members of the household in favour of adopting a Bulldog?

- 🐾 Type of home and whether you have a fenced yard

- 🐾 How will the dog be exercised, how often, and who will supervise the dog while outdoors?

- 🐾 Does your home have stairs that the Bulldog will have to go up and down?

- 🐾 Are your home and car air-conditioned?

- 🐾 Do you have a swimming pool, pond or other body of water near your home?

- 🐾 Where will the Bulldog be kept during the day - and night?

- 🐾 Are any family members at home during the day time?

- 🐾 Do you expect any changes in your family in the next few years?

- 🐾 Do you own any other cats or dogs?

- 🐾 Do all your pets receive regular veterinary care and are they up-to-date on vaccinations?

BCARN also needs rescue volunteers. If you think you are up to the challenge, contact the BCA Rescue network representative nearest you or the co-coordinator for your area of the country. Details can be found on the BCA rescue website at www.rescuebulls.org

Other Bulldog-specific organizations with their own websites include:

California – San Diego Bulldog Rescue www.sdbr.org

Southern California Bulldog Rescue www.socalbulldogrescue.org

Northern California Bulldog Rescue www.norcalbulldogrescue.org

Chicago English Bulldog Rescue (covers the Midwest) www.ebullymatch.com

Detroit Bulldog Rescue www.detroitbulldogrescue.org

Florida: www.floridaenglishbulldogrescue.com

Illinois, Wisconsin and NW Indiana www.adoptabull.org

Illinois English Bulldog Rescue www.ilenglishbulldogrescue.org

Indiana www.indianabulldogrescue.com

Mid Atlantic http://midatlanticbulldogrescue.com

Mideastern States – On the Rebound Bulldog Rescue www.otrbulldogrescue.org

New York and New England http://longislandbulldogrescue.org

NJ, PA, DE and MD www.guidestar.org/profile/20-4677825

Smoky Mountains Bulldog Club Rescue http://smbcarn.org

## Canada

In Alberta and British Columbia contact Kodie Burgess by email: bulldogwrangler@yahoo.com or phone 971-267-0744. In Ontario and Quebec contact Laurette Richin at 631-689-6245.

## UK

**Bulldog Rescue and Rehoming Trust** (Registered Charity number 1115009)

The Trust was set up over 40 years ago and has rehomed around 3,000 Bulldogs as well as giving free advice, memorials and operating a list for lost and stolen Bulldogs. The charity has around 80 volunteers, who travel over 10,000 miles a year checking out new homes and collecting Bulldogs for rehoming and fostering. The total annual veterinary bill can be anything from £20,000 to £30,000.

The most common reasons for a Bulldog needing a new home in the UK is divorce or separation, then a new baby, followed by house moves and emigration abroad. This is what the Trust has to say:

"We are a mainly voluntary organisation, offering a Rescue and Rehoming service for pure bred bulldogs across the UK, who, for whatever reason cannot stay where they are. We are not a dog's home or a shelter and aim to always do our best for every bulldog we are asked to help. We will subsequently stand by him for the rest of his life, offering support, education and advice to his new owners whenever it is required.

"Only a few bulldogs end up in rescue because they have been abused, mis-treated or abandoned, the majority of bulldogs looking for a second chance are simply victims of circumstance – i.e. divorce, new baby or a change in the family situation. All the owner wants is a good pet home and by using our rehoming service they are going some way to ensure the new home is the right home first time. Homes are selected on a system of area and suitability from our extensive waiting list of people across the country, in most cases we are able to work within the dog's own area and find a home that matches his criteria.

"Adoption fees, fund raising and donations are our only means of funding – every bulldog that simply needs a good home will help us to pay for those that require veterinary treatment, transportation or fostering. Our adoption fees are nominal – regardless of how much we had to spend on the dog before we could rehome it.

"Everything is coordinated from one central point and thanks to our dedicated team of volunteers across the UK we can act quickly if necessary, home check potential new homes and supply short stay foster care where required.

"Please feel free to contact us if you would like to know more about Bulldog Rescue and what we do or visit our website at www.bulldogrescue.org.uk"

Visit www.bulldogrescue.org.uk or www.bulldogrescue.co.uk and click on the **Donate** button to help this dedicated band with their tremendous work in giving so many Bulldogs a second chance.

DON'T get a dog from eBay, Craig's List, Gumtree or any of the other general advertising websites that sell golf clubs, jewellery, old cars, washing machines, etc. You might think you are getting a bargain German Shepherd, but in the long run you will pay the price. If the dog had been well bred and properly cared for, he or she would not be advertised on such websites - or sold in pet shops.

Good breeders do not let their dogs end up in these places. You may be storing up a whole load of trouble for yourselves in terms of health or temperament issues, due to poor breeding and environment.

If you visit general dog rescue websites, you cannot presume that all descriptions are 100% accurate. They are given in good faith, but ideas of what constitutes a "lively" or "challenging" dog may vary. Some dogs advertised as "Bulldog" may have other breeds in their genetic make-up. It does not mean that these are necessarily worse dogs, but if you are attracted to the Bulldog for its temperament, intelligence, looks and other assets, make sure you are looking at a Bulldog.

If you haven't been put off with all of the above... Congratulations, you may be just the family or person that poor homeless Bulldog is looking for!

If you can't spare the time to adopt - and adoption means forever - you might consider fostering. Or you could help by becoming a home inspector or fundraiser to help keep these very worthy rescue groups providing such a wonderful service.

How ever you decide to get involved, **Good Luck!**

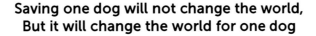

**Saving one dog will not change the world,**
**But it will change the world for one dog**

With thanks to BCARN for assistance with this chapter.

# 16. Caring for Older Bulldogs

Sadly, Bulldogs do not have a long lifespan; eight to 10 years is fairly typical - although some live shorter lives and others longer. Lifespan is influenced by genetics and also by owners. How you feed, exercise and generally look after your dog will all have an impact on his life, but eventually all dogs – even Bulldogs – slow down.

.................................................................................................................................

## Approaching Old Age

How ever fit your older Bulldog is, at some point, he will start to feel the effects of ageing. After having got up early as a puppy, you may find that he now likes to have a lie-in in the morning. He may be even less keen than usual to venture outdoors in the rain and snow.

Physically, joints may become stiffer, and organs, such as heart or liver, may not function quite as effectively. On the mental side - just as with humans - a dog's memory, ability to learn and awareness will all start to dim.

Your faithful companion might become a bit more stubborn or a little less tolerant of lively dogs and children. You may also notice that he doesn't see or hear as well as he used to. On the other hand, your old friend might not be hard of hearing at all. He might have developed that affliction common to many older dogs of *"selective hearing."*

Our old dog Max had bionic hearing when it came to the word *"Dinnertime"* whispered from 20 paces, yet seemed strangely unable to hear the commands *"Come"* or *"Down"* when we were right in front of him!

You can help ease your mature dog into old age gracefully by keeping an eye on him, noticing the changes and taking action to help him as much as possible. This might involve:

- A visit to the vet for supplements and/or medications
- Modifying your dog's environment
- Slowly reducing the amount of daily exercise
- A change of diet

Much depends on the individual dog. Just as with humans, a dog of ideal weight that has been fairly active all of his life is likely to age slower than an overweight couch potato.

Keeping Bulldogs at an optimum weight as they age is important. Their metabolisms slow down, making it easier to put on the pounds unless the daily calories are reduced. Extra weight places additional, unwanted stress on joints and organs, making them have to work harder than they should.

 *We normally talk about dogs being old when they reach the last third of their lives. This varies greatly from dog to dog and bloodline to bloodline. A dog is*

*classed as a "Veteran" at seven years old in the show ring. Some Bulldogs may show few signs of ageing until the day they die, others may start to show signs of ageing at six years old.*

## Physical and Mental Signs of Ageing

If your Bulldog is in or approaching the last third of his life, here are some signs that his body is feeling its age – an old dog may have a few or more of these symptoms:

- He has generally slowed down and is no longer as keen to go out on his walks, or doesn't want to go as far. He is happy pottering and sniffing - and often takes forever to inspect a single clump of grass! Some are less keen to go outside in bad weather

- He gets up from lying down and goes up and down stairs more slowly. He can no longer jump on to the couch or bed; all signs that joints are stiffening, often due to arthritis

- Grey hairs are appearing, particularly around the muzzle

- He has put on a bit of weight

- He may have the occasional *"accident"* (incontinence) inside the house

- He urinates more frequently

- He drinks more water

- He has bouts of constipation or diarrhoea

- He sheds more hair

- The foot pads thicken and nails may become more brittle

- One or more lumps or fatty deposits (lipomas) develop on the body. Our old dog developed two small bumps on top of his head aged 10 and we took him straight to the vet, who performed minor surgery to remove them. They were benign (harmless), but always get the first one checked out ASAP in case they are an early form of cancer - they can also grow quite rapidly, even if benign

- He can't regulate body temperature as he used to and so feels the cold and heat more

- Hearing deteriorates

- Eyesight may also deteriorate – if his eyes appear cloudy he may be developing cataracts, so see your vet if you notice the signs. Unlike humans, many older dogs live quite well with failing eyesight as they have a highly developed sense of smell

- Your dog has bad breath (halitosis), which could be a sign of dental or gum disease. If the bad breath persists, get him checked out by a vet

- If inactive, he may develop callouses on the elbows, especially if he lies on hard surfaces

It's not just your dog's body that deteriorates; his mind may too. Your dog may display some, all or none of these signs of *Canine Cognitive Dysfunction:*

- Sleep patterns change; an older dog may be more restless at night and sleepy during the day. He may start wandering around the house at odd times, causing you sleepless nights

- He barks more, sometimes at nothing or open spaces
- He stares at objects, such as walls, hides in a corner, or wanders aimlessly around the house or garden
- Your dog shows increased anxiety, separation anxiety or aggression
- He forgets or ignores commands or habits he once knew well, such as the Recall and sometimes toilet training
- Some dogs may become clingier and more dependent, often resulting in separation anxiety. He may seek reassurance that you are near as faculties fade and he becomes a bit less confident and independent. Others may become a bit disengaged and less interested in human contact

Understanding the changes happening to your dog and acting on them compassionately and effectively will help ease your dog's passage through his senior years. Your dog has given you so much pleasure over the years, now he needs you to give that bit of extra care for a happy, healthy old age. You can help your Bulldog to stay mentally active by playing gentle games and getting new toys to stimulate his interest.

# Helping Your Dog Age Gracefully

There are many things you can do to ease your dog's passage into his declining years.

As dogs age they need fewer calories and less protein, so many owners feeding kibble switch to one specially formulated for older dogs. These are labelled *Senior, Ageing* or *Mature.* Check the labelling; some are age-specific.

If you are not sure if a senior diet is necessary for your Bulldog, talk to your vet on your next visit. Remember, if you do change brand, switch the food gradually over a week or so, as a dog's digestive system cannot cope with sudden changes of diet.

Years of eating the same food, coupled with less sensitive taste buds can result in some dogs going off their food as they age. If you feed a dry food, try mixing a bit of gravy with it - this works well for us, as has feeding two different feeds: a morning one of kibble with gravy and the second tea-time feed of home-cooked rice and fish or chicken. Rice, white fish and chicken – all cooked – can be particularly good if your old dog has a sensitive stomach.

If you are considering a daily supplement, Omega-3 fatty acids are good for the brain and coat, and glucosamine and various other supplements are available to help joints. We give a squirt of Yumega Omega 3 and half a scoop of Joint Aid in one of the daily feeds.

We had one dog that became very sensitive to loud noises as he got older and the lead up to Bonfire Night was a nightmare. (November 5th in the UK, when the skies are filled with fireworks and loud bangs). Some dogs may also become more stressed by grooming or trips to the vet as they get older.

*There are medications and homeopathic remedies, such as melatonin which has natural sedative properties, to help relieve such anxieties. Check with your vet before introducing any new medicines.*

One of the most important things throughout your Bulldog's life is dental care - either by regular tooth brushing or feeding bones, bully sticks or antlers, etc. to gnaw on. Not only is toothache painful and unpleasant, it can be traumatic for dogs to have teeth removed under anaesthetic after they lose weight due to being unable to eat properly.

If your old friend has started to ignore your verbal commands when out on a walk – either through *"switching off"* or deafness - try a whistle to attract his attention and then use an exaggerated hand signal for the Recall. Once your dog is looking at you, hold your arm out, palm down, at 90 degrees to your body and bring it down, keeping your arm straight, until your fingers point to your toes.

Hand signals worked very effectively with our Max. He looked, understood ......and then decided if he was going to come or not - but at least he knew what he should be doing! More often than not he did come back, especially if the visual signal was repeated while he was still making up his mind.

**Weight** - no matter how old your Bulldog is, he still needs a waist! Maintaining a healthy weight with a balanced diet and regular, gentler exercise are two of the most important things you can do for your dog.

**Environment** - Make sure your dog has a nice soft place to rest his old bones, which may mean adding an extra blanket to his bed. This should be in a place that is not too hot or cold, as he may not be able to regulate his body temperature as well as when he was younger.

He also needs plenty of undisturbed sleep and should not be pestered and/or bullied by younger dogs, other animals or young children. If his eyesight is failing, move obstacles out of his way or use pet barriers to reduce the chance of injuries.

Jumping on and off furniture or in or out of the car is high impact for old joints and bones. He will need a helping hand on and off the couch or your bed - if he's allowed up there - or even a little ramp to get in and out of the car.

We bought an expensive plastic ramp for one old dog as he became hesitant to jump in or out of the car. However, this proved to be a complete waste of money as dogs are tactile and he didn't like the feel of the non-slip surface on his paws. After a couple of tentative attempts, he steadfastly refused to set a paw on it. We ended up lifting him in and out of the car and donating the ramp to a canine charity!

**Exercise** - Take the lead from your dog, if he doesn't want to walk as far, then don't. But if your dog doesn't want to go out at all, you will have to coax him out. ALL old dogs need exercise, not only to keep their joints moving, but also to keep their heart, lungs and joints exercised, and their minds engaged with different places, scents, etc.

**Ears** – Sometimes older dogs produce more ear wax, so check inside the ears regularly. Use clean damp cotton wool to clean out the inner ear and pluck extra ear hair if it's getting waxy.

## Time to Get Checked Out

If your dog is showing any of these signs, get him checked out by a vet:

- Excessive sleeping or a lack of interest in you and his surroundings

- Excessive increased urination or drinking, which can be a sign of reduced liver or kidney function, Cushing's disease or diabetes

- Incontinence, which could be a sign of a mental or physical problem
- Constipation or not urinating regularly, a possible symptom of a digestive system or organ disorder
- Cloudy eyes, possibly cataracts
- Decreased appetite – often one of the first signs of an underlying problem
- Lumps or bumps on the body - often benign, but can occasionally be malignant (cancerous)
- Diarrhoea or vomiting
- A darkening and dryness of skin that never seems to get any better, which can be a sign of hypothyroidism
- Any other out-of-the-ordinary behaviour for your dog. A change in patterns or behaviour is often your dog's way of telling you that all is not well

---

## The Last Lap

Huge advances in veterinary science have meant that there are countless procedures and medications that can prolong the life of your dog, and this is a good thing. But there comes a time when you do have to let go.

If your dog is showing all the signs of ageing, has an ongoing medical condition from which he cannot recover, is showing signs of pain, anxiety or distress and there is no hope of improvement, then the dreaded time has come to say goodbye. You owe it to him.

There is no point keeping an old dog alive if all he has ahead is pain and death. We have their lives in our hands and we can give them the gift of passing away peacefully and humanely at the end when the time is right.

Losing our beloved companion, our best friend, a member of the family, is truly heart-breaking. But one of the things we realised at the back of our minds when we got that gorgeous, lively little puppy that bounded up to meet us like we were the best person in the whole wide world is the pain that comes with it.

We know we will live longer than them and that we'll probably have to make this most painful of decisions at some time in the future.

It's the worst thing about being a dog owner.

If your Bulldog has had a happy life, then you could not have done any more. You were a great owner and your dog was lucky to have you. Remember all the good times you had together. And try not to rush out and buy another dog straight away; wait a while.

Assess your current life and lifestyle and, if your situation is right, only then consider getting another dog and all that that entails in terms of time, commitment and expense. A dog coming into a happy, stable household will get off to a better start in life than a dog entering a home full of grief.

**Whatever you decide to do, put the dog first.**

# Useful Contacts

**North America -**

www.bulldogclubofamerica.org The Bulldog Club of America (BCA)

www.bulldogclubofamerica.org/bca.aspx?id=188 List of BCA registered breeders state by state

www.rescuebulldogs.org The Bulldog Club of America Rescue Network

www.akc.org American Kennel Club

https://marketplace.akc.org/puppies/bulldog? AKC classified ads for Bulldog breeders

www.akcreunite.org Helps find lost or stolen dogs in USA, register your Bulldog's microchip

www.ukcdogs.com United Kennel Club (North America)

www.ckc.ca Canadian Kennel Club

**UK**

www.bulldoginc.co.uk The Bulldog Club Incorporated

www.britishbulldogclub.com British Bulldog Club (UK)

www.bulldogbreedcouncil.co.uk It promotes the health and wellbeing of the breed in the UK

www.bulldogrescue.co.uk UK rescue organisation also helps to find lost or stolen Bulldogs

www.thekennelclub.org.uk The Kennel Club UK

www.thekennelclub.org.uk/services/public/acbr/Default.aspx?breed=Bulldog List of Kennel Club Assured Breeders for Bulldogs

www.thekennelclub.org.uk/services/public/findapuppy/display.aspx?breed=4084&area=0 KC list of breeders with Bulldog puppies available

**General**

www.englishbulldognews.com – Bulldog owners' forum

www.bulldogsworld.com Information website and owners' forum

www.bulldoginformation.com Bulldog information website

www.apdt.com Association of Pet Dog Trainers USA

www.cappdt.ca Canadian Association of Professional Pet Dog Trainers

www.apdt.co.uk Association of Pet Dog Trainers UK

# Disclaimer

This book has been written to provide helpful information on Bulldogs. It is not meant to be used, nor should it be used, to diagnose or treat any medical condition. For diagnosis or treatment of any animal medical problem, consult a qualified veterinarian. The author is not responsible for any specific health or allergy conditions that may require medical supervision and is not liable for any damages or negative consequences from any treatment, action, application or preparation, to any person reading or following the information in this book. References are provided for informational purposes only and do not constitute endorsement of any websites or other sources.

# Pet Care Tracker

Vet's Name: _ _ _ _ _ _ _ _ _ _ _    Groomer's Name: _ _ _ _ _ _ _ _ _ _

Vet's Phone: _ _ _ _ _ _ _ _ _ _    Groomer's Phone: _ _ _ _ _ _ _ _ _ _

Day Care: _ _ _ _ _ _ _ _ _ _ _    Holiday Sitter: _ _ _ _ _ _ _ _ _ _ _

| Pet's Name | Date | Vet Visit | Groomer | NOTES |
|------------|------|-----------|---------|-------|
|  |  |  |  |  |
|  |  |  |  |  |
|  |  |  |  |  |
|  |  |  |  |  |
|  |  |  |  |  |
|  |  |  |  |  |
|  |  |  |  |  |
|  |  |  |  |  |
|  |  |  |  |  |
|  |  |  |  |  |
|  |  |  |  |  |
|  |  |  |  |  |
|  |  |  |  |  |
|  |  |  |  |  |
|  |  |  |  |  |
|  |  |  |  |  |
|  |  |  |  |  |
|  |  |  |  |  |

Made in the USA
Columbia, SC
04 July 2020